Spirit and Nature

Princeton Theological Monograph Series

K. C. Hanson, Charles M. Collier, D. Christopher Spinks,
and Robin Parry, Series Editors

Recent volumes in the series:

Paul W. Chilcote, editor
Making Disciples in a World Parish:
Global Perspectives on Mission and Evangelism

Nathan Montover
Luther's Revolution:
The Political Dimensions of Martin Luther's Universal Priesthood

Alan B. Wheatley
Patronage in Early Christianity:
Its Use and Transformation from Jesus to Paul of Samosata

Eric G. Flett
Persons, Powers, and Pluralities:
Toward a Trinitarian Theology of Culture

Vladimir Kharlamov, editor
Theosis: Deification in Christian Theology, Volume Two

Jon Paul Sydnor
Ramanuja and Schleiermacher:
Toward a Constructive Comparitive Theology

Christian Collins Winn et al., editors
The Pietist Impulse in Christianity

Philip Wingeier-Rayo
Where Are the Poor?: A Comparison of the Ecclesial Base Communities
and Pentecostalism—A Case Study in Cuernavaca, Mexico

Spirit and Nature

*The Study of Christian Spirituality
in a Time of Ecological Urgency*

Edited by
TIMOTHY HESSEL-ROBINSON and
RAY MARIA McNAMARA, RSM

PICKWICK *Publications* · Eugene, Oregon

SPIRIT AND NATURE
The Study of Christian Spirituality in a Time of Ecological Urgency

Princeton Theological Monograph Series 163

Pickwick Publications
An Imprint of Wipf and Stock Publishers
199 W. 8th Ave., Suite 3
Eugene, OR 97401

www.wipfandstock.com

ISBN 13: 978-1-60608-884-5

Cataloging-in-Publication data:

Spirit and nature : the study of Christian spirituality in a time of ecological urgency / edited by Timothy Hessel-Robinson and Ray Maria McNamara, RSM.

cm.—Includes bibliographical references and index.

Princeton Theological Monograph Series 163

ISBN 13: 978-1-60608-884-5

1. Human ecology—Reliogious aspects—Christianity. 2. Environmental ethics. I. Hessel-Robinson, Timothy. II. McNamara, Ray Maria. III. Title. IV. Series

BT695.5 S65 2011

Manufactured in the USA.

For Isaac

Contents

Acknowledgments

THE PROCESS OF PRODUCING A BOOK INCURS MANY DEBTS ALONG THE way, especially when the book is a collection of works written by others. Therefore, we would first like to thank all the contributors whose work appears in the following pages. We appreciate their willingness to engage the questions we have been asking and to share their work with us. We are grateful for their attentive, patient responses to our requests, suggestions, and challenges. This book began, in some ways, during our experience together as doctoral students in Christian spirituality at the Graduate Theological Union. Discovering a common passion for the Earth and for how our scholarship might serve its flourishing, we shared this passion with several other GTU students with similar interests. Two persons deserve special mention because of the sustained conversation we shared about our scholarship and our lives in the context of an ongoing friendship: Nancy Wiens, who contributed to this volume, and Kimberley Whitney. Many other GTU students and teachers contributed to our scholarly and personal formation, as well. We would also like to acknowledge the influence of our teacher Carolyn Merchant at the University of California, Berkeley. Carolyn shared generously with us, inside the classroom and outside of it, helping us to enter the scholarly discourse in environmental philosophy and ethics. Her distinguished work in the field continues to influence ours. Along with these shared expressions of gratitude, we each have individual acknowledgements to make.

Tim Hessel-Robinson: I am deeply grateful to have grown up in the beautiful southern Appalachian Highlands in northeastern Tennessee near the Virginia and North Carolina borders. In that setting there were numerous opportunities for recreation and spiritual nurture in the forests and mountains, in the streams, and on the lakes. I will always be grateful for the people who got me up and into the always visible mountains and made me love them: family, friends, teachers, and especially church youth leaders. I am also blessed to have served as pastor to two congregations where care for God's creation was an intentional focus. Tom Hawley and the SAGE group of Saint Andrew Christian Church (Disciples of Christ), Olathe, Kansas, and Bob Flint, the First Trekkers, and the Earthkeepers group of First Christian Church (Disciples of Christ), Lynchburg, Virginia have inspired me with their commitment to the Earth and their efforts to promote its care among people of faith. I also want to thank several people who contributed to the development of this project. Arthur Holder of the Graduate Theological Union read and offered suggestions on early drafts of the proposal, as well as one of the essays. Lisa Dahill read carefully and offered very helpful suggestions on a draft of my chapter and another one. Susan Smith and Beth Hessel-Robinson also read and offered keen observations about my essay. Sandra Schneiders, whose influence is evident in the following pages, definitively shaped my understanding of the study of Christian spirituality. I am also grateful to my colleagues at Brite Divinity School who have encouraged and supported my scholarship and teaching in this area. My research assistant Dyan Dietz has gone beyond the call of duty in helping us to prepare this manuscript. My friend Ray Maria McNamara has persevered with me in the midst of challenging circumstances, and for her dedicated efforts to this, our shared project, I am indebted. Finally, I offer my deepest gratitude to my son Isaac, to whom I dedicate this book. As an eight year old, he fell in love with cetaceans, and his enthusiasm for creatures of the ocean has been infectious. It was Isaac who suggested I should write about the baiji and he brought its plight to my attention. He loaned me his books and field guides about dolphins, whales, and porpoises to use in my research. Isaac's love of cetaceans, and his zeal for "saving the Earth" inspires my often flagging hopes for the future of the planet and its creatures.

Ray Maria McNamara: As I reflect back on the people whose influence helped shape the work reflected in this book I am aware that the list is a life-time in length. However, there are those who merit particular recognition. I am grateful to my parents who first exposed me to the delight of working in fresh-turned soil and who fostered a young child's fascination in the small creatures who make their homes on the forest floor. I am grateful to the many teachers in my life: science teachers who awakened my passion for the natural world and the faculty at the Jesuit School of Theology and the Graduate Theological Union, both in Berkeley, CA, who helped give intellectual shape and direction to a life-long passion for God. The doctoral program in Christian spirituality at the GTU provided me the opportunity to situate my deepening concerns for the well being of our planet in the face of ecological degradation within the context of the Christian tradition. To the faculty who direct and sustain this program, I extend a heartfelt "thank you." While the process of bringing a co-edited piece of work to being is an arduous one, I am deeply grateful for the opportunity to work with Tim Hessel-Robinson, colleague and friend, whose commitment to the discipline of Christian spirituality and concerns for Earth have been an inspiration to me; our on-going conversations continue to be a source of energy and hope. Finally, I am especially indebted to the members of my religious community, the Sisters of Mercy, who provided me with the time and personal support to do advanced studies in Christian spirituality and whose lives of prayer and service to the most marginalized in our society are a constant witness to the God who dwells within and among all of creation.

Contributors

Brock Bingaman, Assistant Professor of Religious Studies, Wesleyan College, Macon, GA.

Colleen Mary Carpenter, Assistant Professor of Theology at St. Catherine University, St. Paul, MN. Her publications include *Redeeming the Story: Women, Suffering, and Christ.*

Toni Craven, I. Wylie and Elizabeth M. Briscoe Professor of Hebrew Bible at Brite Divinity School at Texas Christian University. Her publications include *Higher Education Reconceived: A Geography of Change* with Sherrie Reynolds, and *The Book of Psalms* in the Message of Biblical Spirituality series.

Melanie L. Harris, Assistant Professor of Religion at Texas Christian University, Fort Worth, TX.

Timothy Hessel-Robinson, Alberta and Harold Lunger Assistant Professor of Spiritual Resources and Disciplines at Brite Divinity School at Texas Christian University. His publications include several articles and essays on ecology and liturgy and Reformed spirituality.

Mary Jo Kaska, PhD candidate in biblical interpretation at Brite Divinity School at Texas Christian University.

Belden C. Lane, Professor of Theological Studies at Saint Louis University. His publications include *Landscapes of the Sacred, The Solace of Fierce Landscapes: Exploring Desert and Mountain Spirituality,* and *Ravished by Beauty: The Surprising Legacy of Reformed Spirituality*

Ray Maria McNamara, RSM, Director of Mission Advancement for The Sisters of Mercy. She formerly taught theology and spirituality at the University of Portland. Her publications include *Interdependence and the God Quest: A Christian Ecological Spirituality.*

John O'Keefe, Professor of Historical Theology at Creighton University. His publications include *Sanctified Vision: An Introduction to Early Christian Interpretation of the Bible* with R. R. Reno.

Robert John Russell, Director, Center for Theology and the Natural Sciences and Professor of Theology and Science at the Graduate Theological Union, Berkeley, CA. His publications include *Cosmology: From Alpha to Omega* and numerous other works on science and theology.

Laura A. Stivers, Associate Professor of Ethics at Dominican University, San Rafael, CA. Her publications include *Disrupting Homelessness: From Charity to Community* and *Justice in a Global Economy: Strategies for Home, Community, and World.*

Nancy S. Wiens, Co-founder and Director of the Center for Nature and Christian Spirituality, Occidental, CA. She holds a PhD from the Graduate Theological Union.

1

Introduction

Timothy Hessel-Robinson and Ray Maria McNamara, RSM

IT IS NOT NEWS THAT OUR PLANETARY ECOSYSTEMS ARE IN CRISIS.
Daily, abundant evidence about threats to water, air, soil, forests, animals, food, and humans is available to any observant person. During the editing of this book, the United States was captivated by live streaming images of raw crude oil spewing from a well on the ocean floor and into the Gulf of Mexico. The BP Deepwater Horizon disaster produced massive pools of oil that formed slicks on the Gulf's surface, closed fisheries, and fouled sensitive wildlife habitat. Images of dead and dying birds, sea turtles, and fish, along with the pleas of desperate Gulf Coast residents whose livelihoods and health were put at risk, aroused anger, sympathy, and grief. The well is now capped, but the clean-up is far from over and the extent of the damage has not yet been fully calculated. The incident, which played out over the course of three months, shows the enormity of the strain we are placing on the biological systems upon which human life and health depends. We are to the point, argues environmental writer Bill McKibben, that the planet has been fundamentally and irreversibly altered by human activity. This is no longer the globe humans have known for most of history. In a clever rhetorical move, McKibben suggests we re-name the planet to emphasize current realties: he calls it "Eaarth." Reversing the damage is no longer possible, according to McKibben. What we must now do is focus on adapting to this new planet by reconfiguring our economic and social arrangements.[1] Such a situation demands that all segments of society consider how they have contributed to the current conditions

---

1. See McKibben, *Eaarth.*

I

and what they might do in response. This especially includes the world's religions and those who study them.

More and more, members of religious communities are responding to our new planetary realities by re-interpreting their sacred texts, revising their liturgies, re-reading their histories, retrofitting their facilities, altering their lifestyles, making public pronouncements, and engaging in social and political actions in defense of nature. In short, people of faith are re-thinking the way their religious traditions conceive of and practice spirituality. Douglas Burton-Christie has written, "Christians today face the immense challenge of reimagining our faith in terms that will help us cherish and preserve the world."[2] In many quarters, this seems to be occurring. This book contains eleven essays by scholars reflecting on various dimensions of Christian spirituality as it is being re-conceived in relation to nature.[3] Speaking about the ecological realities we now face, Mary Frohlich, in her presidential address before the Society for the Study of Christian Spirituality in 2008, pressed the audience to ask what "these times ask of us as scholars of Christian spirituality."[4] Frolich compared the present situation to the biblical Jonah, "broken and ravaged in the belly of the sea monster." The current ecosystemic crisis, she went on to say, presents us with a dilemma similar to Jonah's when he was called to preach to the Ninevites: are we able and willing to transform our fundamental worldviews and patterns of living in response to a new reality which surpasses anything we have previously known? Whereas Jonah's urgent call to prophesy in Nineveh came to him directly from God, the call now extended to humanity, to people of religious faith, and to spirituality scholars, comes directly from the Earth. "Through a crescendo of disturbing information about global warming, species extinction, resource depletion, toxic pollution, and the worldwide breakdown of ecosystemic self-healing systems," humanity is being summoned to a profound transformation of our economic, political, social, and religious arrangements. Such times, said Frohlich, summon those who study and teach Christian

2. Burton-Christie, "Nature," 479.

3. We are aware that terms like "nature," "ecology," and "environment" are contested in the academic discourse of environmental philosophy. We do not think this discussion is unimportant, but a thorough consideration of the issues involved is beyond the scope of our concern here, and we have chosen not to make fine distinctions about terminology.

4. Frohlich, "Under the Sign of Jonah," 27.

spirituality to "place the Earth and its wounds at the center of our attention in very concrete ways."[5]

This task is especially pressing because, while many are re-imagining faith in light of contemporary ecology, there are many others who are skeptical about the genuineness and the urgency of the threats facing the planet. Often, the skeptics rely on faith-based arguments, usually Christian, to justify their suspicion and inaction. A recent article on climate change skepticism among politically conservative groups in the United States reflects this: one person interviewed stated, "I read my Bible . . . [God] made this earth for us to utilize." Another person expressed fear that the concept of climate change is simply a tactic to erode civil liberties: "Being a strong Christian, I cannot help but believe the Lord placed a lot of minerals in our country and it's not there to destroy us."[6] In a recent congressional subcommittee hearing, a United States congress person denied that humans have the capability of effecting climate change, or if so, that it will have any ill effects. He supported his assertions by quoting from Genesis 8 and Matthew 24. "The earth will end only when God declares it's time to be over," he said, adding with conviction that humans have no power to destroy the planet.[7] Such statements seem remarkable, but they indicate that a significant stream of Christian belief has been formed around the assumption that God sanctions unrestrained human exploitation of the rest of creation for the maintenance and comfort of humans. That such ill-conceived religious convictions play a considerable role in shaping public policy is another sign that scholars and teachers of spirituality must find purposeful ways to contribute to the formation of a more ecologically responsible faith.

Scholars of spirituality have many dialogue partners from which to choose as we engage this work. Over the past thirty or forty years almost every area of theology and religious studies has developed a significant literature dealing with ecological concerns. While the field of environmental ethics emerged as an intellectual response to environmental activism in the 1960s and 1970s, Lynn White's classic essay, "The Historical Roots of Our Ecologic Crisis," was the catalyst for scholars to address the place of nature in Christian faith. Theologians spilled a great deal of ink trying to defend the Christian tradition

---

5. Ibid., 27–28.

6. Broder, "Skepticism on Climate Change," A1, A4.

7. Kelly, "God Will Save Us from Climate Change."

against White's claims and to retrieve an ecologically friendly legacy from the Christian past. In biblical studies, scholars attempted to interpret the Genesis creation narratives and other texts in ways that softened the force of dominion theology. Systematic theologians and theological ethicists have reflected on nature as a locus of divine activity and moral considerability. Scholars in various areas of religious studies have extensively engaged the literature of environmental ethics. Dialogue between religion and the natural sciences and technology has become a thriving sub-discipline within systematic theology and religious studies. Feminists like Rosemary Ruether and Sallie McFague have influenced Christian theologians, but have also contributed to the development of ecofeminism generally. A number of recent studies consider the theology, spirituality, and ethics of agriculture and food production and consumption. Overall, there is a voluminous and ever-growing literature in the fields of ecotheology, and ecology and religion.

During roughly the same time period, the field of Christian spirituality has emerged to claim a distinct niche within the academy. With graduate programs, a professional guild, and academic journals, spirituality is now a recognized and respected discipline in colleges, universities, and theological schools North America, Europe and Africa. While many spirituality scholars have shown interest in nature-related issues, there is not a scholarly literature devoted to the integration of ecological issues and spirituality comparable in size to other disciplines in religion and theology. Perhaps this is because spirituality has been busy establishing itself as a discipline, defining the objects of its study, developing distinctive methodologies, and building a disciplinary infrastructure during the period in which nature emerged as a key concern elsewhere. There have been some significant works by scholars of spirituality treating nature, to be sure. Belden Lane's remarkable *The Solace of Fierce Landscapes*, along with his earlier (and later revised) *Landscapes of the Sacred* pioneered the integration of cultural geography and religious experience within various traditions of Christian spirituality.[8] Douglas Burton-Christie has produced several important essays over the last twenty years focusing on spirituality in contemporary nature writing and poetry, and on sacred place.[9] Others are now beginning attend to

8. Lane, *Solace of Fierce Landscapes*; and *Landscapes of the Sacred*.

9. Burton-Christie, "Weight of the World," "Nature," "Spirit of Place," "Into the Body of Another," "Nature, Spirit, and Imagination in the Poetry of Mary Oliver," "Mapping

this issue, but to this point the field of spirituality has not engaged in a sustained, in-depth conversation with either the scholarly literature of environmental history, philosophy, and ethics, and the natural sciences, or the existential threat of environmental calamity. We hope that this book serves as a catalyst for such a conversation.

Ideas for this book emerged over a long period, beginning with the editors' experience together in graduate school, and developing into some conversations about a much more ambitious project. At the American Academy of Religion meeting in 2007, the Christian Spirituality Group and the Religion and Ecology Group co-sponsored a session called "Christian Spiritual Practices for a Sustainable Ecology." That session generated much discussion and gave us encouragement to pursue some of our ideas. Two of the papers presented at that session appear here in revised form. After that meeting we invited several other authors we knew to be interested in the relationship between spirituality and ecology, receiving a somewhat eclectic collection of essays from both established and emerging scholars. We believe this to be part of the volume's strength. We do not claim this to be the definitive word on spirituality and nature; rather, this collection invited scholars to reflect on how ecological concerns might implicate their work, offers examples of how this occurs, and invites others to take up such concerns as well. Our deepest hope is that this work stimulates further conversation about ecological matters within the field of spirituality scholarship.

We did not establish for a uniform definition of spirituality to which all authors were expected to adhere. However, we referred authors to the essays in the *Blackwell Companion to Christian Spirituality*, especially "Approaches to the Study of Christian Spirituality" by Sandra Schneiders.[10] Schneiders' efforts to establish spirituality as an academic field over the past few decades have been immense. Her writings on methodological parameters for the field have been widely influential. Her article on approaches serves as a reference point for several of the authors in this volume, either implicitly or explicitly. Still, Schneiders is not the only figure who has worked to define the field and other approaches are reflected here as well.

---

the Sacred Landscape," "Literature of Nature and the Quest for the Sacred," and "Feeling for the Natural World."

   10. Schneiders, "Approaches to the Study of Christian Spirituality," 15–33.

Several characteristics of spirituality as an academic field of study enumerated by Schneiders are evident, however. The interdisciplinary and multidisciplinary character of work in spirituality is evident throughout this volume. These essays focus on or engage a number of theological and non-theological disciplines including, biblical studies, historical studies, systematic theology, liturgical theology, environmental philosophy, ethics, literature, aesthetics and visual arts, and the natural sciences. Because the study of spirituality is a multi-disciplinary enterprise, and also because the ecological challenges facing us are so complex and diverse, spirituality studies must engage in dialogue with other disciplines in order to come to a fuller understanding of our situation and a fuller articulation of how religious experience is situated within the context of nature. We were intentional about inviting authors from outside the field of spirituality to engage this topic, believing that work in ecological spirituality needs the perspectives of those who specialize in important fields like biblical studies, ethics, and womanist theology.

The self-implicating dimension of scholarship in spirituality is also evident throughout this work. Obvious in Frohlich's challenge to the guild is a call to personal, as well as intellectual, transformation. Historical studies of the desert ascetics, or engagement with Alice Walker's writings, for example, are explicit about seeking resources that inform contemporary religious experience and practice. Work in ecological spirituality is intent on the transformation of authors and readers alike, a transformation toward a clearer perception of God's presence in the natural world and toward more sustainable living. In working with students, we have found that the study of ecological spirituality and environmental ethics is one of the most personally challenging and transforming areas of inquiry in which we engage. Those who get very far into this field find themselves questioning everything from what they eat to what kind of transportation they use. Lisa Dahill is another who has recently argued that spirituality as a scholarly field should prioritize an "orientation toward the earth." Dahill asks, "What is our contribution as scholars in this field to the Great Work of human conversion and survival on Earth?"[11] When framed in this way, it is evident that such work is not "merely academic," but is a matter of crucial, practical importance.

11. Dahill, "For the Life of the World," 290.

Schneiders argues that Christian spirituality is Christian because of its relationship to its "normative texts," and because of the church's communal experience.[12] Of course, that communal experience is characterized by historical, social, cultural, and religious particularity, meaning that there is no uniform "experience" to which we might point, and no single tradition that norms all others. Still, Christians share a relationship to Scripture and to the whole history of the Church meaning that any attempt to describe spiritualities of nature, as Christian, is informed by the generating experiences of historical persons and communities. Scripture and history might be seen as archives of the distinguishing "data" of Christian spirituality. The first few essays in this book look backward, attempting to retrieve the witness of Christian traditions on nature in specific contexts. These essays do not constitute a comprehensive survey, but rather, examples of the way Christian scripture and history can be approached with Earth in mind.

Christian spiritual traditions have never been devoid of reflection on nature or creation. Scripture begins with stories of creation and includes references to the more-than-human world throughout. The lives and imaginations of early Christian monks were shaped by the immediacy of their relationship to the wilderness. St. Francis of Assisi is well known and much beloved largely because of his vibrant relationship to the animals and the elements. John Calvin and his Puritan heirs possessed a vivid sacramental imagination, regarding the Earth and the universe as charged with the presence of God. In recent times, whole religious communities have oriented their lives around the creation spiritualities of Thomas Berry and Matthew Fox.[13] Feminist theologians like Rosemary Radford Ruether, Sallie McFague, and Ivone Gebara have challenged Christians around the world with prophetic visions of global eco-justice. These and other voices appear throughout these essays. The critical retrieval of biblical and historical resources is not limited to focused studies, however, but forms a crucial part of most of the essays included here. However, it is also the case that voices on behalf of the Earth and its inhabitants have often been suppressed within Christianity. It is the task of the scholar to critique such instances and to retrieve and foreground those sources which hold the promise of helping us re-imagine spirituality in more Earth-friendly ways. The later

12. Schneiders, "Study of Christian Spirituality," 25.

13. For example, see Taylor, *Green Sisters*.

essays in this book, engaging various disciplinary perspectives, provide examples of this re-imaginative process. Those essays engage spirituality in dialogue with a variety of sources, literary, artistic, philosophical, ethical, scientific, liturgical, and theological.

This book begins with a careful study of the legacy of creation found in both the Hebrew Bible and the Aprocryphal/Deuterocanonical Books. Biblical scholars Toni Craven and Mary Jo Kaska argue that scripture provides not a single view of nature, but an understanding of creation that is mutable and plural in form and function, thus suggesting that the sacred text can support a change in the way we interpret or understand the human and non-human relationship(s) with G/god(s) and the cosmos. Citing multiple texts they begin by showing the many, and at times contradictory, ways God relates to creation: restricted and non-restricted concerns for members of the Earth community and inclusive/exclusive, positive/negative ways of relating with the Earth community. They continue by examining the question of shared mutuality or non-mutuality between YHWH and members of the Earth community. Through a detailed analysis of the terms "subdue" and "dominion" Craven and Kaska show that an understanding of the human/ non-human relationship based on these concepts has made for a worldview that is anthropocentric, patriarchal, and androcentric. Such a worldview gives license to devalue Earth for the sake of human wants/needs. To counter this interpretation Craven and Kaska suggest that what is needed is a new way of reading the text where the old story of hierarchy, human dominion of nature, is replaced with a hermeneutics of consciousness where ecological justice and mutual subjectivity shape the way we read the text, thus creating a new story of mutuality in which the human person takes responsibility for the care and well-being of creation.

Moving to the early centuries of Christianity, John O'Keefe articulates a way to interpret contemporary sustainable practices by drawing on the ascetic practices of Christian monasticism. Arguing that early Christian ascetics enacted in their bodies the spiritual transformation they sought, O'Keefe sees parallels for those attempting to live more sustainably today. By enacting a kind of eco-asceticism, Christians today might also understand themselves to be participating in and anticipating the eschatological redemption of creation. O'Keefe encourages the adoption of sustainable practices such as eating locally and organically grown foods, reducing energy consumption, driving less, that are not necessarily religious practices. However, when adopted as part of a consciously Christian spirituality, such practices become the means for deepened consciousness of the divine relationship with and intention for the natural world, and a way to participate more fully in God's work within creation. In the same way, O'Keefe argues that historic and specifically Christian spiritual practices, like the Ignatian examen, when viewed in light of God's purposes for creation, can also foster a more ecologically oriented spirituality. The goals of the "ecological ascetic" are to nurture greater intimacy with God in the world, and to live in a way that anticipates the world's renewal.

Belden Lane also looks to a prominent spiritual tradition from the Christian past to inform contemporary ecological spirituality. The Reformed tradition demonstrates a significant connection between beauty and justice, especially in John Calvin and Jonathan Edwards, the two figures on which Lane focuses. For Calvin, the world is a theatre in which God's glorious and beautiful presence is enacted. For Edwards, nature is something to be enjoyed for its great beauty, but the world's beauty always leads to the enjoyment of God, its source. Reformed Trinitarian theology is relational and participative, indicating that God eagerly shares divine beauty with the rest of creation and tirelessly goes outside of the divine self, repairing what has been damaged. At this point, according to Lane, the aesthetic becomes ethical as humanity is called to imitate God's generosity and to treat the Earth as a place that reflects God's beauty. According to Lane's reading of the Reformed tradition the experience of sheer delight in the beauty of creation becomes the foundation for an ecospirituality that includes environmental justice.

Brock Bingaman believes that much contemporary ecotheology is more ecologically driven than theologically driven. He seeks a more explicitly theological foundation for ecospirituality than he often finds. Bingaman looks for resources by turning to two significant figures in Eastern Christianity, John Cassian and Maximus the Confessor, and putting them into dialogue with Jurgen Moltmann. Bingaman creates a conversation among them around five themes: eschatology, *theosis*, ethics, community, and ecumenism. These "congruent elements" of each figure's theology support an "ecological mission," according to Bingaman, that is explicitly theological. Methodologically, Bingaman does not focus on experience or practice, his argument unfolding as work in historical theology. Nevertheless, he uncovers important intellectual resources that serve to undergird the practice of environmental stewardship as a key dimension of Christian spirituality.

Robert Russell's essay, "Contemplation in a Vibrant Universe: the Natural Context of Christian Spirituality," is the only previously published piece in this book. It appeared in print almost twenty years ago, which might seem to make it somewhat dated. In fact, some of the references and sources will indicate its context in time. However, we believe this remarkable essay deserves a wider audience than it received in its original publication in the bulletin of the Center for Theology and the Natural Sciences, which Russell directs. It also represents an early and exemplary effort to integrate spirituality and the natural sciences. Russell is trained as both a physicist and a theologian, and he has been a leading figure in the dialogue between science and theology and continues to produce groundbreaking work in that field.

In this early essay, Russell draws on cosmology, quantum physics, and evolutionary biology to shape a Christian spirituality that is rooted in the Source of all Being while focused outward into our expansive universe. He builds this reflection on St. Teresa of Avila's metaphor for God, the diamond, a gem whose facets each "reflect a glimmer of its central illumination." Russell contends that a contemplation of the multiple facets of the universe through the light of science will draw one into a fuller awareness of the dynamics that constitute the created world, both on a cosmic as well as a quantum scale. Equally important, according to Russell, is the fact that as one moves towards greater understanding of the universe one is ultimately drawn back into a contemplation of divine Life in which all that exists dwells; "the God within is the God throughout." Moving back and forth between scientific knowledge and theological insights, Russell's reflection draws the reader into a world of experience that is as wide as the universe and as intimate as the indwelling of God. Contemplating nature as cosmic fire shows the dependent and fragile nature of reality. From the perspective of quantum physics, according to Russell, matter is like finely spun gossamer, a delicate global veil, a sparkling and spontaneous arrangement of chaotic order," reflecting a God who is ever at work creating and re-creating nature and human experience. The third section of Russell's reflection focuses on nature through the lens of evolutionary biology, reinforcing the notion that all of life is interconnected, that we are "of a piece with all of life, and with the very water of the earth itself." The next perspective contemplates nature as the ecological web of life. Recognizing that God is the source of this ecological web reinforces the responsibility on the human community to sustain its complex of relationships for the sake of the future of all life and in gratitude to God who is the author of life. Finally, contemplating the cosmos from the perspective of its future, Russell, acknowledging the dark unknown inherent in this perspective, encourages a surrender into God who alone can save all that is and in whom all that is finds its ultimate meaning. Russell's anticipated outcome from this inward/outward contemplation of the cosmos and God is a shift in imagination that will enable Christians to "envision better ways to care for the earth as stewards, shepherds, and friends."

Nancy Wiens, a student of Russell's, continues the dialogue between science and spirituality in "Practicing Christian Spiritual Discernment in Light of Natural Science." A skilled spiritual director and a careful scholar, Wiens focuses on the practice of Christian discernment, producing a highly original account of how this ancient and contemporary spiritual exercise is reformulated in light of today's science. Distilling insights from cosmology, evolutionary biology, quantum physics, and neuroscience, Wiens maintains that God is active in the world, but she renders that activity in a way that is consistent with science. God does not override or interfere with Nature's regularities or impinge upon human freedom. Rather, God acts dynamically through the processes of nature. Wiens demonstrates how discernment can be conceived as a lively mutual and simultaneous engagement between the human person and the divine presence. Wiens' engagement with the sciences also shows how religious experience is embedded within natural processes, while, in turn, showing how persons of faith may conduct everyday decision-making in ways that contribute to ecological sustainability.

Tim Hessel-Robinson's essay addresses the important role of worship in locating concern for environmental issues within the context of Christian spirituality. Hessel-Robinson notes that liturgy helps to shape ways of seeing the world around us as well as ways of imagining the future. In light of our current ecological crisis, Hessel-Robinson underscores the important role Christian worship can play in helping worshippers name the forces that are a threat to creation, grieve what is already lost through extension, and take responsibility for acting on behalf of all the vulnerable species on our planet. Focusing specifically on the plight of the Yangtze River dolphin, or baiji, Hessel-Robinson begins his essay within the context of a concrete experience of loss and deep grief. Questioning how a Christian community might pray in light of this event, Hessel-Robinson surveys the role animals play in Scripture and in the literature of select writers from the history of Christian spirituality. Shifting focus, Hessel-Robinson then considers the recent scholarship on lament in biblical studies and in practical theology. The wisdom in his selection of lament as the prayer form for Christian worship in light of ecological issues is best exemplified in his use of the work of Walter Brueggemann. According to Brueggemann, there are three main questions that surface in the biblical lament Psalms: "How long?" "Why?" "Where?" From these questions one can see that the lament Psalms give the worshipping community access to the deepest of human emotions and raise the age-old question of God's presence in the midst of unexplainable tragedy. Hessel-Robinson concludes his essay by suggesting five ways that lament can assist Christians in formulating effective responses to contemporary ecological tragedies. These five suggestions span the scope of human response from naming the forces through expression of grief to claiming responsibility to address and alter the forces that threaten the life-sustaining ecological balance of our planet.

Laura Stivers, an ethicist, engages the spirituality of Latina ecofeminists resisting water privatization and fighting for water justice in Central and South America. Stivers analyzes the efforts by multinational corporations, and backed by the IMF and World Bank, to privatize public water utilities. Privatization is couched in ideals like improved infrastructure and efficiency of distribution, but the end result is water is sold for economic gain to the highest bidder, and the poor are forced to spend more of their income on a necessity. Latina ecofeminist groups, exemplified by the Conspirando collective, resist commodification, insisting that water is a basic right. As such, explains Stivers, ecofeminists view water as the sacred source of life. Their spirituality is grounded in the experiences of oppression, nurtured by ritual, and embodied in relationships. Stivers sees their struggles for water justice as part of a holistic spirituality, grounded in an understanding of interrelatedness within the "sacred body of the cosmos," sustained by water, the "sacred bloodstream of creation."

Melanie Harris's article, "Alice Walker and the Emergence of Ecowomanist Spirituality," uses the lens of womanist critical analysis to show the intersection between womanist concerns and eco-justice. Harris describes womanism as the work of scholars to uncover the voices, wisdom, and lived experiences of women of African descent, giving validity to their lives as reflected in their stories, their writings. Through a critical analysis of this literature, womanist scholars show that issues of race, gender, class, sexual orientation and religion do matter, thus challenging the notion of a "universal woman." Eco-womanism, according to Harris, is an approach to finding solutions to ecological problems using the experiences and voices of women of African descent. It studies the complex ways racism, classism, sexism, and heterosexism operate in environmental injustice. Drawing on the insights and wisdom found in Alice Walker's non-fiction writings, Harris illustrates that it is Walker's "fluid spirituality," a blending of her Christian and Native American spiritual traditions with her own experience as a woman of African descent growing up in the Jim Crow south, that shapes a vision of compassion in the world that includes Earth and all earthlings. Rather than denying or skirting around the devastating impact of oppression and injustice in Walker's own life, Harris' womanist intersectional analysis of Walker's writings shows how her womanist spirituality provides a way of crossing through hatred, prejudice, and oppression into a kind of love that gives rise to an all inclusive compassion towards the whole of creation. Harris concludes her essay by pointing out that oppressions are connected; ecological degradation perpetuates an injustice not only on Earth but on human persons as well, especially people of color.

Colleen Carpenter's essay uses the forest paintings and prose of Canadian artist Emily Carr (1871–1945) to illustrate the redemptive potential in an engaged encounter with the death and destruction that marks our current ecological crisis. Carpenter portrays this shift in imagination by juxtaposing several of Carr's paintings of the forest as wilderness with paintings in which Carr depicts the devastation caused by industrial logging. In these paintings one is able to see Carr's deep love for the wildness of the forest with all its loneliness and danger to humans. However, Carpenter points out that one is best able to see Carr's forest spirituality most powerfully through her paintings depicting the aftermath of industrial logging. Drawing on the work of Belden Lane's spirituality of brokenness in *Solace of a Fierce Landscapes*, Carpenter interprets these paintings of violence in a way that enables one to truly encounter the horror of the destruction while, at the same time, catching glimpses of hope. In the attentive encounter of a landscape in trauma, according to Carpenter, one comes face to face with one's own brokenness, and in that moment finds the God who, according to scripture, was always found among the suffering, lost, and abandoned. In conclusion, Carpenter states that Carr looked at clearcuts and saw both devastation as well as a landscape held in the embrace of God, a shift in imagination from the "terrifying impasse of ecocide towards something entirely new;" resurrection.

Finally, Ray Maria McNamara's essay "Love of Nature and Love of God: A Christian Ecological Spirituality" serves as a fitting conclusion to the volume. McNamara attempts to overcome the dualistic notion that one must choose between the nature-human relationship and the God-human relationship, implying that one diminishes the other. According to McNamara, a Christian ecological spirituality locates the human relationship with God precisely within the context of nature. She turns to two prominent environmental philosophers—Aldo Leopold and Carolyn Merchant—to develop a holistic worldview in which we understand humans as embedded within nature as a part of it, rather than as separate from it. By analyzing Eiseley's remarkable essay "The Flowing River," McNamara shows how direct experience with nature opens the doors of human perception to grasp how we are "plain members and citizens of" the earth, as Leopold asserted. Finally, McNamrara turns to Athanasius' classic text *Life of Antony*, to demonstrate how this understanding of the human-nature relationship coincides with Christian spirituality. In *Life of Antony*, treated also by O'Keefe, the pattern of call, withdrawal, and return summarizes the spiritual life. For McNamara, this pattern parallels Eiseley's experience in many ways, and she sees it as suggestive for Christians attempting to live in closer and more responsible relationships with the rest of nature. Such a contemplative stance toward creation can lead to a transformed view of the world, the holistic view advanced by environmental philosophers. It can also lead to a transformed understanding of God and God's desires for the world.

This book is part of our response to Mary Frohlich's challenge to make the Earth and its plight a central focus in our scholarly work. In putting this together, we also join Frohlich in calling for other spirituality scholars to consider how their work can help persons and communities re-imagine the human-divine relationship in ways that better cherish and preserve Earth's fragile beauty. As we seek to describe the embodiment of the God-quest in the human-nature relationship, we hope that this collection will inspire a larger scholarly conversation about the relationship of spirituality and nature.

Bibliography

John Broder. "Skepticism on Climate Change Is Article of Faith for Tea Party." *New York Times* (October 21, 2010) A1 & A4.

Burton-Christie, Douglas. "A Feeling for the Natural World: Spirituality and the Appeal to the Heart in Contemporary Nature Writing." *Continuum* 2 (1993) 229–52.

———. "Into the Body of Another: *Eros,* Embodiment and Intimacy with the Natural World." *Anglican Theological Review* 81 (1999) 13–37.

———. "The Literature of Nature and the Quest for the Sacred." *The Way Supplement* 81 (1994) 4–14.

———. "Mapping the Sacred Landscape: Spirituality and the Contemporary Literature of Nature." *Horizons* 21 (1994) 22–47.

———. "Nature." In *The Blackwell Companion to Christian Spirituality,* edited by Arthur Holder, 478–95. Malden, MA: Blackwell, 2005.

———. "Nature, Spirit, and Imagination in the Poetry of Mary Oliver." *Cross Currents* 46 (1996) 77–87.

———. "The Spirit of Place: The Columbia River Watershed Letter and the Meaning of Community." *Horizons* 30 (2003) 7–24.

———. "The Weight of the World: The Heaviness of Nature in Spiritual Experience." In *Exploring Christian Spirituality,* edited by Elizabeth Liebert and Bruce Lescher, 142–60. Mawah, NJ: Paulist, 2006.

Dahill, Lisa. "For the Life of the World." *Spiritus* 10 (2010) 288–93.

Frolich, Mary. "Under the Sign of Jonah: Studying Spirituality in a Time of Ecosystemic Crisis." *Spiritus* 9 (2009) 27–45.

Kelly, Cathal. "God Will Save Us from Climate Change: U.S. Representative." *Toronto Star* (November 10, 2010). Online: http://www.thestar.com/news/world/article/888472--god will-save-us-from-climate-change-u-s-representative.

Lane, Belden. *Landscapes of the Sacred: Geography and Narrative in American Spirituality.* 2nd ed. Baltimore: Johns Hopkins University Press, 2001.

———. *The Solace of Fierce Landscapes: Exploring Desert and Mountain Spirituality.* Oxford: Oxford University Press, 1998.

McKibben, Bill. *Eaarth: Making Life on a Tough New Planet.* New York: Holt, 2010.

Schneiders, Sandra. "Approaches to the Study of Christian Spirituality." In *The Blackwell Companion to Christian Spirituality,* edited by Arthur Holder, 15–33. Malden, MA: Blackwell, 2005.

Taylor, Sarah MacFarland. *Green Sisters: A Spiritual Ecology.* Cambridge: Harvard University Press, 2008.

2

The Legacy of Creation in the Hebrew Bible and Apocryphal/Deuterocanonical Books

Toni Craven and Mary Jo Kaska

> The fulfillment of the Earth community is to be caught up in the grandeur of existence itself and in admiration of those mysterious powers whence all this has emerged
>
> —Thomas Berry,
> *The Great Work: Our Way Into the Future* (xi)

IN THIS STUDY, WE MAKE THE CASE THAT THE LEGACY OF CREATION IN the various forms of the Hebrew Bible or Old Testament is richly mutable and plural in form and function. We examine selected representations of creation in Torah, notably the two opening stories in Gen 1:1—2:4a; 2:4b—3:24; and the two flood stories intertwined in Gen 6:5—9:17. Other First Testament texts, and various expansions of the Christian OT canons in the Apocryphal/Deuterocanonical Books are also considered. The Bible says much more on this topic than we can address here. We hope our work will stir you, our readers, to take up examination of these and other biblical representations of creation.

The opening chapters of Genesis record honored textual cosmogonies (theories of the origin of the universe) that reflect communal memories of Israel regarding the identity and agency of God and members of Earth community. These chapters and their expansions in other biblical books are critical to understanding whom God is and what it means to relate to God, to each other within Earth community,[1]

---

1. Except in biblical quotation, we follow the practice of the Earth Bible Team making Earth a proper noun to emphasize its role as a subject. See Habel, *Readings from the*

and to the planetary universe. Together these various passages portray richly diverse beliefs, attitudes, practices, or spiritualities regarding creation and creator.[2] The variety of cultural locations, questions, and consequences of these texts and their associations depict complex characterizations with multifold identities and agencies attributed to God, nature, and living beings, non-human and human alike. Israel's stories of the creation and purpose of the Heavens, Earth, and underworld in Genesis moor YHWH Elohim to creation in more than one way from the start through the telling of differing stories of origin.

In the Genesis 1 story, credited to the Priestly or P author, Elohim is a mysterious figure who arrives alone in the darkness at the narrative's opening as a hovering spirit[3] above the watery depths or primordial ocean, which hides Earth within.[4] Elohim creates light, cosmos, and living beings in six days, with creation of the land beings and human beings the work of the sixth day. Humans—a male and a female—are

---

Perspective of Earth, 34.

2. Our understanding of biblical spirituality is especially indebted to Kugel's article, "Topics in the History of the Spirituality of the Psalms" in which he suggests that the basic "spirituality" of the Psalms, for instance, "might have begun to be 'spiritualized'— that is, decontextualized—from a very early time" (135). It seems that "as the Psalms became Scripture, they did so with an interpretive strategy attached: they were not to be interpreted as a self-standing book of prayers or praises, any more than Proverbs was to be a self-standing collection of wise sayings" (136). Biblical texts derive their spirituality by bringing various parts of the canon(s), other bodies of literature, and the needs of the time into conversation with each other that results in a "history of reinterpretation" for "new conditions" (135). Differing ways of theological thinking are "consonant with the rooting of Israelite society in agriculture, with its elemental interface between human need and labor and the cyclic workings of the cosmos." See Knierim, "Cosmos and History," 63–64, 84–85.

3. "*Elohim*, the waters and Earth" are identified within the primordial darkness (Habel, "Geophany," *Genesis,* 36). The rûah 'ĕlōhîm ("spirit, wind, or breath of God") is "described as *merachepet* ('hovering')" (Ibid., 37). Some interpret this as a gentle "wind that from God that swept over the face of the waters" (NRSV); others as a harsh "mighty storm that raged" over the deep. But Deut 32:11 speaks of a mother raptor or eagle "hovering" over her young and spreading her wings "not in some fierce act of disturbance, but apparently to lift them up in the nurturing act of teaching them to fly" (Ibid.). Habel points out that Schottroff interprets this "mysterious movement deep in the darkness" as that of "a giant mother bird." See Habel, "Geophany," 37 and Schottroff, "Creation Narrative," 24–25.

4. We follow Habel's interpretation in "Geophany" of Gen 1:2 that "Earth is present but hidden from view" (36). "On the third day *erets* rises from the waters, an epiphany from below—a geophany" (41). "The appearance of the earth on the third day is not a rescue operation. It is a revelation of a hidden reality" (42).

made in Elohim's own image (Gen 1:27). Finally, Elohim rests on the last day of this story, (Gen 2:2). Time, holiness, and divine affirmation mark all creation in this story.

In the spirit of Judaism of a period much later than Genesis 1, yet traceable to a strand of this story, Heschel links the rest of the seventh day to the concept of life eternal:

> While Jewish tradition offers us no definition of the concept of eternity, it tells us how to experience the taste of eternity or eternal life within time. Eternal life does not grow away from us; it is "planted within us," growing beyond us. The world to come is therefore not only a posthumous condition, dawning upon the soul on the morrow after its departure from the body. The essence of the world to come is Sabbath eternal, and the seventh day in time is an example of eternity. The seventh day has the flavor of the seventh heaven and was given as a foretaste of the world to come; *ot hi le-ʿolam*, a token of eternity.[5]

Whatever its origin, Sabbath observation is "participation in the rhythm of the divine life itself" and "the nearest approximation to *unio mystica*" in Hebraic thought.[6]

In the second origin story (Gen 2:4b—3:24), YHWH Elohim is an immanent being who walks, talks, fashions creation, is concerned about human companionship, and repairs divine misfired action when the animals do not fulfill like-partnership with the first human.[7] This version of creation, often credited to the Yahwist or J author, portrays YHWH Elohim as first creating an individual human being (*hā ʾāḏām*) out of the dust of the ground (*hāʾăḏāmâ*) and breathing into its nostrils the "breath of life." The first creature keeps a garden, which YHWH Elohim populates with animals whom the first creature names. At this story's end, YHWH Elohim creates male and female as distinctive human

---

5. Heschel, *Sabbath*, 74.

6. Levenson, "Jerusalem Temple," 32. Generally speaking, more than a century of study and proposals about the origin and function of Sabbath has produced "No hypothesis whether astrological, menological, sociological, etymological, or cultic [that] commands the respect of a scholarly consensus" (Hasel, "Sabbath," *ABD* 5:851). *Jub.* 2:30 states that only Israelites, not other people, observe the Sabbath.

7. Westermann, *Genesis 1–11*, comments as he quotes H. Gunkel who writes, "'God makes an experiment that is futile. The Melanesians too tell of a number of attempts to create humans which misfire' (similarly A. Menes, F. Schwally, G. J. Thierry, K. Budde, L. Köhler)" (225) that "The narratives often tell of the creator god reflecting as to how he [*sic*] can repair his creatures (Frazer, p. 8f.)" (226).

beings, recognized by the first human, now minus the traditional rib or side, as at last "bone of my bones and flesh of my flesh" (Gen 2:23).

Each culture in the ancient world assigns creation to the actions of their G/god(s) based on the particularity of their story.[8] Life as sacred service, either as slave or free, is at the heart of the various understandings of divine, non-human, and human identity along with agency. Ecology in our sense is not a major concern in any of these ancient cultures, including Israel; nor are the 'scientific' beliefs expressed in these texts anything like our own. Nonetheless, there are in Israel's holy books and those of others, deep concerns for human and non-human relationship(s) with G/god(s) and cosmos. While we will focus on ancient Israel's mytho-poetic statements regarding creation, they share in a wider set of cosmological understandings. Israel's stories incorporate some things borrowed from neighboring cultures and others things rejected.[9] How the universe is understood to work is affected by many variables. Usually, Israel honors Elohim, and YHWH as creator and sustainer of the world and its continuing story.

God's restricted or non-restricted concern for members of Earth community—Israel only or all the nations and world—differentiates a major variation in representations of relationship with the divine. Shared mutuality or non-mutuality between YHWH and the members of Earth community—human and non-human—constitutes another key distinction in identity and agency. Hierarchy, exercised by a controlling group in the formal organization of the world, is the dominant mode of relationship, though other relational strategies are depicted in some texts.

God relates to Earth community in inclusive and exclusive, positive and negative ways as the following examples illustrate. Exodus

8. On the origin stories of surrounding cultures including those of Egypt, Syria, Assyria, Babylonia, Persia, and Greece, see Davies and Rogerson, *Old Testament World*, esp. chaps. 8, 16, and 17.

9. From Babylonia, e.g., bits and pieces of the *Enuma Elish*, with its Gilgamesh Epic (Tablet XI) seem to have influenced parts of the Gen 1 creation story and the flood story. Many hold that Babylonian belief in a world created from parts of the carcass of Tiamat (mother Earth) was incorporated into Gen 1. Virtually all reject the idea that Israel adopted creation of the universe from Marduk's vanquishing of another God (his mother, Tiamat) in Gen 1, even though in Pss 68:21–23; 74:12–17; 89:5–14 (esp. 9–10); Isa 51:9–13, God defeats the forces of chaos as part of creation. Egypt had a concept of afterlife, which Israel seemingly rejected for itself, until under later Greek influence, afterlife provided a useful answer to how and when the righteous are rewarded (Wis 3:1–9).

makes clear that from the beginning of its story God restricted special regard for the people Israel as their deliverer: "I am YHWH Elohim who brought you out of the land of Egypt, out of the house of slavery: you shall have no other Elohim ('G/gods') before me" (Exod 20:2–3; Deut 5:6–7). Yet sometimes YHWH is more than deliverer of only the chosen people. YHWH is the unrestricted savior of *all living beings*, "humans and animals alike" (Ps 36:6). In other instances, YHWH Elohim is supreme over all creation and all cultures—all people, all matter, all spirits, all other G/gods[10] are caught up in the maintenance of relationship with the God of Israel.[11] God's global judgment and punishment of the surrounding nations as well as Israel and Judah (Amos 1–3) make the case of God's concern for all people. As does Josiah's reform (2 Kgs 23:1–25), which "constituted a temporarily successful attempt by the king to impose a specific cultus, clergy, and mode of Yahwism on all territories under his direct military control."[12]

When God is "grieved" as in the great flood story (Gen 6:7), YHWH Elohim can also be destroyer of all life (save those on the ark who are necessary to regenerate creation). YHWH is maker of heaven, moon, and stars, who has created a human being "little lower than Elohim" (G/gods), giving the human dominion, putting all things under his feet—domesticated and wild animals, birds of the air, fish of the sea, and whatever passes along the paths of the seas (Ps 8:3–8). YHWH Elohim, clothed in "light as a garment," stretches "out the heavens like a tent," rides "on the wings of the wind," and makes "winds messengers, fire and flame ministers" (Ps 104:2–4). Who God is and what God

---

10. Psalms 65–68 depict God as universally providing "covering" or "atoning for" human iniquity (65:3); watering Earth and clothing meadows with flocks (65:9–13); accepting the joyful noise of "all the earth" (66:1–4); keeping an eye on "the nations" (66:7); so that "all the people" and "all the ends of the earth revere" God (67:2, 7); for YHWH "daily bears us up" (68:20).

11. There are twelve references in all in the Psalms to other G/gods. *Elohe*, a masculine plural noun in construct, appears in Ps 96:5, "all the G/gods of the people are idols." *Elohim*, grammatically a masculine plural noun for ("G/gods") other than YHWH appears in Ps 96:4, YHWH "is to be revered above all G/gods" and also in Pss 82:1, 6; 84:7; 86:8; 95:3; 97:7, 9; 135:5; 136:2; and 138:1. References to the God of Israel using this same noun, predominantly although not exclusively in its masculine plural form, appear a total of 440 times in the Pss (only 72 of these usages are forms of *El*, the masculine singular form). See Craven, *Psalms*, 61.

12. Zevit, *Religions*, 668.

does changes in the First Testament and Apocryphal/Deuterocanonical Books. God's identity is fluid, not immutable.

Non-human and human identities are also mutable. Hayes holds that a "compelling image of the mourning earth, turned to barren wilderness because of the acts of its inhabitants, is reflected" in Jeremiah's prayer for retribution against those whose treachery results in prosperity at great cost to Earth. "How long will the earth mourn, and the grass of every field wither? From the evil of those who dwell in it, the beasts and birds are swept away" (Jer 12:4).[13] In this example, disorder is set right by a world-view that envisions one with ears to hear and a voice to protest "the mourning earth" (Jer 12:4). In other instances, divine promises signal a radical, fresh start with a "new heaven and new earth" (Isa 65:17; 66:22), or the assurance of "a new heart" (the decision making organ) for humanity created by God's own spirit (Ezek 36:26).

God's utter destruction of the Levitical leader, Korah, and all who rebelled against Moses in the wilderness, occurs when Moses says that Korah, Dathan, and Abiram and their families will face an unnatural fate, that YHWH has "something new" in store for them. Then, "The earth opened its mouth and swallowed them up, along with their households—everyone who belonged to Korah and all their goods. So they with all that belonged to them went down alive into Sheol; the earth closed over them, and they perished from the midst of the assembly" (Num 16:32–33). In another instance, an unexpected stay of execution diverts impending disaster at the last minute when the angel of YHWH whom David saw standing between heaven and earth ready to destroy Jerusalem was commanded by God to sheath his sword (1 Chr 21:15–27). Occasionally, God and cosmos, humans and non-humans alike, seem to get relationship right. All Earth makes a "joyful noise to God," singing "All the earth worships you; they sing praise to you, sing praise to your name" (Ps 66:1–4). All people gratefully thank God, who has "kept us among the living, and has not let our feet slip" (Ps 66:9–10). The psalmist testifies that God has "listened" and "given heed to the words of my prayer" (Ps 66:20). When things are right, God's blessing is available to Israel (Ps 67:1–2), "the nations" (Ps 67:4), and Earth itself (Ps 67:6).

---

13. Hayes, *Earth Mourns*, 1. Hayes traces the image of the "mourning earth" in nine prophetic passages in the Hebrew Bible: Amos 1:2; Hos 4:1–3; Jer 4:23–28; 12:1–4, 7–13; 23:9–12; Isa 24:1–20; 33:7–9; and Joel 1:5–20.

The Genesis creation stories vary in what they say about mutuality and non-mutuality of Earth community. In Gen 1:1—2:4a, the seven-day story, everything that Elohim creates is "good," that is, everything is created with the agency to fulfill its purpose and everything shares in the sacredness or holiness of Elohim. Genesis 1 repeats the word "good" seven times in stylistically similar phrases: "Elohim saw" that something "was good," or "very good" (1:4, 10, 12, 18, 21, 25, 31). The last act of creation in Gen 1 is creation of humanity—male and female—made in the divine image and blessed by Elohim (1:27–28).

Three blessings occur in the first creation story. First, in Gen 1:22, Elohim blesses the water beings and winged ones to "be fruitful and multiply, and fill the waters in the seas, and let birds multiple on the earth." Second, in Gen 1:28, Elohim similarly blesses the female and male humans, giving them moral sovereignty to subdue Earth and have dominion over all other living beings. Third, in Gen 2:3, Elohim blesses the seventh day and makes it holy.

In the case of human living beings, their "blessing" problematically states that they are to "be fruitful and multiply, and fill the earth and *subdue* it, and have *dominion* over the fish of the sea and over the birds of the air and over every living being that moves upon the earth" (1:28). "See," says Elohim on the sixth day, "I have given you (human living beings) every plant yielding seed that is upon the face of all the earth, and every tree with seed in its fruit; you shall have them for food" (1:29). Likewise, all non-human living beings on the land are also to eat "all green vegetation" (1:30). And "Elohim saw everything . . . and indeed, it was very good" (1:31).

Arguably, all is not "very good" (*ṭôb měʾōd*) for non-human beings and nature who are no longer subjects alongside humans, but rather objects for human living beings who now possess moral hegemony as male and female living beings created in the "image of Elohim" and given the right by Elohim to "subdue" Earth and have "dominion" over all other non-human living beings. The only restriction in Gen 1 that affects the behavior of all earthly living beings—human and nonhuman alike—is that they eat vegetation, not each other (1:29–30).

In 1949, von Rad argued that nonhuman beings benefit from humans' likeness to God. Von Rad seemingly overlooked or missed the mutuality implied in the first six divine declarations of creations' own goodness (1:4, 10, 12, 18, 21, 25) and the agency accorded non-human beings as participants in creation.

> Just as powerful earthly kings, to indicate their claim to dominion, erect an image of themselves in the provinces of their empire where they do not personally appear, so man [sic] is placed upon earth in God's image as God's sovereign emblem. He [sic] is really only God's representative, summoned to maintain and enforce God's claim to dominion over the earth. The decisive thing about man's similarity to God, therefore, is his function in the non-human world. The expressions for the exercise of this dominion are remarkably strong *rādā*, "tread," "trample" (e.g., the wine press); similarly *kābaš*, "stamp." Thus man's creation has a retroactive significance for all nonhuman creatures; it gives them a new relation to God. The creatures, in addition to having been created by God, receive through man a responsibility to God; in any case, because of man's dominion it receives once again the dignity belonging to a special domain of God's sovereignty. [14]

Thus on the sixth day God given dominion opens the door to human objectification of Earth community.

In Gen 2:4b—3:24, the creation story in the garden, eight additional references to "good" add other connotations to the meaning of this word: "Out of the ground YHWH Elohim made to grow every tree that is pleasant to the sight and good for food" (2:9), also YHWH Elohim made "the tree of the knowledge of good and evil" (2:9b). The gold of the land of Havilah is "good" (2:12).[15] YHWH Elohim commands the first human not to eat of "the tree of the knowledge of good and evil" (2:17), introducing death as penalty for this action. YHWH Elohim also says, "It is not good" (2:18) that the first human is alone, wanting to make an *ʿēzer kĕnegdô*, a partner suitable for the

---

14. von Rad, *Genesis*, 60. "Man" for von Rad, "was not created alone but designated for the 'thou' of the other sex. The idea of man, according to P, finds its full meaning not in the male alone but in man and woman" (ibid). Confusion over mutuality affects understanding of human and non-human beings. Ironically, von Rad's usage of "man" and "he" prophetically points to another set of language problems between the sexes, which privilege human males as the top of the hierarchy.

15. If the information about the river that flows out of Eden dividing into four branches (2:10–14) is a later addition to the text, as we think it is, and if these verses are removed, then Gen 2–3, like Gen 1, repeats the word "good" seven times.

first.[16] The serpent likened the knowing of "good and evil" to being like Elohim (3:5). "The woman saw that the tree was good for food" (3:6). And finally, "YHWH Elohim said, 'See, the human has become like one of us, knowing good and evil'" (3:22).

"Good" in the story of life in the garden means more than the usual "fulfilling the purpose for which it was made." "Good" adds moral values primarily to the human senses of beauty, taste, worth, limitation, and knowledge—both positive (as in the human need for a like companion) and negative (as in the human's not eating of the "tree of the knowledge of good and evil"). Thus, the serpent and God know that "good" affects behavior and has ethical dimensions, as the human beings will soon learn. God's involvement and contact with all creation bestows holiness upon it.

As twenty-first century readers, we interpret the two Genesis stories of creation through a hermeneutic of "consciousness" that "sees" or "beholds," in the sense of Genesis 1:29 and 3:22, that ecological justice demands that Earth and all living beings—non-human and human, female and male—are mutual subjects in the text. Having once "seen," we know that what happens to one part of the planet affects the web of all its parts. In Berry's words, "Earth is a community of subjects, not a collection of objects."[17] The sacredness and holiness of all life and human and non-human interests are served in differing ways by Genesis' fourteen or fifteen uses of the word "good" in the two creation stories.[18] Though Elohim's involvement with all creation bestows holiness upon it, human beings seemingly benefit more than others, in the short term at least, from Elohim's command, "fill the earth and subdue it, and have dominion over the fish of the sea and over the birds of the air and over every living being that moves upon the earth" (1:28). Von

16. Trible, *Rhetoric of Sexuality*, 90.

17. This signature quotation from one of the leading theological and environmental thinkers in North America is foundational in most of Berry's work. See his major studies *The Dream of the Earth*, *The Universe Story* (coauthored with Brian Swimme), and *The Great Work*. In *Evening Thoughts: Reflecting on Earth as Sacred Community*, chapter 1 is titled "Our Way into the Future: A Communion of Subjects," in which Berry says two things are needed at this time: (1) alarm about the cultural consequences of the present devastation of the planet; and (2) fascination with the future "if only we respond creatively to the urgencies universe is composed simply of 'mind and mechanism,'" 18.

18. The question, "Whose vested interest is voiced here?" are the words of Brueggemann in "That the World May Be Redescribed," 362.

Rad is accurate in pointing out that "*rādā*, 'tread,' 'trample'" and "*kābaš* 'stamp'"[19] are harsh expressions. Together they compound in severity. In fact, these two verbs appear jointly only in Gen 1:28 and are never used together elsewhere in the Hebrew Bible.

Consciousness, personal and communal, charges us "to take up the cause of justice for the Earth and to ascertain whether Earth and Earth community are oppressed, silenced, or liberated"[20] by the Bible and our readings of these sacred texts. According to Mary Evelyn Tucker, Thomas Berry believed that for the first time, "a central question we face is whether humans themselves are an endangered species."[21] Berry sees us as caught

> between stories—namely, between a scientific description of evolution and a biblical account of creation . . . resulting in the alienation of humans from the Earth and in their inability to see the Earth as a sacred community. Berry suggests that a new story is needed, one that integrates the material and spiritual dimensions of evolution. This story, he conjectures, will provide an enlivening orientation for a new ecological period for the human-Earth community.[22]

Norman C. Habel unequivocally makes the case

> that as Western interpreters we are heirs of a long anthropocentric, patriarchal, and androcentric approach to reading the text that has devalued the Earth and that continues to influence the way we read the text; to declare, before reading the text, that we are members of a human community that has exploited, oppressed, and endangered the existence of Earth community.[23]

Questions about human responsibility and mutuality are being addressed particularly by those working in the relatively new field of biblical ecological study,[24] which owes a great debt to the dedicated work

---

19. See von Rad, *Genesis*, 60.

20. Habel, *Exploring Ecological Hermeneutics*, 1.

21. Tucker, "Editor's Preface" to *Evening Thoughts*, 9.

22. Ibid., 10.

23. Habel, *Readings from the Perspective of Earth*, 34.

24. Like "theology" (study of God), the word "ecology" is a compound word from the ancient Greek words *oikos* (house or living relations) and *logia* (sciences or study of), meaning the science or study of the living relationships within environments or study of organisms and their environments.

of Habel, Vicki Balabanski, Peter Trudinger, Shirley Wurst, and the team of international scholars who have contributed to the Earth Bible Project.[25]

Each of the Earth Bible's five volumes opens with a challenging "Foreword" from Archbishop Desmond Tutu who identifies the theological dimensions of ecojustice and its spiritual challenges this way: "We all need to come to terms with the forces that have created this crisis and the resources within our traditions that can motivate us to resolve the crisis. One of those traditions is our biblical heritage."[26] The Archbishop proposes that we read with a "critical but empathetic eye" and "identify with Earth and the suffering Earth community."[27] Just as "feminists have forced us to confront the patriarchal orientation of much of the biblical texts," the Archbishop argues, ecojustice demands that we face the question: "Does the text de-value Earth by making the self-interest of humans its dominant concern?"[28]

As ecofeminists and biblical literary critics, both of us bring our own questions about how the creation stories and their legacy give and/or take away agency of Earth and members of Earth community. What about mutual kinship within Earth's sacred community? What

---

25. The Earth Bible Project now located in the Centre for Theology, Science, and Culture associated with Adelaide College of Divinity and Flinders University of South Australia has published five volumes: *Readings from the Perspective of Earth*; *The Earth Story in Genesis*; *The Earth Story in Wisdom Traditions*; *The Earth Story in the Psalms and the Prophets*; *The Earth Story in the New Testament*. The bibliographies in these volumes are especially helpful.

26. Tutu, "Foreword," *Readings from the Perspective of Earth*, 7–8.

27. Ibid., 8.

28. Ibid., 7. Toward this new ecological hermeneutic, the Earth Bible Project developed six ecojustice principles that "were refined in consultations and workshops concerned with ecology in general, and ecological concerns linked to theology and the Bible more specifically." 1. The principle of intrinsic worth: The universe, Earth and all its components have intrinsic worth/value. 2. The principle of interconnectedness: Earth is a community of interconnected living things that are mutually dependent on each other for life and survival. 3. The principle of voice: Earth is a subject capable of raising its voice in celebration and against injustice. 4. The principle of purpose: The universe, Earth and all its components are part of a dynamic cosmic design within which each piece has a place in the overall goal of that design. 5. The principle of mutual custodianship: Earth is a balanced and diverse domain where responsible custodians can function as partners with, rather than rulers over, Earth to sustain its balance and a diverse Earth community. 6. The principle of resistance: Earth and its components not only suffer from human injustices but actively resist them in the struggle for justice. Habel, *Exploring Ecological Hermeneutics*, 2.

parts of the biblical story continue to legitimate both human power over and human power with other human and non-human beings? Are the creation stories thoroughly hierarchical (top down), more mutually heterarchical (networked and interdependent), or some combination of the two ways of recognizing and maintaining authorization and order? Hierarchy is linear, with someone or thing at the top of the power pyramid identified as an ultimate authority holding formal precedence over those beneath. Heterarchy, on the other hand, proceeds from emergent authority that results from mutual interactions between simple non-linear behaviors of beings within a multi-agent complex set of interactions that may seem chaotic, especially at first.[29] Peter Schwartz and James Ogilvy describe change from hierarchy to heterarchy as "the rule by one to several rules by some."[30]

Hierarchy is usually partnered with the Bible's androcentrism in which males are culturally entitled to patriarchal dominance and power. Yet within the Bible's transforming visions of the care, mystery, and holiness of God, Earth, and all living beings—non-human and human alike, insiders and outsiders—we find a world where hierarchy sometimes gives way to the emergence of the unexpected. When "the wolf dwells with the lamb" (Isa 11:6) and a servant of YHWH does not break "even a bruised reed" (Isa 42:3) hierarchy and androcentrism are eclipsed. Those who do justice are promised,

29. Reynolds and Craven, *Higher Education,* 21. Reynolds and Craven discuss "how we sometimes use the expression, 'I have my ducks in a row' as a metaphor for individual mastery or control. Interestingly, though not correctly, our figure of speech suggests belief that ducks flying overhead are being led by a head duck in charge of the formation. However, in a 1986 computer-generated model of coordinated animal motion using boids (generic simulated flocking creatures), Craig Reynolds demonstrated that the same results could be obtained if each boid autonomously follows simple local rules about where to fly with respect to the nearest animal. Flockmates steer to maintain three rules: separation to avoid crowding, alignment to the average heading of local flockmates, and cohesion related to the average position of local flockmates. Order emerges from these local rules; it is not dictated by a supreme commander or some hierarchical authority. It isn't even the intent of ducks to fly in a row (it is actually geese who fly in a v-shaped formation, though our colloquial expression about having 'ducks' in a row is popularly understood as described). There is no one duck at the head of a pyramid keeping the others in order. Rather, interactions between simple nonlinear behaviors of individuals produce emergent group behaviors. This kind of system is multi-agent and offers a metaphor for the global behavior of interacting autonomous agents. Though unpredictable, such behaviors are not random, as witness any tightly organized V-shaped row of birds overhead."

30 Schwartz and Ogilvy, *Emergent Paradigm,* 13.

> YHWH will guide you continually, and satisfy your needs in parched places, and make your bones strong; and you shall be like a watered garden, like a spring of water, whose waters never fail. Your ancient ruins shall be rebuilt; you shall raise up the foundations of many generations; you shall be called the repair-er of the breach, the restorer of streets to live in. (Isa 58:11–12)

In Third Isaiah all who serve YHWH—including foreigner and eu-nuch—are welcome in Elohim's house of prayer:

> All who keep the Sabbath, and do not profane it, and hold fast my covenant—these I will bring to my holy mountain, and make them joyful in my house of prayer; their burnt offerings and their sacrifices will be accepted on my altar; for my house shall be called a house of prayer for *all* people. (Isa 56:6d–7)

Those who honor the Sabbath "take delight in YHWH," feeding on the "heritage" of the ancestors (Isa 58:14).

Those who wish to exploit Earth have no trouble finding biblical texts like the following that legitimate hierarchy and dominion. Because YHWH had blessed the tribe of Joseph,

> Joshua said to the house of Joseph, to Ephraim and Manasseh, "You are indeed a numerous people, and have great power, you shall not have one lot only, but the hill country shall be yours, for though it is a forest, you shall clear it and possess it to its farthest borders; for you shall drive out the Canaanites, though they have chariots of iron, and though they are strong." (Josh 17:17–18)

In such instances divine blessing sanctions dominion and hierarchy, and ironically we call this taking of the land of others a "gift" from God. Displacement as divine right is a ruthless standard, even if there is no single explanation about how Israel acquired the land.

Memories of being Pharaoh's slaves in Egypt surface throughout the First Testament. Remembrance of God's presence with the people of Israel mitigates, but does not erase, the suffering acknowledged as part of life. Nor does Israel's slavery seem to sensitize them to the suffering of other people as slaves. "I am YHWH your Elohim who brought you out of the land of Egypt to be their slaves no more; I have broken the bars of your yoke and made you walk erect" (Lev 26:13).[31] Yet as Lev 25:44–46 (NRSV) makes clear, this promise was not extended to all in slavery:

> As for the male and female slaves whom you may have, it is from the nations around you that you may acquire male and female slaves. You may also acquire them from among the aliens residing with you, and from their families that are with you, who have been born in your land; and they may be your property. You may keep them as a possession for your children after you, for them to inherit as property. These you may treat as slaves, but as for your fellow Israelites, no one shall rule over the other with harshness.

The Bible is conflicted regarding restriction of blessings to community insiders only and openness to all. For instance, God tells Abraham, "I will bless those who bless you, and the one who curses you I will curse; and in you *all* the families of the earth shall be blessed" (Gen 12:3). Abraham, Sarah, and their descendants are blessed to be a blessing for *all* peoples. But by the post-exilic restoration of Ezra-Nehemiah, the practice of endogamy (marriage to community insiders) fosters separation. Blessings are for insiders only. Exogamy (marriage to community outsiders) and children of these marriages are expelled from the community of Israel without one word of concern for their well-being or survival (see Ezra 10 and Neh 13:23–27).[32] Alongside Ezra-Nehemiah, and possibly also dated to the post-exilic, the story of Ruth a faithful foreigner may takes shape. This Moabite woman is a model of *hesed* who deals kindly with grace and mercy to all in her story. Ruth integrates into the Jewish community twice through faithful marriage to Mahlon (1:4) and then Boaz (4:13), and is steadfast in her care for Mahlon, Naomi, and Boaz. From her descendants with Boaz, come David (4:22) and Jesus (Matt 1:5). Community that permits inclusion of all, legitimates this foreigner.

---

31. We subscribe to the position that Leviticus took shape across a long period of time and that this passage in the Holiness Code is likely written during the Babylonian exile on account of the reference in Lev 26:44 to being in "the land of their enemies."

32. Ezra's edict of community purity singles out marriage to foreign women as "breaking faith with God" and finds "hope" in the divorce of these women and expulsion of them and their children from the community (Ezra 10:2–3). Nehemiah's call for an oath that will put an end to intermarriage, which he describes as a "great evil" and a "treacherous act against God" (Neh 13:27). Nehemiah is concerned about Jewish daughters as well as Jewish sons who have married foreigners (Neh 13:25b).

Full welcome to God's community is also extended to the post-restoration foreigners (or proselytes) who join themselves to YHWH, yet fear exclusion saying, "YHWH will surely separate me" from the sacred community or like the eunuch who claims, "I am just a dry tree" (Isa 56:3). In such instances, acceptance of outsiders or those normally shunned, as well as community insiders are based on Elohim's acceptance of Sabbath worship and covenant observance (Isa 56:5), not nationality or sexuality. God says to all these persons, "I will give, in my house and within my walls, a monument and a name better than sons and daughters; I will give them an everlasting name that shall not be cut off" (Isa 56:5).[33]

In like manner, the two differing stories of how God created Earth community (Gen 1:1—2:4a; 2:4b—24)—the seven day story and the garden story—make evident that differing memories of Israel, especially those regarding mutuality and non-mutuality, acceptance and rejection, carry special importance in establishing foundational traditions. Located "in the beginning" (NRSV 1:1) or "when God began to create" (NJPS 1:1), these two stories reveal subtle Hebrew grammatical features that are lost in most English translations, that allow full inclusion to the active participation of all Earth.

Genesis 1, which is broad and cosmic in its scope, highlights surprising shared agency, voice, and a commonality of goodness among the interconnected parts of the cosmos. The *rûaḥ ʾĕlōhîm* (God's "breath," "wind," "spirit") sweeps over a dark, watery, expanse in Gen 1. Effortlessly and non-combatively, Elohim's first word brings forth light (1:3) and "causes to separate" (a *Hipʿil* imperfect causative verb, 1:4) light from darkness.[34] Repetitions of "then Elohim said," (1:3, 6, 9, 11, 14, 20, 24, 26, 29) give an impression that the successive acts of creation

33. Israel's Holocaust Memorial, *Yad Va Shem*, "A Monument and a Name" is taken from Isa 56:5.

34. Elohim does not create darkness in Gen 1. Darkness and the watery deep, *"tĕhôm"* are already present. Rashi points out that this is not creation out of nothing. God's creative word is also given prominence in Ps 33:6, 9 and 2 Esd 6:38. Genesis 1:3 brings forth light on the first day, even though it is the fourth day before lights are created in the dome of the sky to give light upon the earth (Gen 1:14—17). The martyred mother of seven sons assertion to her youngest child that he "look at the heaven and the earth and see everything that is in them, and recognize that God did not make them out of things that existed" is sometimes understood as *creatio ex nihilo* or more likely in our opinion as a reference to Elohim's use of unformed matter, "formlessness and chaos," in Gen 1:2.

come into being through the spoken word of God, but grammatical features of Hebrew nuance divine speech with active participation of various members of Earth community in a shared process of creation. Elohim delegates agency to the Firmament[35] in Gen 1:6 to separate waters from waters (see the *Hipʿil* m. s. participle *maḇdîl*, "separate").[36] On the second day, God says, "Let there be a Firmament in the midst of the water, and let it divide water from water" (Gen 1:6).[37]

Elohim then cues Earth (grammatically, a Hebrew feminine singular noun) to "cause to bring forth" (*taḏšēʾ*, a *Hipʿil* imperfect 3 f. s. verb)[38] vegetation and seed bearing trees (Gen 1:11), and Earth does so (Gen 1:12). Thus on the third day of creation, Earth participates in a series of consequent actions that initiate and ensure the cycle of life. At Elohim's instruction, Earth "causes to brings forth" (*dešeʿ*, 1:11, a *Hipʿil* imperfect, 3 f. s. verb) vegetation, plants seeding seed (*mazrîaʿ* 1:11, a *Hipʿil* participle m. s.), and fruit trees making fruit (Qal active participle m. s.). Literally, "Earth causes to sprout sprout[s] of plants" and fruit trees making fruit, so that life will continue (1:11). The cosmos participates in a symphony of creation. Sun and moon give light

35. Mary Jo Kaska first presented her case for non-human agency in creation indicated by the use of *Hipʿil* and jussives verbs in Gen 1 in a 2005 paper, "An Ecojustice Reading of Genesis 1:1–24a," during her doctoral studies in Hebrew Bible at Brite Divinity School. Her argument is contra Westermann, who says of Gen 1:24, "Let the earth bring forth," "The earth has part in the creation of the land animals just as it does in the creation of the plants" . . . "One should not press these differences. When P says "Let the earth bring forth" in v. 24, then that cannot mean a direct participation of the earth in the creation of the animals. . ." (*Genesis 1–11*, 142). On the *Hipʿil*, see Gesenius, *Hebrew Grammar*, 321 and van der Merwe, Naudé, Kroeze, *Biblical Hebrew Reference*, 86–90, which helpfully refers to Waltke and O'Connor §27 and Jouon-Muraoka §54.

36. Elohim's world Earth is created as ancient readers would have understood it from a Babylonian model, a three-storied universe composed of the firmament or sky/heaven, the land and seas, and what would later be understood as the under-world, Sheol in Hebrew, or Hades in Greek, the abode of the dead.

37. We capitalize Earth and those other non-human living beings in the story who have roles as subjects or agents in causative actions.

38. Waltke and O'Connor, *Biblical Hebrew Syntax*, devote chap. 27 to the *Hipʿil* Stem. Drawing upon the work of Ernst Jenni, they show that the *"Piel signifies to bring about a state, and the Hiphʿil, to cause an event"* (433). According to Jenni, *Hipʿils* "cause actively." We hold that in Gen 1, a special relationship exists between the principal subject, God, and the undersubjects of the actively caused actions: Firmament (vv. 6–7), Earth (v. 11), Vegetation (v. 11), Plants (v. 11), Fruit Trees (an exception that we will discuss later, v. 11), Lights (v. 14). Undersubjects are responsible for causing an event or action in the case of *Hipʿil* verbs (445).

and rule the day and night, while stars mark the seasons and years (Gen 1:14–17). To an ancient Israelite agrarian audience the celestial bodies are not G/god(s) that control humans—as in Babylonian belief—but luminaries that participate in the network of life upon which all life depends.

Thus in Gen 1, Elohim is like a conductor and an instrumentalist who both plays a part in a musical ensemble and calls forth the participation and entrance of other players. Just as Iona Brown conducted the Academy of St. Martin in the Field while playing her own part on the violin, Elohim in Gen 1 conducts and participates in creation. Firmament (1:4–7), Earth (mentioned 23 times in 1:1—2:4a), and Elohim each share roles in the score as prompted by Elohim who speaks or conducts in jussives, third person commands with a sense of desiring something of the subject:[39] "Let there be light" (1:3). "Let there be a Firmament in the midst of the waters that cause separation of waters from waters" (1:6). "Let the waters be gathered under the heaven and let the dry land appear" (1:9). "Let the earth cause to spout sprouts of green" (1:11). "Let there be Lights in the Firmament that cause separation between the day and the night, as signs for the season, the days, and the years (1:14)." "Let the waters swarm with (or teem forth) living beings (*nepeš ḥayyā*) and let the birds (literally and inclusively, 'all winged ones') fly" (1:20, 22). "Let the earth cause to bring forth living beings" (*nepeš ḥayyā* 1:24); and so Elohim made the living ones of the earth (*ḥayyat hāʾārĕṣ* 1:25).

As the last act of creation in Gen 1, Elohim creates humanity (*ʾādām*)—male and female—in the divine image (1:26-27; see also 5:1), and blesses them with five imperatives, "*Be fruitful* and *multiply*, and *fill the earth* and *subdue* it; and *dominate/have dominion* over the fish of the sea and over the birds of the air and over every living creeping [being] upon the earth" (1:28; cf. 9:1–2). Five imperatives addressed to the human couple spell out human dominion as a divine blessing of hierarchy (1:28). Five *Hipʿil* forms divinely delegate participatory causative actions resulting in the Firmament, the Earth, Lights sharing in Elohim's work of separation (Elohim causes the light to separate from the darkness, 1:4; the Firmament or Heaven causes the separation of the waters under the firmament from those above it, 1:7; Earth causes vegetation to bring forth of plants and fruit trees, 1:11a–12; Lights in the heavens

---

39. Gesenius, *Hebrew Grammar*, 321.

cause separation of night and day, 1:14–15; a greater light and a lesser light cause separation between light and darkness, 1:16–18).

Voluntative and jussive verbal forms, mentioned above, underscore Earth community's participation in Elohim's work of creation. The five scattered *Hipʿil* actions and the five concentrated imperatives generate tension in the plot and meaning of the first creation story. Reconciliation of "conflict that has no obvious solution," brings the story to a heterarchical-hierarchical impasse.[40] Two clashing ideas about relationship have been articulated. The first part of the story (1:1–25) asserts that non-human living beings of the Earth participate with Elohim and are blessed by Elohim to be fruitful and multiply and fill the waters (1:22), according to a heterarchical, networked model through which Elohim creates them with the ability to participate in bringing forth an orderly blessed universe (1:22). The second part of the story (1:26—2:4a) affirms that human living beings as Elohim's representatives, made in Elohim's own image, though not emergent from Earth or Waters (1:27), are blessed by Elohim to be fruitful and multiply and fill Earth (1:28).[41] This hierarchical, pyramid-like model, ordering those beneath them with God-given authority to subdue and have dominion is a conflict that will be intensified in the flood story.

Finishing heaven and Earth on the sixth day, Elohim saw that all creation was "very good" (1:31). Elohim rested on the seventh day, setting it apart from all other days, blessing it and making it holy (2:3, the third blessing in the story; cf. 1:22, 28). Terrence Fretheim comments that,

> This very temporal framework, a work/rest rhythm, inheres as a part of the created order of things. . . . When all the world rests on the Sabbath (a sign that all are in right relationship with the Creator—Exod 31:12–17), Elohim's created order will once again be complete, will be realized as at the beginning. . . . The divine act of blessing the Sabbath is an unspoken report of God's act of giving power and potentiality to a particular temporal order, in the sense that human honoring of the work-rest

---

40 40. See J. M. Powell, *How to Create Tension in the Plot.*

41. See Habel, *Earth Story in Genesis*, 45–47. "Human beings, unlike all living things, do not emanate from Earth as the logic of the story would seem to dictate, but are created by fiat of *Elohim* in council" (46).

rhythm has the capacity of deeply affecting life itself (as does its neglect). [42]

This restorative work/rest rhythm is essential for the well-being of the entire Earth community's needs, not only God and human beings (cf. Exod 20:8–11; 23:10–12). Sabbath (the seventh day), sabbatical (the seventh year), and jubilee (the fiftieth year) are reminders that all land, time, crops, and livestock belong to God (Lev 25:1–55). The people of Israel are aliens, tenants, and servants of YHWH, free yet bound to divine service by God. In theory, if not in practice, all leases, loans, sales, and produce belong to God. There is no evidence that jubilee was ever carried out, but practice of a sabbatic year is mentioned in 1 Macc 6:49, 53. Covenant obligations attest, at least in principle, to limits in human dominion over creation.

Genesis 2:4b—3:24, a second creation story, is more focused on human life in a particular garden. The narrative opens in an arid world, because YHWH Elohim has not yet caused rain and never does within this story (Gen 2:5; this verse uses the tetragrammaton—YHWH—for the first time in the Bible).[43] When the mist goes up from Earth and saturates it, YHWH Elohim is able to fashion the human (*hā ʾādām*) from the soil of the ground (*hā ʾădāmā*), a Hebrew pun based on the similarities of the sounds of these otherwise unrelated words) blowing into its nostrils the breath of life that makes it a "living being" (*nepeš ḥayyā* Gen 2:7), the same Hebrew phrase first used for the life teeming from the waters in Gen 1:20. Most English translations (e.g., NAB, NIV, NKJV, NJB, NJPS, and RSV) use "living being," (*nepeš ḥayyā*) for the first human (Gen 2:7) and "living creatures" or "animals" for the same *nepeš ḥayyā*(Gen 1:20, 24) that refer to non-human life, thus creating a distinction not found in the Hebrew text between human "beings" and non-human "creatures." We have translated *nepeš ḥayyā* identically throughout Genesis in reference to human and non-human "living beings," since it is the same Hebrew expression and accents parity of identity.[44] Thus *hā ʾādām*, marine life, and life forms on the land bear a

---

42. Fretheim, "Genesis," 346–47.

43. YHWH is the name for God revealed to Moses in the burning bush story (Exod 6:2–3, 6–8).

44. A related term "living of earth" (*hayyat hāʾārĕs*) occurs five times, in Gen 1:25, 30; 9:2, 10 (twice). It is often translated as "animals of the earth" (NRSV), "beasts of the earth" (NKJV), and "wild animals" (NIV, NAB).

common description as "living beings" (see also Gen 1:21, 24, 30; 2:19; 9:10). YHWH Elohim plants a garden and places the human in it, "to serve it and to watch over it" (*lĕʿobdāh ûlĕšomrāh*, Gen 2:15). Jewish environmentalists use this phrase "to serve/work/till it and watch over/ protect/tend it" as a trigger to set into motion actions on behalf of ecojustice.[45] Concerned that it is not good for the human to be alone and wanting to make an *ʿēzer kĕnegdô* ("g"),[46] YHWH Elohim shapes more *nepeshayyā* from the soil (*hā ʾăḏāmā*), specifically "the living of the fields" and the "winged ones in the sky," and brings them to the human who gives names to all these beings (Gen 2:19). When "none is found" (Gen 2:20) a suitable helper or partner for the human living being, YHWH Elohim causes a deep sleep to fall upon this first human and creates in a different way. Taking one of its sides, not soil, YHWH Elohim fashions a woman (Gen 2:21). YHWH Elohim brings her to the first human, who in recognizing his partner finds voice to speak in sentences for the first time, saying, "This at last is bone of my bone and flesh of my flesh, this one will be called woman (*ʾiššā*), for from a man (*ʾîš*, another pun in Hebrew based of the sound of gendered endings of the same noun) this has been taken" (Gen 2:23). With this second attempt, YHWH Elohim is successful in making a partner corresponding (*kĕnegdô*) for the first with whom it is possible to "become one flesh" (Gen 2:24), "naked and unashamed" (Gen 2:25).

After Genesis 3 tells more of the story about being in and outside of the garden (Gen 3:1–24) comes the first usage of the word "sin" (Gen 4:7), Cain's murder of Abel (Gen 4:1–16), the growth of culture (Gen 4:17–26), and the ten generations from Adam to Noah (Gen 5:1–32). Death, burdensome work, enmity between the *nepeshayyā*, including a murder in which the victim's blood has voice to cry out to YHWH Elohim from the soil (*hā ʾăḏāmā*, Gen 4:10–11) mark and mar life. By Gen 6:5–7, corruption not goodness has spread throughout creation. This state of transgression results in YHWH's saying, "I will blot out from the face of the earth *hā ʾāḏām* I have created—*hā ʾāḏām* together with the beasts (*bĕhēmā*) and creeping ones, birds of the air—for I am

45. See *To Till and To Tend: A Guide to Jewish Environmental Study and Action*, which is available online http://www.coejl.org/~coejlor/resources/bib_basic.php with other resources. Jewish environmentalists transliterate this phrase as "*l'ovdah ul'shomra*" and translate it variously, "to serve/work/till it and watch over/protect/tend it." There is no one fixed translation for this important phrase.

46. Trible, *Rhetoric of Sexuality*, 88–94.

sorry that I have made them" (Gen 6:7). Such is the effect, we argue, of the "blessing" of *hā ʾāḏām*, "Be fruitful and multiply and fill the earth and subdue it, have dominion/domination over the birds of the air and over every living being that moves upon the earth" (Gen 1:28).

The Hebrew verb *kbš*, pronounced "kabash" in its lexical form, is used a total of fifteen times in the Masoretic Text (MT of the Hebrew Bible), including Gen 1:28, and is translated variously as "subdue," "subject," "assault," or "ravish." It is likely the source of the contemporary expression, "to put the kibosh on," as in "to dispose of finally, finish off."[47] Six times *kbš* refers to "subjugation" of the land and its people (Num 32:22, 29; Josh 18:1; 2 Sam 8:11; 1 Chr 22:18; 2 Chr 28:10) and four times to "subjugation" of slaves and enemies (Jer 34:11 [2x], 16; Zech 9:15). The remaining four uses make varying claims: in Mic 7:19, God will "stomp out" (*kbš*) "our iniquities and cast all our sins into the depths of the sea"; in Esth 7:8, King Ahasuerus confronts Haman's actions with the question, "Will he even 'assault' (*kbš*) the queen in my presence, in my own house?" (*Kbš*) is used twice in Neh 5:5, the second occurrence suggesting sexual assault.

In the resettlement of Yehud following the Babylonian exile, oppressed Yehudites take their complaint to their governor, Nehemiah: "Our flesh is the same as that of our kindred; our children are the same as their children; and yet we are 'forcing' (*kbš*) our sons and daughters to be slaves, and some of our daughters have been 'ravished' (*kbš*); we are powerless, and our fields and vineyards now belong to others" (Neh 5:5). "Subdue" implies hierarchal entitlement to control, with the possibility of obliteration (Mic 7:19). The uses of the verb *kbš* across the canon are the antithesis of relationships that value intrinsic worth, mutual custodianship, or the emergent networked order of heterarchy.

The eighteen uses of *rdh*, unlike the two in Gen 1:26 and 28 that depict ruling over non-human living-being, uniformly depict people ruling over people, either collectively or individually. *Rdh* refers to nations ruling over enemy nations (Lev 26:17; Num 24:19; Isa 14:2, 6; Ezek 29:15; Ps 68:28; Neh 9:28). *Rdh* also depicts Israel's kings ruling over other nations (1 Kgs 4:24 = 5:4; Pss 72:8; 110:2), shepherds (=kings) of Israel ruling Israel with undue harshness (Ezek 34:4), priests ruling unjustly (Jer 5:31); owners' ruling over slaves (Lev 25:43, 46, 53; 1 Kgs

---

47. "Cabash," *Oxford English Dictionary Online,* 2nd ed. Oxford University Press, 1989. Etymology, "Origin obscure. It has been stated to be Yiddish or Anglo-Hebraic."

9:23), and overseers' ruling over workers (1 Kgs 5:16–30; 2 Chr 8:10).[48] In many instances, "rule by humiliation" is implied. In all cases hierarchy dominates.

Context makes some of these uses of *rdh* exceedingly violent. The tribe of Benjamin "rules" over a victory parade (Ps 68:28, *rdh*) in which Israel's warriors return with enough enemy blood to bathe their feet and satisfy their dogs (Ps 68:23). In Ps 110:2 *rdh* appears in a prayer for the installation of a new king that includes the violent demise of unspecified "enemies":

> YHWH says to my lord,
> "Sit at my right hand
> until I make your enemies your footstool."
> YHWH sends out from Zion
> your mighty scepter.
> Rule (*rdh*) in the midst of your foes.

"My lord" in Ps 110:1 is presumably the king whose victory is graphically portrayed in Ps 110:5–6:

> The Lord is at your right hand;
> he will shatter kings on the day of his wrath.
> He will execute judgment among the nations,
> filling them with corpses;
> he will shatter heads over the wide earth.

Psalm 72, is a prayer for an ideal, righteous king, assigned by the superscription to Solomon, who will deliver the downtrodden and judge with God-given justice and righteousness. This psalm has been employed in the defense of the benevolence of dominion theology. "May he rule (*rdh*) from sea to sea, and from the river to the ends of the Earth" (Ps 72:8). Habel counters,

> The focus of the Genesis text [Gen 1:28] lies on the power of human beings over nature. The thrust remains anthropocentric. Moreover, to soften the force of the verb, 'rule' to mean 'take care of' does not follow from the text of Ps 72. When the verb for 'rule' does appear in Ps 72:8, it refers explicitly to ruling over

---

48. Two uses of the same verbal root in Judg 14:9 refer to Samson scraping honey from the carcass of a lion. A use of *rdh* in Joel 4:13 is "tread." MT numbers the verses differently; 1 Kgs 5:4 is 4:24 in NRSV, 1 Kgs 5:30 is 5:16 in NRSV.

a domain in which all the conquered foes have been forced to
lick the dust [Ps 72:8]. This is hardly an image of caring![49]

To summarize, none of the uses of "have dominion, rule" (*rdh*) are
consistent with the visions of justice and shalom found elsewhere in
the Hebrew Bible. Those who have dominion are not "repairers of the
breach" (Isa 58:12) or doers of righteousness. All of the "rule over" texts
carry deprivation or physical harm to those dominated. Pairing *kbš*
and *rdh* as in Gen 1:28, further intensifies the non-benevolent power
over creation that humans have been given by God. "The plain sense
of the text is that this 'first commandment' is issued to both female and
male."[50] This is God's doing, and one would hope that rather than trying
to rescue these terms *kbš* and *rdh* as benevolent, greater attention to
God's repairing activity might be examined. When something does not
fulfill its purpose, the text of Gen 2 shows an alternative way: repair the
misfired action. The "suitable partner" (2:18) for the first living being
is a woman, not the animals (God's first attempt). The heart of God
can change. The negative overtones of *rdh* ("have dominion/dominate")
and *kbš* ("subdue"), especially in Gen 1:28, introduce conflict and division into the created order and foreshadow the wickedness, corruption,
and violence that subsequently fills Earth in the time of Noah and his
unnamed wife, three sons (Shem, Ham, and Japeth) and their unnamed
wives.

The prologue to the Yahwist flood story (Gen 6:5–8) opens with
YHWH's considered punishment of human sinfulness and then follows
with the Priestly introduction to the same story (Gen 6:9-22), replete
with the details of the building of the ark.

> YHWH saw that the wickedness of *hā 'ādām* was great in the
> earth, and that every inclination of the thoughts of their hearts
> was only evil continually. And YHWH was sorry to have made
> *hā 'ādām* on the earth and sick at heart. So YHWH said, "I will
> blot out from the earth *hā 'ādām* I have created—*hā 'ādām* to-
> gether with animals and creeping ones and birds of the air—for
> I am sorry that I have made them." But Noah found favor in the
> sight of YHWH. (Gen 6:5–8)

---

49. Habel, *Readings from the Perspective of Earth*, 31.

50. Eskenazi, "Genesis Notes," 8.

> Now the earth was corrupt in Elohim's sight, and the earth was
> filled with violence. And Elohim saw that the earth was corrupt;
> for all flesh had corrupted its ways upon the earth. And Elohim
> said to Noah, "I have determined to make an end of all flesh, for
> the earth is filled with violence because of them: I am going to
> destroy them along with the earth (Gen 6:11–13).

God's destructive way of "repair" results in an undoing of creation.
According to the Yahwist or J author it rained forty days and forty
nights upon the earth (Gen 7:12), with swelling water for five months.
According to the Priestly or P author (Gen 7:24), as the ark rose high
above the earth on account of the rising waters (Gen 7:17–20), "All flesh
perished that moved on the earth" including "all human beings" (Gen
7:21). All with "the breath of life in its nostrils died" (Gen 7:22). The
destructive results are very similar. God is a destroying God who saves
only one family.

When Noah and family exit the ark only three of the five commands of Gen 1:28 are repeated: "be fruitful," "multiply," and "fill" Earth
(9:1). The commands of 1:28 to "have dominion over" (*rdh*) and "sub-
due/tread upon" (*kbš*) are replaced with what could be interpreted as
effects.

> Elohim blessed Noah and his sons, and said to them, "Be fruit-
> ful and multiply, and fill the earth. *The fear* (*môraʾ*) *of you* and
> *the terror* (*ḥat*) *of you* will be upon all the living of the Earth
> (*köl-ḥayyat hāʾāreṣ*), and on every bird of the air, on every thing
> that creeps on the ground, and on all the fish of the sea; into
> your hand they are given. Every creeping one that lives, shall be
> food for you; and just as I gave you the green plants, I give you
> everything (for food)." (Gen 9:1–3)

Living beings are in the hands of Noah and his sons, and now these
living beings find those hands fearful and terrifying. They are food for
humans. Their blood, but not their lives, is protected.

Elohim prohibits the consumption of any living-being's blood, and
human or non-human murder of other humans made in the divine image (cf. Gen 1:27; 9:4–6).

> Only you shall not eat flesh with its life, that is, its blood. From
> your own lifeblood I will surely require a reckoning: from every
> living (being) I will require it and from [literally] *ʾhā ʾādām'*
> from the hand of a man—his brother, I will require a reckoning

for *nepeš hā ʾāḏām*. The shedder of the blood of a human, by
a human shall that person's blood be shed for in the image of
Elohim, *hā ʾāḏām* was made. (Gen 9:4–6)

Genesis 9:7 echoes the blessing of 1:28, again omitting *kbš* and *rdh*:
"And you, be fruitful and multiply, teem on the earth and multiply in it"
(9:7; cf. also 9:1).[51]

With Noah and his sons, all living beings, and all future generations, Elohim makes a new covenant. The wife and three daughters-in-
law of Noah are not explicitly mentioned, though they must be included
because of their role in bearing future generations. Women exist anony-
mously in this post-flood, androcentric, hierarchical world. A bow in
the sky, aimed at the heavens, memorializes Elohim's promise to never
again destroy all life with a flood:

> Then Elohim said to Noah and his sons with him, "As for me, I
> am establishing my covenant with you and your seed after you,
> and with every living being (cf. Gen 1:20, 21, 24) that is with
> you, the winged ones, the beasts, and every living [being] of the
> earth with you, as many as came out of the ark. I establish my
> covenant with you that never again shall all flesh be cut off by
> the waters of a flood and never again shall there be a flood to
> destroy the earth." (Gen 9:8–11)

This new covenant, entirely hierarchical in character, does very little for
women other than make them procreators. The other living beings do
not benefit much from now knowing "fear" and "dread" of Noah and
his sons (Gen 9:2).

Human dominion/domination in Gen 6–9 does not result in mutual custodianship. Dominion is clearly not the solution. Relationships
of another sort, as yet untold are necessary. In the post-diluvian setting,
unlike that of the seven day story in which male and female share the
image of God (Gen 1:27), human females here are simply overlooked.
Male humans and all other living beings belong to the Noachic covenant by virtue of meriting God's attention. Human females belong by
virtue of being unmentioned mates of Noah and his sons. Genesis 6–9
is not the story from which an integrative, non-hierarchical alternative
story emerges. A hermeneutic of consciousness allows readers of both
flood stories—the Yahwist and the Priestly—to see the limiting nature

---

51. "Be fruitful and multiply" is repeated recursively (with variations) in Gen 1:22
and 1:28 and again in Gen 9:1 and 9:7.

of male superiority over female and consider fear and terror as a metaphor for human subordination of "every living [being] on Earth, on all the winged ones in the sky, on all that creeps on the ground, and upon all the fish of the sea" (Gen 9:2a). The Priestly adds, "they are placed in your (m. p.) hands" (Gen 9:2b).

Beyond Genesis, the verb "to create" appears in a variety of contexts. God is always the creator, though often conceived differently than the classic Genesis texts. For instance, Isa 45:7 claims that YHWH makes everything even darkness and evil:[52] "I form light and create darkness making shalom and creating evil. I am YHWH, maker of all these." Psalm 104:29–30 explains YHWH's control over *all* creation, "Hide your face, they are terrified, take away their breath, they perish and turn again into dust; send back your breath, they are created and you renew the face of earth."

The Wisdom of Solomon, also an Apocryphal/Deuterocanonical book, took its shape in Alexandrian Judaism as an attempt to put Hebrew thought in Greek garb. Wisdom contains repeated exhortations to depend upon and follow wisdom's ways (*ḥokmā* in Hebrew; *sophia* in Greek). God does not make death according to this way of thinking, but creates all things that they might exist in wholesomeness, with "no destructive poison in them" (Wis 1:14). Wisdom builds upon and goes beyond Gen 1 in many ways including an ascription of goodness to all creation and in linking righteousness with immortality for the very first time (Wis 1:15). God not only makes humanity in the divine image (cf. Gen 1:26–27), but God also creates humans for incorruption (Wis 2:23). The Most High promises that the righteous will live forever (Wis 5:15) and that God "will arm all creation to repel" enemies of the divine (Wis 5:17). "Creation" will fight with God against God's "frenzied foes" (Wis 5:20). This agency and networking of creation for the purpose of attack is reminiscent of the assignment of roles to various parts of creation in Gen 1 with the resultant agency shared with non-human beings.

Wisdom is personified as God's companion during creation, "I will tell you what Sophia is and how she came to be, and I will hide no

---

52. In Gen 1:3–5, God does not create darkness; it is simply there. God creates the light, sees that is good, separates it from the darkness, and names the light Day, and the darkness Night. In Isa 45:7, God forms light and creates darkness; makes weal and creates woe. YHWH is maker of all aspects of the natural world and all events of human history. See also Sir 39:16–35 in the Apocryphal/Deuterocanonical books where destructive forces are created for God's vengeance.

secrets from you. But I will trace her course from the beginning of creation, and make knowledge of her clear, and I will not pass by the truth" (Wis 6:22). Solomon's prayer (Wis 9:1–18) praises God for humankind's "dominion over" God's creatures (Wis 9:2), speaks of Wisdom who "sits by your [God's] throne" (Wis 9:4), who was "present" when God made the world (Wis 9:9), asking that Wisdom "may labor" at God's side (Wis 9:10) to guide and guard Solomon (Wis 9:12). No one but Wisdom knows the ways of God; it is she who "saves" (Wis 9:18). The line between God and Wisdom is blurred by this unsurpassed idealization of Woman Wisdom. Wisdom "protected the first-formed father of the world when he alone had been created" (Wis 10:1), "delivering him from his transgression" (10:1), and giving him strength to "rule all things" (10:2). Wisdom's saving power was also with the unrighteous Cain (Wis 10:3; cf. Gen 4:1–16), and seven other righteous men, including though unnamed in Wisdom, Noah (Wis 10:4; cf. Gen 5:28—9:29), Abraham (Wis 10:5: cf. esp. Gen 22), Lot (Wis 10:6–8; cf. Gen 19:23–26), Jacob (Wis 9–12; cf. Gen 25:19—49:33, esp. Gen 28), Joseph (Wis 10:13–14; cf. Gen 39; 41:39–47), and the holy prophet Moses (Wis 11:1) who led the "holy" (Wis 10:15, 17) and "righteous" (Wis 10:20) people.

Revisionist in nature, this historical catalogue (Wis 10:1–11:4) does not mention one righteous woman, although Wis 11:23 says God is "merciful to all" and Wis 12:1 makes the claim that God's "immortal spirit is in all things." Wisdom 11:17–18 states that God "created the world out of formless matter" (cf. Gen 1:2), adding mention of "newly-created unknown beasts full of rage." Wisdom 13:3, 5 hail God as the "author" and "creator" of "beauty." Even heathen idols, though thoroughly ridiculed as worthless, are "part of what God created" (Wis 14:11). Creation "serves" God who "punishes the unrighteous" (Wis 16:24). "For the whole creation in its nature was fashioned anew, complying with your [God's] commands, so that your children might be kept unharmed" (19:6). In Wisdom of Solomon, God is unquestionably creator of all. The new insights in this book are immortality of the righteous (hinted at, but undeveloped in 2 Macc 7 and Dan 12; more fully developed in 2 Esd 2:45; 7:113; 119 and 4 Macc 9:22; 14:5; 16:13; 17:12) and the information that Wisdom, a female, has been God's close agent from the beginning to the present. God, who is now assumed male, becomes "Father" of our fathers, such as was not done in the Genesis accounts of creation.[53]

Creation is associated with the number seven (cf. Gen 1:1—2:4a) and likened to an inspiring dance for those facing persecution in 4 Macc 14:7, "O most holy seven, brothers in harmony! For just as the seven days of creation move in choral dance around godly faith, so these youths, forming a chorus, encircled the seven-fold fear of tortures and dissolved it." Their mother watches each son die, knowing that their souls are destined for immortality and her actions have been motivate on account of religion (4 Macc 16:13; cf. 7:3; 14:6; 18:23 on immortality).

At the conclusion of Judith's chapter long prayer before undertaking her mission against Holofernes and the Assyrians, this wise, beautiful widow states that God's "strength does not depend on numbers" nor God's "might on the powerful" (Jdt 9:11). Twice she prays that her "deceitful words" (Jdt 9:10, 13) will overcome those who have planned cruelty against the Temple and covenant (9:10). Addressing God with ten titles (Jdt 9:11–14), the last two of which specifically point to God as creator, she concludes, "You are the God of the lowly, helper of the oppressed; upholder of the weak, protector of the forsaken, savior of those without hope. Please, please, God of my father, God of the heritage of Israel, Lord of heaven and earth, Creator of the waters, King of all your creation, hear my prayer!" Actually, the last three titles offer praise of "the Lord of heaven and earth, Creator of the waters, and King of all your creation." Belief in God's protection of those without resources grounds Judith's petition, "Let your whole nation and every tribe know and understand that you are God, the God of all power and might, and that there is no other who protects the people of Israel but you alone (Jdt 9:14).

In Judith 13:11, when Judith returns Home from the enemy camp after decapitating Holofernes, she shows the enemy general's head to the people (Jdt 13:15–16), and the Bethulians with one accord bless God (Jdt 13:17). Then Uzziah, one the leaders of the town of Bethulia, praises Judith and God the creator, saying, "O daughter, you are blessed by the Most High God above all other women on earth; and blessed be the Lord God, who created the heavens and the earth, who has guided you to cut off the head of the leader of our enemies" (Jdt 14:18). Judith sings a "new song" (Jdt 16:1, 13) to God their creator

53. See Wis 2:16; 9:1, 12; 10:1; 11:10; 12:6, 21; 14:3, 15; 18:6, 9, 22, 24.

"who spoke, and they were made. You sent forth your spirit, and it formed them; there is none who can resist your voice. . . . To those who fear you, you show mercy" (16:14–15). Memory of Judith's actions and beliefs produces a community in which, "No one ever again spread terror among the Israelites during the lifetime of Judith, or for a long time after her death" (Jdt 16:25).

Ben Sira, or Jesus son of Eleazar son of Sirach of Jerusalem (Sir 50:27), sage, traveler (Sir 34:12–13), and teacher (Sir 24:30–34; 33:16–18), believed that Wisdom was created by God (Sir 1:9) "before all things" (Sir 1:4). He looked to Israel's past to support his belief in the superiority of Jewish beliefs to Greek philosophy. His book, like Proverbs, opens with praise of Wisdom includes striking tree similes that "her branches are long life" (Sir 1:20), and that safe shelter is found for children who lodges under her boughs" (Sir 14:26). Only Adam's creation is described (Sir 40:1; 49:16), though Eve, nameless in the text, is implicitly held at fault for the first sin and human death in the first biblical reinterpretation of this sort: "From a woman sin had its beginning, and because of her we all die" (Sir 25:24). God is addressed "father" (Sir 23:1, 4; 51:10) as in Wisdom of Solomon, and only men make Sirach's listing of Jewish heroes from Enoch to Simon (Sir 41–50). Praise of the famous ancestors is praise of human males alone (Sir 41–50). A benediction thought to be the inspiration for the hymn "Now Thank We All Our God" closes Ben Sira's listing of famous men (Sir 50:22–24).

The biblical legacy of creation is impressively and richly diverse. The texts we have sampled show a plurality of ideas about the mysterious unpredictability of God's agency, both splendid and disappointing. Human agency—female and male—is unexpectedly mutual at times but more frequently hierarchical, with men in control. Certain gynocentric (women-centered) stories reverse this norm, such as the courageous Hebrew mother who encourages each of her seven martyred sons as they face torture and death (4 Macc 8:1—14:10; 2 Macc 7:1–42), who is far more rational than the Greek king (2 Macc 7:40; 4 Macc 14:11–17: and boldly jumps into the fire rather than be defiled by a Greek touching her body (4 Macc 17:1). Also of this sort is the story of a pious widow, Judith, who is more concerned about prayer and being on God's side than making an alliance with the town leaders, who prays twice that God make her a good liar (Jdt 9:10; 13), chops off the enemy general's head (Jdt 13:8), and refuses to remarry

(Jdt 16:22). The agency of non-human beings in the First Testament and Apocryphal/Deuterocanonical Books is surprisingly frequent, from the very first chapter of Genesis to familiar Psalms, certain texts clearly envision power as the domain of non-human beings. Earth is a living organism who mourns (Jer 12:4) and swallows a whole family alive (Num 16:32–33). God can hear the voice of Cain's brother's blood crying out from the ground (Gen 4:10), and Earth sings praise to the divine name (Ps 96:1).

God's concerns are restricted and non-restricted, sometimes favoring Israel, other times open to all peoples. God frees Israel from slavery, but never destroys the practice of slavery, allowing people of other nations to be enslaved by Israelites. Hierarchy and heterarchy, mutuality and non-mutuality, community insiders and outsiders, androcentrism, patriarchy, and gynocentrism—all find expression in these texts. It is as if the Bible says in its wisdom, "Look to me for how the story can go wrong" even as it proclaims, "O sing to YHWH a new song; sing to YHWH, all the earth" (Ps 96:1).[54]

In order to find a new story, we must "sing a new song" of the Earth community—non-human and human—together across disciplines, including insights from scientist and theologian, student of sacred texts and philosopher, economist and politician, environmentalist and parent raising children, business leader and clergy of all faiths, farmer and animal rescuer, believer and non-believer alike. *All* Earth and heaven, winged-ones and fish of the sea must find full welcome; *none* should fear exclusion from the sacred community where all must commit to respect for each other.

In this essay, we have tried to bring to consciousness some of what creation bequeaths to us in the First Testament and the Apocryphal/ Deuterocanonical Books. Our new story has to have room for what we know consciously as well as for thoughts, dreams, vision, and imagination, born in the unconscious. Creation happens in that place of darkness where God hovers over all potentiality (cf. Gen 1:1). Bateson helps

---

54. In addition, on "sing a new song," see Pss 33:3; 40:3; 98:1; 144:1; 149:1. Stuhlmueller claims that the phrase "new song" occurs only in exilic and postexilic hymns where what is "new" may include "literary, a new role is given to ancient hymns; or pastoral, a new deliverance by God; or ritual, a spontaneous shout or song of the people; or best of all, theological, in that God's redemptive acts are actualized in their full effect within a new generation of Israelites"

us comprehend that in unconscious thought map and territory are the same, whereas conscious thought deals only with the map.[55]

The unconscious is both a source of thought and a repository for it. It is, as Bateson suggests, the source of our direct experience of ourselves and our world. It is where intuition and information are processed. Unconscious thought sees and hears *new* things in *new* ways, with room for surprises, seemingly random connections, and the emergence of ideas that form themselves into new relationships. So in the end, we want to encourage practice of both a hermeneutic of conscious thought about what the Bible says regarding creation, as well as practice of a hermeneutic of unconsciousness that relies upon an inner sense of resonance and creativity to shape a "new story" (or "song") that we will recognize in its unintended disclosure of the biblical legacy of creation, a new way of understanding the work of creation, and a new appreciation of the beauty of creation. Or as Berry says, "The fulfillment of the Earth community is to be caught up in the grandeur of existence itself and in admiration of those mysterious powers whence all this has emerged."[56]

Bibliography

Bateson, Gregory. *Mind and Nature: A Necessary Unity.* New York: Hampton, 2002.

Berry, Thomas. *Evening Thoughts: Reflecting on Earth as Sacred Community.* San Francisco: Sierra Club Books, 2006.

———. *The Great Work: Our Way into the Future.* New York: Bell Tower, 1999.

Brueggemann, Walter. "That the World May Be Redescribed." *Interpretation* 56 (2002) 359–67.

Craven, Toni. *The Book of Psalms.* A Michael Glazier Book. Collegeville, MN: Liturgical, 1992.

Davies, Philip R., and John Rogerson. *The Old Testament World.* 2nd ed. Louisville: Westminster John Knox, 2005.

Eskenazi, Tamara Cohn. "Genesis Notes." In *The Torah: A Women's Commentary,* edited by Tamara Cohn Eskenazi. New York: URJ Press and Women of Reform Judaism, 2008.

Fretheim, Terrence E. "The Book of Genesis." In *The New Interpreter's Bible,* vol. 1, edited by Leander E. Keck et al., 320–674. Nashville: Abingdon, 1994.

Gesenius, H. F. W. *Gesenius' Hebrew Grammar.* 2nd ed. Oxford: Oxford University Press, 1910.

---

55. Bateson, *Mind and Nature.* Also, see Reynolds and Craven, *Higher Education Reconceived,* 40–41.

56. Berry, *The Great Work,* xi.

Habel, Norman C., editor. *The Earth Story in the Psalms and the Prophets*. Sheffield, UK: Sheffield Academic, 2000.

———. "Geophany: The Earth Story in Genesis 1." *The Earth Story in Genesis*, edited by Norman C. Habel and Shirley Wurst. Sheffield, UK: Sheffield Academic, 2000.

———, editor. *Readings from the Perspective of Earth*. Sheffield, UK: Sheffield, Academic, 2000.

Habel, Norman C., and Peter Trudinger. *Exploring Ecological Hermeneutics*. Symposium Series 46. Atlanta: Society of Biblical Literature, 2008.

Habel, Norman C., and Shirley Wurst, editors. *The Earth Story in Genesis*. Sheffield UK: Sheffield Academic, 2000.

Hasel, Gerhard F. "Sabbath." In *The Anchor Bible Dictionary*. 6 vols. Edited by David Noel Freedman, 849–56. New York: Doubleday, 1992.

Hayes, Katherine M. *"The Earth Mourns": Prophetic Metaphor and Oral Aesthetic*. SBL Academia Biblica 8. Boston: Brill, 2002.

Heschel, Abraham Joshua. *The Sabbath: Its Meaning for Modern Man*. New York: Farrar Straus & Giroux, 1951.

Knierim, Rolf P. "Cosmos and History in Israel's Theology." *HBT* 3 (1981) 59–123.

Kugel, James L. "Topics in the History of the Spirituality of the Psalms." In *Jewish Spirituality: From the Bible Through the Middle Ages*, edited by Arthur Green, 113–43. New York: Crossroad, 1986.

Levenson, Jon D. "The Jerusalem Temple in Devotional and Visionary Experience." In *Jewish Spirituality from the Bible through the Middle Ages*, edited by Arthur Green, 32–59. New York: Crossroad, 1986.

Powell, J. M. "How to Create Tension in the Plot." Online: http://webcache. googleusercontent.com/search?q=cache:GhzHGxn9zFUJ:files.meetup. com/167930/How%2520to%2520Create%2520Tension%2520in%2520the%25 20Plot.doc+Creating+tension+in+plot&cd=1&hl=en&ct=clnk&gl=us&client= safari.

Reynolds, Sherrie, and Toni Craven. *Higher Education Reconceived: A Geography of Change*. Fort Worth, TX: TCU Press, 2009.

Sarna, Nahum M. *The JPS Torah Commentary, Genesis*. Philadelphia: Jewish Publication Society, 1989.

Schottroff, Luise. "The Creation Narrative: Genesis 1.1—2.4a." In *A Feminist Companion to Genesis*, edited by Athalya Brenner. Feminist Companion to the Bible 1. Sheffield, UK: Sheffield Academic, 1993.

Schwartz, Peter, and James Ogilvy. *The Emergent Paradigm: Changing Patterns of Thought and Belief. VALS Report No. 7*. Menlo Park, CA: Values and Lifestyles Program, 1979.

Simon, Uriel. *Jonah: The Traditional Hebrew Text with the New JPS Translation*. Translated by Lenn J. Schramm. Philadelphia: Jewish Publication Society, 1999.

Stuhlmueller, Carroll. *Psalms 2*. Old Testament Message 22. Wilmington, DE: Michael Glazier, 1983.

To Till and To Tend: A Guide to Jewish Environmental Study and Action. New York: Coalition of the Environment and Jewish Life, 1994.

Trible, Phyllis. *God and the Rhetoric of Sexuality*. Philadelphia: Fortress, 1985.

van der Merwe, Christo H. J., et al. *A Biblical Hebrew Reference Grammar*. Biblical Languages: Hebrew 3. Sheffield, UK: Sheffield Academic, 2000.

Von Rad, Gerhard. *Genesis: A Commentary.* Translated by John H. Marks. Philadelphia: Westminster, 1972.

Waltke, Bruce K., and M. O'Connor. *An Introduction to Biblical Hebrew Syntax.* Winona Lake, IN: Eisenbrauns, 1990.

Westermann, Claus. *Genesis 1–11: A Commentary.* Translated by John J. Scullion. Minneapolis: Augsburg, 1984.

Zevit, Ziony. *The Religions of Ancient Israel: A Synthesis of Parallactic Approaches.* New York: Continuum, 2001.

3

Spiritual Practice and Sustainability:
Resources from Early Christian Monasticism

John O'Keefe

Monastic Bodies

WHEN EARLY CHRISTIAN ASCETICS WENT OUT INTO THE DESERTS OF Egypt and Syria to begin their training, they were enacting with their bodies the spiritual transformation that they hoped to achieve. The classic example is St. Antony, who, after years of rigorous asceticism finally emerged from seclusion glowing and radiant. Unlike those who had spent their lives in less rigorous pursuits and eating their fill, Antony presented to observers a man who was spiritually fit, full of a life and vigor unavailable to those living more sated lives in towns and cities. According to Athanasius in *The Life of Antony*, Antony spent "nearly twenty years" pursuing the ascetical life. During that time his reputation grew considerably, though no one had seen him. Finally, because they desired to follow his way of life "some friends came and tore down and forcefully removed the fortress door" that had ensured his seclusion. "Antony came forth as though from some shrine, having been led into divine mysteries and inspired by God." What is most remarkable is that "his body had maintained its former condition, neither fat from lack of exercise, nor emaciated from fasting and combat with demons." He had become a heavenly man: "the state of his soul was one of purity, for it was not constricted by grief, nor relaxed by pleasure, nor affected by either laughter or dejection. From this point and so transformed, Antony began a ministry of healing and preaching.[1]

Those who study this literature know better than I do that the ambition of early Christian monasticism was more than to enact literally Jesus' moral exhortation to the rich young man to go and sell all of his possessions and give them to the poor,[2] although that was certainly a part of it. The monastic project itself was eschatological. These individuals strove to reveal in the present world the reality that Paul had predicted: Jesus was the first-born of the new humanity and this new humanity was the promised future of all of his followers.[3] Given that the redemption of the human race had occurred in Christ, many reasoned that the fruits of that redemption ought to be realizable here in this life. Ascetical training and ascetical practice were seen as a way to release this transformed self and to live now in anticipation of the promised fulfillment. Thus, the monk modeled with body and practice a deep confidence in the promise that God through Christ would make us all into a new creation.

To be more specific, we can say that ancient monks practiced celibacy because they were sure that Jesus did not lie when he responded to the Sadducess that in the resurrection people "neither marry nor are given in marriage, but are like angels in heaven."[4] The new humanity, it seems, would have no need for sex. Many monks ate a vegetarian diet as a way to anticipate the heavenly banquet at which, Isaiah promised, "the wolf and the lamb will lie down together" and animals will no longer be forced to eat each other. If heavenly wolves do not eat lambs, neither do heavenly humans.[5]

These ancient ascetical practitioners sought to be "divinized." Psalm 82:6 had declared "I say, 'you are gods, children of the Most High, all of you; nevertheless, you shall die like mortals, and fall like any prince.'" Ancient interpreters read this, along with others texts hinting at the nature of the resurrected life, as an indicator that one of the fruits of the incarnation was the restoration of the divine quality of pre-lapsarian humanity. God became a human being so that human beings

1. Athanasius, *Life of Antony and the Letter to Marcellinus*, 42.

2. Matt 19:16–30.

3. See 1 Cor 15:27; 2 Cor 5:17; Col 1:15; Phil 3:21.

4. Mark 12:23.

5. Leyerle, "Monks and Other Animals," 150–71.

could share in the life of God and be, as it were, divinized. For these early Christians, divinization did not mean that human beings were turned into God or that the difference between God and created human nature was erased.[6] Rather, divinization referred to the restored and immortal physicality of the resurrected person. A divinized person was free from decay, what Paul called "corruption." Belief in divinization arose, in part, through an extended meditation on Romans 8:20–21: "for creation was subjected to futility, not of its own will but by the will of the one who subjected it, in hope that creation itself will be set from its bondage to decay and will obtain the freedom of the glory of the children of God."[7] Ancient ascetical practices were designed to concretize the ideal of divinization. Through their spiritual practice the monks claimed that it was possible to begin in this life to experience what they were seeking. They believed that through their asceticism they would be like Antony: their earthly bodies would begin to resemble the bodies of the saints inhabiting a world renewed.

In my view, it is precisely this sense of a deep connection between eschatological vision and religious practices that should to be revived in any effort to develop Christian practices that foster sustainability. Just as the monks asked "what is the body for" and "where is it bound," we need to have some idea in our minds about how to answer the question "what is the earth for and where is it bound" if we are going to develop practices that both help to reveal it and provoke in us a desire to move toward it. The answer to these questions inevitably involves eschatology. Unlike ethics, which primarily responds to the question "how should I live," eschatology is the branch of theology best suited to answer the question "why should I live." Even in the secular environmental movement there is an embedded eschatology: we should live well and lightly on the earth so that the project of life can continue. For many people of this mindset, the eschatological impulse may go even deeper. Such individuals may have a sense that even though their own lives will end, they are mystically participating a larger purpose. "The Circle of Life" in the Disney film *The Lion King* is an example of this kind of secular eschatological imagination. Before he can be king, the young lion Simba must

6. For a full discussion of the theology of divinization, see Russell, *Doctrine of Deification in the Greek Patristic Tradition*.

7. For a discussion of the importance of this text in patristic Christology, see O'Keefe, "Persistence of Decay," 228.

learn both about his true place in the web of living things and about his spiritual connection to his own ancestors who were themselves part of this mystical web of life. If Christians desire to develop a compelling vision for sustainable living, they must be intentional and conscious about eschatology. That is, they must, like Simba, be able to articulate answers to questions about what their lives are for and what the earth is for, and they must do so precisely as Christians.

The Persistence of Platonism

However, answering these questions in a way that is useful for Christian ecological practice turns out to be difficult. One of the reasons for this is the language of the tradition itself. Since the publication of Lynn White's essay "The Historical Roots of our Ecologic Crisis,"[8] ecologically-minded Christians have been on the defensive. White seemed to point to nearly insurmountable flaws in the Christian worldview, flaws that made it especially prone to develop spiritual traditions that were, at base, anti-material. Christianity, White and others after him argued, has long imagined the earth as something that God had given humans to use as they saw fit. From this perspective, Christianity, following Gen 1:28–30, recommends that humans dominate the earth (literally have dominion over) rather than live in harmony with it. If the earth has any enduring spiritual value, again following this critique of Christianity, it is as an instrumental tool, assisting humans on their journey toward spiritual transcendence. Although White himself suggested in his essay that Christians might look to the example of St. Francis as a source for an ecologically-minded alternative Christian worldview, that recommendation has tended to be subsumed beneath the momentum of his larger critique.[9]

In his book *The Travail of Nature*, Lutheran theologian H. Paul Santmire aptly traces the history of Christian theological engagement with the material creation.[10] The story he tells is for the most part a negative one. According to Santmire, although the Church firmly rejected the anti-cosmic theology of Gnosticism, with few exceptions was Christian theology able to escape from a worldview that understood

8. White, "Historical Roots of our Ecologic Crisis," 1203–7.

9. Ibid., 1206–7.

10. Santmire, *Travail of Nature*.

salvation in the way that White's critique suggests. Historically, most Christian thinkers have understood salvation as involving a movement from coarse material existence to rarified spiritual existence. Thomas Aquinas is typical. Although he writes eloquently about the goodness of the world, it is clear that for him the material creation has no ultimate value beyond its service to human beings. For example, in the supplement to the *Summa Theologica,* question 91, Thomas take up the question "whether the plants and animals will remain in [the] renewal [of the world]." In the course of the argument, we learn that since humans will then have spiritual bodies and no longer need food, the purpose of the earth as the sustaining environment for humans will have been fulfilled and it will pass away. Aquinas explains:

> Since the renewal of the world will be for man's sake it follows that it should be conformed to the renewal of man. Now by being renewed man will pass from the state of corruption to incorruptibility and to a state of everlasting rest, wherefore it is written (1 Cor 15:53): "This corruptible must put on incorruption, and this mortal must put on immortality"; and, consequently the world will be renewed in such a way as to throw off all corruption and remain for ever at rest. Therefore it will be impossible for anything to be the subject of that renewal, unless it be a subject of incorruption. Now such are the heavenly bodies, the elements, and man. . . . [But,] dumb animals, plants, and minerals . . . are corruptible both in their whole and in their part . . . and thus they are in no way subjects of incorruption. Hence, they will not remain in this renewal.[11]

If one is convinced, as Aquinas and many others were, that the human person is bound to some transcendent other place, then one would develop spiritual practices to facilitate that crossing. It is hardly revolutionary to note that many spiritual practices of the Christian church have at their root the ambition of assisting in our personal transition to transcendence. Environmentally-minded observers of Christian theology and spirituality, like Paul Santmire, frequently point to the pervasive presence of Platonism as the root cause of this problem. According to these observers, the platonic notion that matter and spirit stands in a relationship of unreal to real makes it impossible for Christianity to really value the materiality of the world. According to this argument, when the spiritual traditions of Christianity rely upon vertical imagery

11. Aquinas, *Summa Theologica,* Supplement., Question 91, Article 5.

to describe the spiritual life, they reveal how deeply beholden they are to a platonic vision of ultimate reality.

Even the titles of the Christian spiritual classics suggest this Platonic polarity. Examples abound: St. John Climacus's *The Ladder of Divine Ascent,* St. John of the Cross's *The Ascent of Mount Carmel,* and Thomas Merton's *Seven Story Mountain* come immediately to mind. Indeed, one could argue that most of the classic works of Christian spirituality describe the spiritual life in terms of the soul's ascent from matter toward spirit. In this spiritual tradition, the world may be a good place because God made it, but it is seen primarily as the staging ground for humans plotting their exit strategies.

The origin of this spirituality of ascent is relatively easy to trace. In late antiquity Platonism reigned virtually unchallenged as the dominant descriptor of the nature of reality. Philosophers reasoned not only about the nature of wisdom and truth, but also about the nature of the universe itself. Platonic metaphysics included a cosmology, which the intellectuals of the ancient world accepted as an accurate account of the reality they encountered every day. The material world occupied a space literally below the spiritual world, and humans, uniquely among sentient beings, lived partly in the world of matter and partly in the world of spirit. Because the creation narratives of the Bible, in contrast to the sophistication of Greek wisdom, seemed quaint and foolish, the emerging Christian intellectual tradition had to respond to the challenge that the conflicting accounts put before them. In this effort they were not unlike modern theologians who attempt to reconcile scientific and theological reasoning.

In the third century, the theologian Origen rose to this challenge. Although Origen was condemned posthumously at the Second Council of Constantinople in 553, his influence was enormous. During his prolific career, Origen carved out the essential features of a Christian Platonism that made possible the reconciliation of platonic metaphysics and Christian revelation. For Origen, the material creation exists as a kind of pedagogical camp for souls journeying back to God. Origen believed that souls were created but enjoyed a spiritual existence prior to their fall and embodiment. Tragically, these souls that originally enjoyed a vision of God turned away from God and in turning fell. Rather than allow them to fall all the way to nothingness, God provided the material creation as a mechanism for their reconciliation and return.

The material creation came into existence in order to prevent fallen human souls from tumbling into oblivion. In other words, for Origen, when souls, which were primarily spiritual, fell, they fell down the chain of being[12] and literally became solid.[13] Their solidity arrested the fall. Embodiment made a return to spirit possible. Thus, for Origen the material creation was good because it provides a context for salvation, but it was also temporary. When redemption is completed and when humans no longer need the material creation, it will pass away, its purpose exhausted.

Origen believed that this was the best way to interpret the two creation narratives at the beginning of Genesis. One story refers to the creation of the spiritual world and the other to the creation of the material world. Origen saw an allegorical reference to the spiritual creation in Gen 1:26–27 of the first account, when God says "Let us make humankind in our image, according to our likeness . . . So God created humankind in his image . . . male and female he created them." Likewise, he saw an allegorical reference to the material creation in the second account, where Gen 2:7 says "then the Lord God formed man from the dust of the ground, and breathed into his nostrils the breath of life." Origen's posthumous condemnation was in part related to his belief in the creation of human souls before human embodiment, but his idea that there was a spiritual creation that was superior and distinct from the material creation enjoyed wide support and acceptance. Although somewhat jarring to modern readers, Origen's allegorical style was unremarkable in the pre-critical exegetical world that he inhabited.[14]

Gregory of Nyssa provides another excellent example. Gregory was heavily influenced by Origen, but he has always been considered to be orthodox by the tradition. In his influential work *The Life of Moses*, Gregory reflects upon the allegorical meaning of Gen 3:21. After the fall, "the Lord God made garments of skins for the man and for his wife, and clothed them." According to Gregory, these "garments of skins" were "placed around our nature at the beginning" when we found ourselves naked before God. These "garments" must be removed before we can

12. On the idea of the "chain of being," see Lovejoy, *Great Chain of Being*.

13. See Dawson, *Christian Figural Reading and the Fashioning of Identity*, 19–80.

14. For a full discussion of early Christian biblical interpretation, see O'Keefe and Reno, *Sanctified Vision*.

have a full and complete vision of God.[15] We know from other texts of Gregory that he did not share Origen's idea that soul pre-exists embodiment, but his interpretation of the "garments of skins" suggests that our current materiality cannot and should not survive our redemption.

Gregory's views are hardly unique. Indeed, it is difficult to overstate the impact that Origen's reconciliation with Platonism had on the subsequent Christian intellectual tradition. Beginning in the third century, Origen's project was enhanced by Christian appropriation of the work of Plotinus. Plotinus's "neo-Platonism" provided the intellectuals of emerging Christian culture with yet another means to embrace Christ while being true to the best philosophical knowledge that their culture could offer. Famously, in *The Confessions* Saint Augustine wrote about how his encounter with "the books of the Platonists" allowed him to see a way to embrace faith in Christ that was not intellectually foolish.[16] The protracted discussions in the fourth century about the nature of God that resulted in the Nicene Creed operated within this intellectual orbit, as did the Christological discussions held at the councils of Ephesus and Chalcedon. The fifth-century Christian neo-Platonic author known as Pseudo-Dionysius ensured that Platonic insight impacted directly the development of medieval mystical traditions, especially the apophatic tradition. The Gothic ambition to channel the light of heaven into material space though stained glass, light, and height carried the mark of Pseudo-Dionysian neo-Platonic spirituality. Even the modern practice of centering prayer, which has been heavily influenced by the anonymous medieval work *The Cloud of Unknowing*, can trace its intellectual pedigree back to Pseudo-Dionysius's seminal neo-Platonic speculation.[17]

Most contemporary authors with an interest in sustainable spirituality recognize that although this Platonic vision has served as a foundation for Christian spiritual reflections for millennia, it can do so no longer. The strong contrast between matter and spirit and the tendency to see the material creation only as the stage upon which the divine and human drama is acted out are rightly understood to be antithetical to a religious vision that is ecologically meaningful. In contrast, they would argue, we need a spirituality that wraps itself in material reality

15. Gregory of Nyssa, *Life of Moses*, 59
16. Augustine *Confessions* 7.9.13.
17. For a good discussion of this, see Luibheid, *Pseudo–Dionysius*, 11–46.

and understands the human spiritual project not as an ascent out of matter, but as somehow a deep communion with it. For many authors, the effort to ground spiritual insight and practice in the earthly and the material seems to require the abandonment of traditional Christian doctrine and insight precisely because of its thick association with Platonisim. Thomas Berry, Rosemary Radford Ruether, Sallie McFague, and Michael Dowd, to mention but a few names, all significantly modify core Christian doctrine in an effort to make Christianity more ecologically friendly. Although it is easy to understand the frustration of these authors, these modifications often produce changes to traditional Christian doctrine that some find problematic.[18] For example, one could legitimately ask if it is possible to redefine the Incarnation to mean that the world is God's body (as with McFague) or interpret the resurrection to mean mystical participation in the project of life (as with Berry), and still claim that these redefined doctrines have sufficient Christian theological coherence. The redefinitions certainly solve the problem of Platonism, but they potentially introduce other problems into the internal narrative of Christianity that are difficult to overcome.

In his book *Nature Reborn,* Paul Santmire provides a helpful typology for understanding the various ways in which Christian theologians are attempting to respond theologically to the challenge the ecological crisis poses to Christians. According to Santmire, eco-theologians tend to be either reconstructionists, apologists, or revisionists. Reconstructionists argue that the problems with traditional Christianity are so severe that "a new edifice of thought must be designed, from the ground up, with new foundations and new categories." Santimire continues, "these thinkers take it for granted that traditional Christian thought offers no—or few—viable theological resources to help people of faith respond to the ecological crisis."[19] Authors such as Rosemary Ruether, Thomas Berry, and, possibly, Sallie McFague exemplify this type. Apologists, according to Santmire, are in some ways the opposite. These authors "have sought to underline what they consider to be [the tradition's] positive ecological implications, above all the tradition's encouragement of 'good stewardship' of the earth."[20] Authors

---

18. Berry, *Dream of the Earth*; Ruether, *Gaia and God*; McFague, *Body of God*; Michael Dowd, *Thank God for Evolution.*

19. Santmire, *Nature Reborn*, 6.

20. Ibid., 7.

like Terry Wimberley, from a Protestant perspective, or even the U.S. Catholic Bishops, are good examples of this approach.[21] The revisionist, or third approach, which reflects Santmire's and my own, tends to work "mainly within the milieu of classical Christian thought, as defined by the ecumenical creeds,"[22] and to look for solutions and lost resources from within the tradition itself. Thus, in this essay, rather than reject the classic tradition as a whole because of its fifteen-hundred-year association with Platonism, my effort is largely an attempt to reclaim resources from the past that have a rich potential for assisting in the construction of an ecologically sustainable and recognizably Christian spirituality. To that end, let us turn to the work of Irenaeus of Lyons.

Irenaeus and Pre-Platonic Christianity

At first glance, such a project may seem like a massive waste of time. Given all of the problems with the classic Christian tradition, it may seem odd that I would recommend a return to the spiritual insights of monasticism for inspiration in the creation of an ecologically friendly Christian spirituality. The oddness seems to grow when we note the strength of the resistance to Platonism in emerging Christian eco-theology. It seems an even greater stretch when we realize how much language of Christian spirituality since Origen has tended to be dominated by both Platonic cosmology and Platonic views on the value (or lack of value) of matter. Indeed, the recommendation seems quite absurd as we observe that many of these spiritual traditions were developed by monks who were themselves influenced by Platonism. However, this recommendation can make sense if we recognize that the earliest monastic traditions that emerged in Egypt and Syria were driven by a different strand of ancient Christianity than the neo-Platonic one that came to dominate after Origen. This strand, to which I alluded at the beginning of this essay, displayed a remarkably physicalist tendency. Monastic practitioners sought, through ascetical rigor, to construct in this world bodies that anticipated the bodies of the saints inhabiting the New Jerusalem. Just as citizens of modern Western cities labor in

---

21. See, for example, Wimberley, "Conservationism, Preservationism, and Environmentalism," and the statement of the U.S. bishops "Global Climate Change: A Pleas for Dialogue, Prudence, and the Common Good."

22. Santmire, *Nature Reborn,* 7.

gyms to construct six-pack abs and "ripped" biceps, citizens of the desert cities of Christian antiquity, to paraphrase the great Derwas Chitty, labored for their own particular form of fitness.[23]

In my view, the intellectual source of this particular monastic vision dates back to a pre-Platonic form of Christianity associated with the theologian Irenaeus. I first became aware of the importance of Irenaeus many years ago in a conversation with the late patristics scholar Lloyd Patterson. During the conversation Patterson said something like this: "there is a great Irenaean thread that runs through the entire fabric of early Christian thought." Although I knew very little about the development of Christian theology at that time I heard Patterson says this, the statement seemed, somehow, right. Patterson did not explain to me the exact nature of this Irenaean thread, but the passage of time and the deepening of my own understanding of Christian antiquity have convinced me that this thread is made of matter and that Irenaeus was, deep down, a materialist. For Irenaeus, the created word, in all its detail, exists because God intended it to be the native place for humans and all other creatures. Unlike Origen, who lived a generation later, Irenaeus attempted no deals with Platonism. In fact, Irenaeus believed that excess fascination with philosophy was one of the primary errors of his Gnostic opponents. Irenaean theology, then, offers us a glimpse of Christian self-understanding in the second century, before the rapprochement with Platonism.

The struggle with Gnosticism defined Irenaeus' efforts as both a bishop and theologian. Gnosticism was a dualistic, anti-cosmic, and anti-material religious worldview. Although the doctrines of individual Gnostic teachers differed in detail, they all shared a fundamental disdain for the world of matter. The cosmos, indeed all material reality, existed as a massive deception designed to keep spirits from awakening to their true identities. Gnostics were convinced that the Old Testament, including the creation narrative, testified to the malevolent presence of an evil ruler of the cosmos intent on keeping us ignorant of our spiritual natures. For Gnostics, the primary goal of the spiritual life was to weaken the material bonds that blind us to our true nature and allow our spiritual identities freedom to return to our native place outside the world.

23. Chitty, *Desert a City*. See also the thorough discussion of early monasticism in Harmless, *Desert Christians*.

Irenaeus combated Gnosticism through an extended and complex series of exegetical arguments. In his opinion, although the Gnostics used the Bible, they used it badly. Like film editors in the modern world, Irenaeus claimed that Gnostics took the stories of the Bible—what a filmmaker would call "the footage"—cut them in to pieces and edited them to form a perverse narrative. The analogy he actually used, however, was taken from his own culture. Gnostics were akin to someone who had destroyed the mosaic portrait of a king by mixing up the tesserae and then rearranging "the stones to make the image of a dog or a fox, declaring that this badly composed image is that good image of the king made by a skillful artist."[24] Thus, Irenaeus explains, "[the Gnostics] try to draw their proof not only from the Gospels and the writings of the Apostle, changing the interpretations and twisting the exegesis, but also from the law and the prophets."[25]

Irenaeus believed that the Bible contained a coherent narrative. He understood that the full details of that narrative were not self-evident and required editorial assembly. However, he believed that he, not the Gnostics, understood how to put the pieces together in such a way that they formed a coherent Christian vision. He called that pattern the *divine economy*. In our book *Sanctified Vision*, R. R. Reno and I discuss the way this concept functioned in the theology of Irenaeus: "The word *economy* expresses a concept central to patristic theology." It has nothing to do with the modern usage in association with markets and commerce. "Economy can refer to the well-run household, as well as a well-constructed story." This is how Irenaeus used it: "the true and accurate reading of scripture, he argues, must follow the divine economy by which God has put together the mosaic of scripture."[26] For Irenaeus, the Church, not the Gnostics, was in possession of the true and accurate reading. It alone presented to the world the authentic narrative of salvation. It alone preserved the wonder of what Christ had accomplished by his incarnation, death, and resurrection.

In one of the most famous passages from all of early Christian literature Irenaeus explains. It is worth quoting in full. Grant's fairly literal translation preserves the relentless energy of the original text:

---

24. See Grant, *Irenaeus of Lyons*, 66. As a selection of primary texts in translation, Grant's book provides an excellent introduction to the thought of Irenaeus.

25. Ibid., 62.

26. O"Keefe and Reno, *Sanctified Vision*, 37.

The church, dispersed throughout the world to the ends of the earth, received from the apostles and their disciples the faith in one God the Father Almighty, "who made heaven and earth and sea and all that is in them" (Exod 20:11), and in one Christ Jesus, the Son of God, incarnate for our salvation, and in the Holy Spirit, who through the prophets predicted the dispensations of God: the coming, the birth from the Virgin, the passion, the resurrection from the dead, and the ascension of the beloved Jesus Christ our Lord in the flesh into the heavens, and his coming from the heavens in the glory of the Father to "recapitulate all things" (Eph 1:10) and raise up all flesh of the human race, so that to Christ Jesus our Lord and God and Savior and King, according to the good pleasure of the invisible Father, "every knee should bow, of beings in heaven and one earth and under the earth, and that every tongue should confess him" (Phil 2:10–11), and that he should render a just judgment on all and send to eternal fire the spiritual power of iniquity, the lying and apostate angels, and men who are impious, unjust, iniquitous, and blasphemous, while on the contrary he should give life imperishable as a reward to the just and equitable who keep his commandments and persevere in his love (some from the beginning, others since their conversion), and surround it with eternal glory.[27]

As this passage suggests, Irenaeus' understanding of the content of the Christian narrative is fairly straightforward. God created a good world, which he intended to be a material world. God created human beings to live in this material creation along with the other creatures of land and sea. Human beings sinned against God and broke their relationship with the good creation, introducing sin and decay into our lives and, in a way, infecting all of the creation with our bilious nature. Desiring to repair the damage, God sent Christ into the world to reverse the perversion of decay and to restore the possibility of communion with God by re-divinizing our fallen nature. Irenaeus uses the word recapitulation to capture the redemptive work of Christ. By this he means that Christ takes up the failures of the old humanity, recasts them, and reorients them to found the new humanity. Where Adam was the first born of the old humanity, Christ is the first born of the new. Where Adam was disobedient, Christ was obedient. Where Adam introduced

---

27. Grant, *Irenaeus of Lyons*, 70–71.

decay, Christ restores life.[28] For Irenaeus, the final salvation of all things would happen at the end of the world when Christ would return, raise the dead and literally enact the millennial promises predicted in the book of Revelation. As Irenaeus explains toward the end of *Against the Heresies,* "none of this can be taken allegorically," as the Gnostics take it, "but everything is solid and true and substantial, made by God for the enjoyment of just men." Indeed, we will "really rise from the dead, and not allegorically," and we will "exercise imperishability and grow and be strong in the times of the kingdom."[29]

Despite the persuasive power of Irenaeus' rhetoric, his theological synthesis was not without problems. Like modern fundamentalists, Irenaeus made no effort to reconcile the details of his eschatological imagination with the "scientific" wisdom of his culture. He was, in many ways, a literalist. This accounts, at least in part, for the greater attraction of Origen's synthesis among ancient Christian intellectuals. It also helps explains why, despite his heroic efforts to combat Gnosticism, and despite his enormous influence on the emerging Christian doctrine, Irenaeus' body of work has been inconstantly preserved.[30]

Because of this strong literalism, especially the millenarian dimension, it is difficult to assess the impact of Irenaeus' vision on the later tradition. It was clearly less influential than Origen's. Origen, after all, spoke the language of Platonism, the great intellectual synthesis of antiquity. He seemed to offer a way forward that permitted the reconciliation of the Bible and Philosophy, while Irenaeus seemed to ignore the latter in defense of the former. Still, as Scott Moringiello has persuasively argued, Irenaeus is best understood as a theologian making a rhetorical argument against Gnosticism rather than a philosophical one.[31] Indeed, as already noted, Irenaeus believed that over-fascination with philosophy was one reason Gnostics found themselves traveling a path that led to ruin. Moreover, the vision that Irenaeus rhetorically protects represents one of the oldest Christian visions about which we know.

---

28. Grant, *Irenaeus of Lyons,* 46–53.

29. Ibid., 184.

30. For example, his most important books are lost in the original Greek: *Against the Heresies* survives primarily in Latin translation and *Proof of Apostolic Preaching* is preserved only in Armenian translation. For a discussion of the theological impact of Irenaeus, see O'Keefe and Reno, *Sanctified Vision,* 114–39.

31. Moringiello, *Irenaeus Rhetor.*

Because of this, it seems at least possible that we could return to Irenaeus not as a source of inspiration for how to reconcile philosophy or science and Christian revelation, but as the source of a rhetorically dense and extremely old Christian vision. It is a vision that is profoundly, even radically, positively disposed toward the material creation. Although space does not permit development of this here, I have argued elsewhere that traces of the commitment to the positive value of matter show up in unlikely places in the Christian tradition, including the theological controversies that produced the Nicene Creed and the Christological formula of Chalcedon.[32] Thus, although something of a minority report in the later tradition, Irenaeus' vision of the redemptive work of Christ impacted the wider tradition significantly.[33] The persistence of this rhetorically dense subtext in the unfolding theological tradition is significant and meaningful both as an enhancement of our grasp of the past and as an inspiration for our current discourse.

Thus, what is needed for environmental theology and spirituality is, I would argue, a recovery of the rhetorically charged Christian materialism of Irenaeus. The anti-Gnostic and pro-material worldview that he preached and that the early monks enacted with their bodies could serve as one possible source of inspiration by which Christians desiring to cultivate a spirituality of sustainability can re-conceive the understood purpose of their spiritual practice. Sustainable living requires significant effort, and for us to be willing to adopt sustainable practices, we need to have some conviction about why we should be doing them at all.

Christian Spiritual Practice and Sustainability

Moving from theory to practice is tricky. It is certainly true that theory and practice exist in tandem. For example, the practice of Western medicine is intimately tied to the ideology of Western medicine. Oncologists deploy chemo-therapy because they believe that the root cause of cancer is a cellular disorder rather than, say, a blocked chakra. Likewise, it is also the case that the liturgical and the sacramental traditions of the Church reinforce the worldview of Catholics in the same way that the iconoclastic ritual spaces of Protestant communi-

32. O'Keefe, "Persistence of Decay."
33. Santmire, *Travail of Nature,* 31–54, 175–88.

ties reinforce that of Protestants. Theory and practice tend to develop together and to influence each other. Yet, theory and practice are not tied together absolutely. Individuals with very different understandings of reality can use the same practices to achieve different ends. Thus one person might attend Yoga classes at the YMCA in an effort to increase flexibility and a different person might practice the same asanas as part of an effort to achieve spiritual illumination. Similarly, Christians who practice centering prayer have been influenced by techniques historically connected with eastern mediation, but they have not necessarily adopted an eastern religious metaphysics. The practices, in these cases, are relatively neutral.

I am not arguing here that theory and practice can be radically separated. In real and fundamental ways we become what we do. A Buddhist who does not meditate has little hope of experiencing freedom from craving, and the Catholic who does not attend mass will not experience the liturgy's subtle teaching about the nature of the community that unites the human and divine communions. Practices are necessary to make religious ideas concrete and livable. I am arguing, however, that even though practices concretize and actualize ideas and doctrines, they do not, by themselves, carry the ideas and doctrines. Thus, recovering the materially dense Christian spiritual imagination that I detailed above is not dependent upon, say, deciding to take vows of celibacy, poverty, and obedience. Many people who take these ancient vows no longer remember the ancient eschatological context that shaped early monasticism and the practices do not magically infuse this into them.

What then, exactly, are the practices that characterize a sustainable Christian spirituality and that can help us live into the eschatological vision of the redeemed creation? My answer to this is two-fold. First, I suggest that the practices that will foster a sustainable Christian spirituality are the very same practices that have sustained Christian living for two millennia. These practices need not be abandoned; they simply need to be re-imagined in the light of a new ecological awareness. Second, I suggest that concrete practices for a sustainable Christian spirituality are emerging from within the sustainability movement itself. Although these practices are not in themselves Christian, they can be used by Christians and by that usage they can become Christian spiritual practices.

I turn initially to the second of these. Consider the many exhortations that flow from modern proponents of ecological living: We should forego the 3,000 miles salad and eat locally. Since fisheries are collapsing, we should be careful about fish. We should not eat genetically-modified crops. We should beware of the food industry. We should buy organic. We should grow more of our own food. We should raise chickens and plant a garden. We should leave the car at home and take public transportation, or better yet we should bike to work. We should use less energy, maybe even turning everything off once a week. We should reduce our carbon footprint. We should install solar panels and wind turbines. We should use smart meters. We should buy geothermal heat pumps. We should fight the coal industry. We should condemn mountain-top removal. We should produce less trash. We should not use plastic. The list goes on and can be, at times, profoundly overwhelming.

Now, if we consider this long list of practices recommended by people who are serious about living sustainably, there is nothing on it that is specifically Christian or spiritual. We can do these things whether we are Hindu, Buddhist, Muslim, Christian, or nothing at all. The practices presume a sense of environmental crisis, but they do not presume any particular spirituality. Yet, because, as I have suggested, practices are somewhat neutral, if they are adopted by Christians trying to live a sustainable spirituality, they can become Christian spiritual practices that have the power to help foster Christian ecological consciousness and create Christian spiritual insight. From this point of view, when we eat locally and bike to work we are not simply encouraging local agriculture and saving energy; we are also trying to reveal with our bodies and our actions some glimpse of God's promise of a world renewed. If I plant a garden and raise chickens I may do so because I wish to resist the industrial food industry, but I may also do so as a way to both model and experience a deeper sense of the relationship God intended between humans and the rest of creation. When I install a geo-thermal heat pump I may do so to save money and to reduce my carbon footprint, but I may also do so as a conscious act of making more concrete the kind of world that God intended.

The many practices recommended by the sustainability movement are a form of asceticism, and, it seems to me, we can receive them as such and think about them precisely as a form of spiritual training. Like the ancient monks who labored through their ascetical practices to reveal the divine promise that they perceived, so also Christians attempting to live sustainably can, through their labor, reveal the divine promise of creation renewed that they perceive. The reverse is also true; the practices not only reveal, they also help to make the vision real to the practitioner. Thus, like the ancient monks who gradually experienced the reality they sought because they embraced the monastic way of life, modern Christians who live sustainably can become increasingly conscious of God's intimacy with creation precisely because they have embraced a sustainable way of life. Thus, although these practice are, in themselves, spiritually neutral, they possess enormous spiritual potential.

Despite the importance of cultivating these emerging sustainable practices, however, a Christian spirituality of sustainability must be based upon more than the re-appropriation of a particular set of lifestyle choices. Christians need not abandon their own history. Many of the great spiritual traditions of the Church can be recovered and reoriented for use in intentional ecological living. Although these traditions developed in another age before the human community sensed the first hints of ecological peril, their insights into the ways of the human heart remain valid. Indeed, I would argue that without them the raw asceticism outlined above can quickly lead either to self-righteous elitism or bitter disappointment. Christian spirituality has always insisted that active striving must lead to interior transformation and deeper conscious awareness of what motivates us. Human beings working to make the world more environmentally stable are no less susceptible to the same temptations as our non-ecological forebears. We may think we are motivated by altruistic desire but secretly be driven by thirst for power. Ecological ascetics can still misuse, and abuse. They can still be greedy and petty. They may ruin their personal relationships in pursuit of the purity of their vision. All of these things are familiar to those with long experience in the Christian life, and they are not changed by a shift in the direction of our eschatological imaginations or by an increase in the zeal of our sustainable practice.

In a way, what we are talking about here is finding the proper balance between action and contemplation. All of the traditions of Christian spirituality include some form of active engagement with the world. This is true even of those traditions most closely associated with the contemplative life, such as Benedictine monasticism. As a student of the spiritual traditions of the church, I know that the relative balance between a life of action and contemplation has more to do with the personality of the practitioner than it does with the superiority of a particular form of life (although there have certainly been moments in Christian history where one form of life has been hailed as more perfect than another). The contemplative side of the tradition has always had as its object the creation of a space for interior awareness while the active side has been about the work of promoting the reign of God. A Christian spirituality of sustainability must balance its active labor for ecological transformation with the age-old practices that lead to interior awareness.

It is beyond the scope of this essay to trace out in detail the ways in which the individual spiritual traditions of the Church should modify their practices to promote active sustainable spiritual living in a way that also cultivates interior wisdom. However, I will mention one with which I have some familiarity. For twenty-five years I have been actively practicing Ignatian spirituality. Although associated with the Jesuits, this tradition maintains a balance between contemplation and action—between the interior life and the work of transformation—that is readily adaptable to the life of a layperson. In my case, I have been trying to do this as a theologian, husband, and father of four. For most of the time that I have been practicing this spiritual tradition my fellow Ignatians have focused their active lives on the work of the social gospel. That is, there has been a strong and consistent emphasis on the idea that the work of the gospel must include active labor to reform the unjust social structures that conspire to oppress the poor all over the world. Liberation eschatology envisioning a renewed human community actively operates within this tradition as a key reason for our striving. Among the traditions of Christian spirituality, Ignatian spirituality is among those most self-consciously concerned with action.

On the other hand, also according to this tradition, the quality of this action rises and falls according to the quality of our interior life. Ignatian spirituality insists that to do God's will we must "discern" our own desires. We need to learn to distinguish between desires that come from ourselves and are self-serving, and desires that come from God and serve God's reign. A kind of spiritual boot camp called the Spiritual Exercises provides basic training in this way of seeing and listening. However, the key to moving from basic training to competence rests in a little practice called the examen. The examen is nothing more than a daily period of contemplation in which the practitioner clears a space for listening for God's will by attending to the movement of one's own interior desires.

On the one hand, at the level of their structure, grounding practices, like the examen, that have developed over two millennia of Christian history need not change to accommodate our newfound hunger and thirst for a more sustainable world. In the case of Ignatian spirituality, for example, coming to understand that the eschatological hope of Christians is not just a hope for the redemption of the human community, but also a hope for the redemption of the whole creation does not change or eliminate the need for a the daily practice of the examen. I still need a tool to help me discriminate between temptation and holy desire. Our humanity has not changed because we are now concerned with sustainability. If our humanity has not changed, neither have the particular obstacles to spiritual transformation, which the ancient practices of the Church evolved to combat.

On the other hand, it is clearly essential that our contemplative practice, like our active practice, be reoriented toward the project of revealing the new creation. Thus, I should adopt in some serious way the active (and ascetical) struggle to create a world that is both more sustainable and that more fully reveals God's future. At the same time I need to clear an interior space from which I can discern how God is calling me to care more deeply for the whole of creation. If the model of early monasticism is to serve as an analogy, God's work for the redemption of the world has already taken place in Christ even though the full realization of that promise must wait for its full eschatological realization. If the ancient monks sought to mystically carry on their own ascetical bodies the first fruits of the transformed life yet to come, the Christian ecological ascetic seeks through sustainable practices both contemplative and active to live in anticipation of a world renewed.

Bibliography

Aquinas, Thomas. *Summa Theologica*. Online: http://www.newadvent.org/summa/5091.htm#article5.

Athanasius. *The Life of Antony and the Letter to Marcellinus*. Translated with Introduction by Robert Gregg. New York: Paulist, 1980.

Augustine. *Confessions*. Translated with Introduction by Henry Chadwick. Oxford: Oxford University Press, 1991.

Berry, Thomas. *The Dream of the Earth*. San Francisco: Sierra Club, 1990.

Chitty, Derwas. *The Desert a City*. Crestwood, NY: St. Vladimir's Seminary Press, 1966.

Dawson, David. *Christian Figural Reading and the Fashioning of Identity*. Berkeley: University of California Press, 2002.

Dowd, Michael. *Thank God for Evolution*. New York: Penguin, 2007.

Grant, Robert. *Irenaeus of Lyons*. London and New York: Routledge, 1997.

Gregory of Nyssa. *The Life of Moses*. Translated by Everett Ferguson and Abraham J. Malherbe. New York: Paulist, 1978.

Harmless, William. *Desert Christians: An Introduction to the Literature of Early Monasticism*. New York: Oxford University Press, 2007.

Leyerle, Blake. "Monks and Other Animals." In *The Cultural Turn in Late Ancient Studies: Gender, Asceticism, and Historiography*, edited by Dale B. Martin and Patricia Cox Miller, 150–71. Durham, NC: Duke University Press, 2005.

Lovejoy, Arthur. *The Great Chain of Being: A Study of the History of an Idea*. Cambridge, MA: Harvard University Press, 1936.

McFague, Sallie. *The Body of God: An Ecological Theology*. Minneapolis: Fortress, 1993.

Moringiello, Scott D. "Irenaeus Rhetor." PhD diss., University of Notre Dame, 2008.

O'Keefe, John. "The Persistence of Decay." In *The Shadow of the Incarnation: Essays on Jesus Christ in the Early Church in Honor of Brian E. Daley, S.J.*, edited by Peter W. Martens, 228–45. Notre Dame, IN: University of Notre Dame Press, 2008.

O'Keefe, John, and R. R. Reno. *Sanctified Vision: An Introduction to Early Christian Interpretation of the Bible*. Baltimore: Johns Hopkins University Press, 2005.

Pseudo-Dionysius. *The Complete Works*. Translated with Introduction by Colm Luibheid. New York: Paulist, 1987.

Ruether, Rosemary Radford. *Gaia and God: An Ecofeminist Theology of Earth Healing*. San Francisco: HarperSanFrancisco, 1992.

Santmire, H. Paul. *Nature Reborn: The Ecological and Cosmic Promise of Christian Theology*. Minneapolis: Fortress, 2000.

———. *The Travail of Nature: The Ambiguous Ecological Promise of Christian Theology*. Philadelphia: Fortress, 1985.

U.S. Conference of Catholic Bishops. "Global Climate Change: A Plea for Dialogue, Prudence, and the Common Good" (2001). Online: http://www.usccb.org/sdwp/international/globalclimate.shtml.

White, Lynn, Jr. "The Historic Roots of our Ecologic Crisis." *Science* 155:3767 (1967) 1203–7.

Wimberly, Terry. "Conservationism, Preservationism, and Environmentalism." *Journal of Religion and Society*. Supplement 3 (2008). Online: http://moses.creighton.edu/JRS/2008/2008–14.html.

4

A Reformed Vision of the World

Trinitarian Beauty and Environmental Ethics

Belden C. Lane

IN THE SUMMER OF 1938, WHEN GEORGE MACLEOD ARRIVED ON THE Island of Iona with a group of students and unemployed laborers, he had two visions in mind. One was to restore the beauty of its thirteenth-century Benedictine abbey, lying in ruins off the rugged western coast of Scotland. The other was to bring together a diverse band of people who had suffered through the Depression—from out-of-work craftsmen with socialist sympathies to divinity students working with delinquent kids from the hard streets of Glasgow. It was a strange notion at the time—that the ancient beauty of a reclaimed monastery and lively discussions over politics and economics could mesh together so well. But it worked. The struggling Presbyterian community was accused of standing half way between Rome and Moscow, but its vision of bestowing beauty as a form of justice was a natural expression of its Calvinist heritage.[1]

MacLeod knew that the wild splendor of the island itself offered a healing, if unnerving beauty. From the windy heights of Dun I on the north end, overlooking the abbey, to the rocky shores of St. Columba's Bay on the south, a harsh glory fills the place. Colorful puffins nest in the rocks. Highland cattle set their shaggy faces into the wind. The roots of hardy wildflowers like the burnet rose help bind the sand of the dunes. In a place ruled by wind and sea, everything not firmly rooted is quickly washed or blown away. Yet a haunting beauty remains.

---

1. See Ferguson, *Chasing the Wild Goose*. George F. MacLeod (1895–1991) was a Church of Scotland minister actively engaged in issues of poverty and pacifism.

Edmund Burke would call it sublime, not beautiful. He described the sublime in nature as that which suspends the mind in astonishment. It borders on a sense of terror, stopping the heart with the intensity of its presence.[2] Such is the untamed beauty of Iona. It awakens wonder, stirs a deep vulnerability, and lends itself to a worship that exults in justice. As George MacLeod soon learned, the mean streets of Glasgow more than met their match in the wild expanse of Iona. There he found the earth's commanding beauty summoning the soul to a praise that calls forth beauty everywhere.

Beauty is a central theme in Reformed spirituality, increasing in prominence from John Calvin to Jonathan Edwards. For theologians like these, the beauty of the earth discloses a God of the beautiful and sublime, alluring a dislocated creation back to its Maker. The human imagination may be limited in its capacity to appreciate and interpret this beauty aright. But the world itself, despite the damages of human sin, is chock-full of radiance. The goal of this essay is to identify the connection between beauty and justice in the Reformed tradition, showing how a delight in the earth's beauty can lead to a concern for environmental justice.

Calvin's Theater Metaphor and the Nature of Beauty

Calvin's notion of the world as a theater of God's glory draws on the colorful imagery of Psalm 104.[3] There God becomes the director and principal actor of a traveling theatrical troupe, as it were. The actors and stage crew erect a huge tent in every community to which they come along their way. Under the tent of the heavens, with its stage lit by glimmering stars, God steps out from behind the curtain as the lights go up. This spellbinding actor performs with all the colorful creatures of the company, frequently changing costumes so as to entice the audience to enter the drama and participate themselves in the cosmic dance of God's glory.[4]

2. Edmund Burke, *On the Sublime*, 58.

3. "This world is like a theatre, in which the Lord presents to us a clear manifestation of his glory," Calvin wrote in his commentary on 1 Corinthians 1:21. All quotations from Calvin's commentaries are taken from the *Corpus Reformatorum* (Brunswick: A. Schwetchke and Son [M. Bruhn], 1863–1900) vol. 49, 326. Hereafter referred to as CO. Translations are from the Calvin Translation Society, 1843–1848, reprinted as *Calvin's Commentaries* vol. XX, 85. Hereafter referred to as CTS.

4. Calvin says in his commentary on Ps 104:31, "It is no small honor that God

God "irradiates the whole world by his splendor," Calvin declared. "This is the garment in which He, who is hidden in himself, appears in a manner visible to us." The earth is the canvas on which God paints the mirrored glory of God's Trinitarian life. Even as the Eucharist connects us directly with the vivified humanity of Christ, the mysteries of the universe constitute a dramatic/liturgical performance that stretches our capacity for wonder. "We must cast our eyes upon the very beautiful fabric of the world in which [God] wishes to be seen by us," Calvin insisted.[5] Only then can the earth—singing glory for all it's worth—reveal the full extent of its possibilities for beauty.

This metaphor of the world as a theater of God's sublime mystery begins with Calvin in the Reformed tradition and passes on through numerous Puritan preachers and commentators to Jonathan Edwards in colonial Massachusetts. They all perceived nature as a spectacle one enjoys, a mirror one gazes into, a book one reads, a school one attends. But always they recognized the world as pointing to God's glory, awakening desire for a beauty that transcends every earthly charm, even in drawing everything earthly to itself.

This is the beginning point, I would suggest, for an environmental ethic in the Reformed tradition. Edwards insisted that God's beauty is something that must be shared. Its nature is to replicate itself in the beautifying of others. "God is God, and distinguished from all other beings, and exalted above 'em, chiefly by his divine beauty," said the Northampton theologian.[6] He saw this beauty as leading far beyond the appreciation of individual theater-goers to the extension of God's beautifying life in creative action, enhancing the wellbeing of all existing things.

We dare not locate it in the decorative and ornamental alone, said Edwards, but in the celebration of being itself, in the affirmation of God's own diverse and interwoven splendor—eagerly communicating itself to others. This is how the beauty of holiness completes itself in doxology. Beauty prompts the praise of God and God's praise engenders

---

for our sake has so magnificently adorned the world, in order that we may not only be spectators of this beauteous theatre, but also enjoy the multiplied abundance and variety of good things which are presented to us in it." CO 32:96; CTS VI:169. See also Lane, "Spirituality as the Performance of Desire," 1–30.

5. Calvin's Commentary on Ps 104:1, CO 32:85; CTS VI:145.

6. Edwards, *Religious Affections*, 298. References to the Yale Edition of Edwards's works are hereafter referred to as YE.

the beautification of all God's works. It adorns itself, at last, in justice. Hence, if the earth is indeed the theater of God's glory, we ought to treat it as such.

Some have argued that Calvin (and even Edwards) lacked any aesthetic impulse, absorbed as they were in the mysteries of a transcendent God.[7] This is hard to fathom for either one of them. Having been trained as a humanist, for example, it would have been difficult for Calvin to reject art as such. Admittedly, he warned of the danger of idolatry in breaking the second commandment. Representational art, in his opinion, seldom offered the reliable witness to God's beauty that one finds in the natural world. Yet he himself was a gifted artist with words. He introduced silk weaving to Geneva as an artistic craft able to help the local economy. He expressed delight in the loveliness of gold and silver, ivory and marble in sculpture and architecture. The Genevan reformer took note of the first appearance of art in Scripture, celebrating the happy invention of the harp and other musical instruments in the tents of Jubal. He even urged that fine wine be drunk, "not only in cases of necessity, but also to make us merry." All these gifts, he observed, "minister to our pleasure rather than our necessity."[8] They should never be considered superfluous, much less condemned. Beauty is a gift that glorifies God and ennobles our lives.

Yet the Reformed tradition reminds us that none of these gifts— from sculpture to music to the beauty of the earth itself—provide lasting aesthetic pleasure if they are not also part of a beautiful life. We discover their deepest meaning in moving beyond the casual relishing of loveliness to the sustained task of extending God's beauty throughout the cosmos. This is central to grasping the theological significance of Calvin's image of the world as a theater of God's glory. From his perspective, the traveling theatrical troupe in Psalm 104 has no desire to dazzle the audience's aesthetic sense through a parade of comely appearances. Their goal is to trigger compassion for the beauty of being itself, urging the audience (in praising God) to seek the wellbeing and interconnectedness of everything to which God has given existence.

---

7. On the centrality of beauty to Edwards's theology, see Delattre, *Beauty and Sensibility in the Thought of Jonathan Edwards.*

8. Calvin, *Institutes*, 3.10.2 and 1.2.12; Calvin's Commentary on Gen 4:20–21 (CO 23:99–100; CTS I:218); Calvin's Commentary on Ps 104:15, CO 32:90–91; CTS VI:157.

The depth of God's investment in the work of making ugly things beautiful is found in the beauty of the cross, says Calvin. Here the theater of God's glory is revealed most perfectly. The whole of creation discovers its longed-for correction and hope in this "splendid theater" of Golgotha. "The glory of God shines, indeed," Calvin affirmed, "in all creatures on high and below, but never more brightly than in the cross."[9] There is a point in the cosmic drama when eyes are suddenly turned to a rough-hewn cross thrown up on stage. The immense suffering marring the world's loveliness is not only disclosed in that moment, but acted out, shared and embraced. God assumes (in the mystery of the divine vulnerability) the pain of an anguished world, exercising an incomparable love. Because of this pivotal event at the heart of the performance, the redemption awaited by the whole of creation is assured at the conclusion of the final act.

Beauty, then, is the quality of a life that practices compassion—a "beautifying" life that vigorously seeks the well-being of others, participating in the suffering of those it embraces. It isn't a refined "artistic taste" so much as a way of relating to the world with aesthetic sensitivity, akin to the Navajo understanding of "walking in beauty," moving in harmony with everything that lives.[10] A Reformed environmental ethic similarly emphasizes a divine beauty that creates harmony throughout the created order. It recognizes (and restores) shimmering webs of interconnectedness at every turn as it moves through the world.

God's Trinitarian Beauty as a Lens for Perceiving the World

Both Calvin and Edwards emphasized that the beauty of the Trinity is never simply absorbed in its own splendor. It remains intensely participative, realized in the loving exchange of Father, Son and Holy Spirit and naturally over-flowing into a hunger for ever wider and deeper relationships. It longs to be shared in every possible way throughout the whole of creation.

Richard Rohr says that where we start in speaking of the mystery of the Trinity usually determines where we end. Christian thought about the Trinity in the West has traditionally begun with detached

9. Calvin's Commentary on John 13:31, CO 47:317, CTS XVIII:73.

10. For reflections on this conception of beauty as harmony with the world, see Gunn et al., *Hozho—Walking in Beauty*.

and abstract questions about God's *being*—the nature of the One, the essence from which all things come. Its tendency, as a result, has been to remain static, focusing on an undynamic monotheism, with God's "power" as the chief attribute of divinity. In the East, by contrast, the Cappadocian fathers started with God's *loving*, with the exchange of desire among the persons of the Trinity, putting stress on the movement, dynamism, and "beauty" of God's shared being. When we begin with the One, says Rohr, we end up perceiving the universe as a monarchical pyramid. When we start with the Three, we become more attentive to the flow of energy as it moves in circles of sharing.[11]

Calvin and Edwards stand squarely in the latter tradition of emphasizing the relational, participative character of God as Holy Trinity.[12] The most important thing we can say of God, Edwards urges, is to stress God's communicative nature, eagerly sharing the divine beauty within God's self and with every possible "other" as well. If beauty within the Trinity tends naturally to be shared, bestowing its luster on others, then God remains restless until the entirety of creation is restored to its original wholeness. The impulse to "distributive beauty" found within God's innermost being thus gives rise to the "distributive justice" that has to be exercised in sharing that beauty with others. The aesthetic has to lead to the ethical.

The nature of true virtue, as Edwards would say, is not to love individual things because of their outward beauty, but to love all things because of God's beauty hidden within them.[13] If we can see the world as God sees it, out of an overwhelming desire to bestow beauty wherever possible, our perception of everything changes dramatically. We

---

11. See Rohr, "Divine Dance." See also Gunton, *One, the Three and the Many*.

12. Calvin insisted that God "proclaims himself as the One in such a way that he presents himself to be contemplated distinctly in three Persons. Unless we hold fast to these it is merely a naked and empty name of God, without the true God, that flutters in our brain." *Institutes*, 1.13.2. Edwards similarly emphasized the dynamic exchange within God's being as Father, Son, and Holy Spirit. "These three, God, and the idea of God, and the inclination, affection and love of God, must be conceived as really distinct." *Discourse on the Trinity*, YE 21:131–32. Yet at the same time, Calvin and Edwards were careful to show how their ontological distinctions of three persons in God was different from tritheism.

13. "True virtue primarily consists, not in love to any particular beings, because of their virtue or beauty, nor in gratitude, because they love us; but in a propensity and union of heart to Being simply considered." Edwards, "Nature of True Virtue," in YE 8:544.

discern connections that suggest endless possibilities for interrelationship, looking continually for opportunities where beauty can alter the ugly face of injustice.

But in this, as in everything else, what we see is what we get. When we perceive the world as God perceives it, we discover an extraordinary correlation between God's glory, what the world naturally reflects of that glory, and how we can live out the beauty of both in our lives. Everything depends on how we perceive it. Clarity of perception is prerequisite to any responsible ethical action. The way we act in every situation depends on the habits of discernment we bring to what we see. Calvin argued, for example, that the ability to grasp God's glory in the universe requires a "quickening" (*vivificatio*) of consciousness, something more than intellectual understanding alone. "Only a supernaturally-heightened consciousness can achieve the requisite speed and agility to perceive as 'the glory of God' the kaleidoscope of rushing lifefulness which everywhere meets the eye," says Margaret Miles, summarizing Calvin's thought.[14]

Jonathan Edwards similarly spoke of a "new spiritual sense" that allows believers to perceive the world with an expanded sensitivity. Going beyond any natural ability to experience the world and its beauty, it enables them to make connections they wouldn't otherwise draw. He described it as "a taste or relish of the amiableness and beauty of that which is truly good and holy." It values what others may dismiss as insignificant, conveying a gift of "relishing and feeling" the sensuous delight of things.[15]

This new graced quality of perception offers a "sensible knowledge, in which more than the mere intellect is concerned." Yet it involves an "opening of the mind" as well—to the imaginative power of metaphor and analogy, for example, and to the harmony of interrelated ideas. As it increases the affective and cognitive sensitivities of believers, it enhances also their attention to embodied experience and improves their capacity for radical amazement. It teaches them, in short, how to exercise desire—how to discover a new aesthetic taste in savoring beauty and a new ethical impulse to make the world beautiful.[16] How, then, can

14. Margaret Miles, "Theology, Anthropology, and the Human Body," 304.

15. See Lane, "Jonathan Edwards on Beauty, Desire, and the Sensory World," 44–72.

16. Edwards said the new sense "opens a [whole] new world to its view . . . showing the glory of all God's works." See Edwards, "Religious Affections," YE 2:272–81.

we describe more fully the characteristics of this new spiritual perception that shares in God's own passionate desire to communicate love?

The rest of this essay is an effort to spell out six specific dimensions of an enhanced spiritual awareness, drawn not only from Edwards's description of the "new sense," but from the larger Reformed tradition as well. Together they constitute a Reformed way of perceiving the world. They show how an ethical life (bestowing beauty on others) naturally unfolds from an apprehension of God's communicative beauty as Holy Trinity. This is a radically theocentric ethic, focusing on God's glory, not on human needs, as the end of creation. It suggests that only a theocentric approach to ecological responsibility can avoid the errors of anthropocentrism on the one hand (seeing humans as all that count) and the extremes of a radical biocentrism on the other hand (a Deep Ecology unable to distinguish the value of cancer cells from the little girl in whom they dwell). We can properly assign value and exercise compassion only as we see the world through the eyes of God's own longing for shared relationship.

Interdependence—If the universe is a vibrant, over-flowing communication of the Trinity's beauty, then our perception of the world will value unity as well as diversity, honoring the interdependence and interpenetration of all systems of life.

To perceive the world with God's sensitivity to interdependence is to participate in the life of God's astounding beauty as Holy Trinity. This doctrine has nothing to do with number or abstract "being." It is all about shared delight. It identifies God as an interpenetrating unity of persons—loving and needing each other, while remaining separate and diverse in themselves. God is never happy alone. Hunger for relationship lies at the core of God's being.

Early theologians in the Eastern church employed the word *perichoresis* in describing this relationship within God's being, as it overflows into God's restless love for the world. The word comes from the etymological root "to dance around" and is usually translated "interpenetration."[17] The image suggests interpenetrating lines of

---

17. See Boff, *Trinity and Society*, 6, 134–36; and Harrison, "*Perichoresis* in the Greek Fathers," 53–65.

dancers in a nineteenth-century Shaker meeting house, moving in and out of each other as they form (and re-form) perfect circles of shared praise. If God (in the heart of the divine being) is a lively exchange of interdependent synergy and love, we find echoes of this relationship mirrored in the creation that flows from God's hand. Perceiving the world through God's eyes, we naturally notice interconnectedness everywhere we look.

Listening for echoes of Trinitarian *perichoresis* in the phenomenal world, we grasp more readily the unity-in-diversity that characterizes natural systems, learning to honor the differences in species and forms that make up larger patterns of interrelatedness. In each of these ways, we apprehend sensuous snatches of God's wild beauty in the cosmos, discovering parallels between God's shared longing and the biosphere's own passion for relationship.

Everything connects in a world created by an avidly communicative God. We glimpse Trinitarian patterns of connectedness in the vast network of common bonds that characterize any given ecosystem. Identifying these points of connection is central to the work of permaculturists like Bill Mollison.[18] They try to mimic the patterns of nature in developing sustainable methods of food production and waste management. Taking note of the mutuality of living systems, for example, they point to "plant guilds" growing naturally in interactive harmony.

The Three Sisters of maize, squash, and beans constitute such a guild. Growing side by side, the cornstalks offer a trellis for the bean vines to climb, the large squash leaves inhibit weeds and keep the ground moist, and the beans provide nitrogen-fixing bacteria to fertilize the soil.[19] Such patterns of interlocking connectedness mark the life of the universe at every turn, even as they echo the mutually-sustaining diversity that constitutes the Trinity itself. Even quantum theory affirms that things never exist in themselves, only in relation to each other. Everything's gotta dance.

If our perception were more sensitive to natural patterns of interconnectedness, we would copy what nature itself does so well—practicing "biomimicry," as Janine Benyus describes it.[20] We would organize

18. See Mollison and Slay, *Introduction to Permaculture.*

19. Hemenway and Todd, *Gaia's Garden.* The White Oak guild similarly connects white oak trees with ten other plants that cooperate in mutually beneficial ways.

20. Benyus, *Biomimicry,* 291–92. She finds models for a sustainable economic

loops of recurring interactivity (on biological, industrial, and city-planning scales) so as to reduce waste and limit energy loss within ever more complicated systems. This happens in the design of low impact, sustainable housing projects like Crystal Waters Village near Brisbane, Australia. Crystal Waters received a World Habitat Award for its pioneering work in creating a viable community where commerce, light industry, and green technologies cooperate with existing patterns native to the bioregion. The success of projects like this depends on an attentiveness to configurations of interdependence within nature itself, noting where life-enhancing connections naturally occur.

Reverencing diversity (and its convergence in community) is a natural consequence of Trinitarian theology. Thomas Aquinas celebrated the immense number of creatures in the world, seeing God's glory to be enhanced by their boundless heterogeneity. In his thinking, each species manifests a peculiar aspect of God's wisdom and goodness in a way that others cannot.[21] God dances in the endless color and variety of Florida manatees, desert bandicoots, and maidenhair ferns. Unfortunately, however, God no longer dances in passenger pigeons, dodo birds, lotus blue butterflies, and golden toads, all now extinct because of human impact on the environment. Our perception of God's variegated beauty is diminished as a result.

Yet the dance goes on—and in wild abundance. "In a handful of typical healthy soil," Cornell ecologist David Wolfe observes, "there are more creatures than there are humans on the entire planet." Life underground is as exuberant as it is unfathomed by us.

> We are beginning to realize what 'surface chauvinists' we have been in our myopic vision of life on the planet, blind to all but the most obvious of subterranean creatures. The latest scientific data suggest that the total biomass of the life beneath our feet is much more vast than all that we observe aboveground.[22]

Life flourishes everywhere, and with it continual signs of God's iridescent splendor.

---

system in prairies, coral reefs, and oak-hickory forests everywhere. They develop cooperative strategies as organisms spread out into largely non-competing niches, fostering weblike food chains in which all participants "play their parts in closing the loops so resources won't be lost."

21. Aquinas, *Summa Theologica*, 1.47.1 and 1.44.4.

22. Wolfe, *Tales From the Underground*, 1, 3.

Moreover, says Thomas Berry, our very ability to imagine God's multifaceted beauty depends upon such diversity. We live in a kaleidoscopic world that induces wonder.

> If we have powers of imagination, these are activated by the magic display of color and sound, of form and movement, such as we observe in the clouds of the sky, the trees and bushes and flowers, the waters and the wind, the singing birds, and the movement of the great blue whale through the sea. If we have words with which to speak . . . it is because of the impressions we have received from the variety of beings about us. If we lived on the moon, our mind and emotions, our speech, our imagination, our sense of the divine would all reflect the desolation of the lunar landscape.[23]

Living in a dappled world allows us to marvel at a God who is ever beyond our comprehension. Indeed, we require the rest of creation as a spur to the imagination, lest we fail to appreciate the vast unity-in-diversity that is God's own deepest mystery.

Enjoyment—*If God's chief characteristic is beauty (a sensuous beauty eager to share itself with others), then an equally sensuous enjoyment will be the means by which we know God, as well as the form our gratitude should take in response to God's gift.*

Perceiving the world as God's gift—sharing in the same raucous enjoyment that God takes in it—is another quality of perception that derives from a Trinitarian theology rooted in the Reformed tradition. Edwards continually emphasized the inseparability of "knowing" and "enjoying" holy things. The properly-trained mind not only "speculates and beholds, but relishes and feels."[24] Epistemology and enthrallment naturally go together. Knowing God (and God's works) is inescapably a matter of delighting in God. It demands a capacity to marvel, far more than a "head" knowledge aimed at mastering concepts. As Calvin himself argued, "The Word of God is not received by faith if it flits about in the top of the brain, but when it takes root in the depth of the heart."[25]

---

23. Berry, *Dream of the Earth*, 11.

24. Edwards, *Religious Affections*, 2:272.

25. *Institutes*, 3.2.36.

To experience God is to comprehend the magnitude of God's uncontainable delight. The eagerness of the Holy Trinity to share a common joy is a theme repeated in thousands of Reformed sermons, from John Calvin and Richard Sibbes to John Cotton and Jonathan Edwards. They reiterate the extent to which happiness is God's goal for all of created life. They stir the affections, elicit a zealous longing for union with Christ, and continually ring the changes on a fervent spirituality of desire.[26] God's power is far more often perceived as winsome attraction than as naked force.

God's absolute pleasure in communicating beauty fills the earth. Everything else is response—an echo of God's enjoyment, an endless rippling effect of shared attraction and delight. Calvin realized that God could have made a bland world in which necessities alone predominate, a mechanistic cosmos stripped of delight and enjoyment. God might have produced a universe with minimal interaction among all of its parts. But the desire of the Trinity required extravagance, resulting in a heaven and earth riddled with desire.

"All things [are] created for God's pleasure," Edwards declared. As creation responds to the divine longing that gives it birth, "God provides . . . for the satisfaction of the appetites and desires of every living thing."[27] The world, in short, turns on the aching distance between requited and unrequited love. Desire makes the world go round.

Physicist Brian Swimme reflects, for example, on the wide range of allurements that operate at every level of the cosmos—from the attraction of gravitation to electromagnetic interactions, from chemical attractors to allurements in the biological and human worlds. All are joined by a common fascination with the "other," whether discerned in galaxies, families, atoms, or ecosystems. Jeffrey Masson, in his study of the emotional lives of animals, tells of gorillas singing together as a means of cementing social connections and whales expressing affectionate, playful behavior in rearing their young. Elephants grieve over

26. This theme is developed more fully in the author's book entitled *Ravished by Beauty: Nature and Desire in Reformed Spirituality*, where he traces the development of a spirituality of desire in Reformed Christianity from Calvin to Edwards. This work explores the danger of misplaced desire and the frustration of unfulfilled longing in Puritan spirituality, showing how desire for the "other" always remains illusive, capable of provoking delight but never of being possessed.

27. Edwards, *Miscellanies*, #448, in YE 13:496; and *Miscellanies*, #1205 in YE 23:26. See Gerrish, *Grace and Gratitude*, 22–31.

a dead member of the herd and a falcon will mourn the loss of its mate, even when grief has no particular evolutionary or survival value. A pleasure in common bonds simply pervades the natural order of things.[28]

Social ecologist Chaia Heller perceives shared delight as a phenomenon cutting across species in general. She reminds us that as early as 1890, Peter Kropotkin criticized bourgeois theorists for overemphasizing Darwin's conception of the *competitive* character of evolution, at the expense of the *cooperative* dimension that he also identified as central to species survival. Kropotkin noticed that mutual aid was a significant factor in the evolution of species. We readily think of the symbiotic linkage of fungus and algae that constitutes the cooperative life of the lichen, for example. The latent sociability of animals suggests that they, too, take pleasure in associating with each other, even beyond the satisfaction of physical needs for survival.[29]

The world yearns for an emerging sense of interactive community, Heller contends. The goal of human beings is to create social and political structures that allow members of all species to participate constructively in the larger process of natural evolution, nurturing consciousness and cooperative action in every possible sphere. Social ecology strengthens the attractions that naturally bind human and more-than-human species in mutual support. The entire process is fed by reciprocal desire.

If God as Trinity delights in the shared enjoyment of the Other, and if the world naturally echoes that delight in its own display of mutual attractions, then our contemplation of God's beauty requires a similar capacity for intense enjoyment. Our enchantment with the world is, in fact, prerequisite to the task of restoring and protecting its wild beauty. "We will not fight to save what we do not love," said evolutionary biologist Stephen Jay Gould.[30] People naturally love what they have come to relish and realize they might also lose.

Contrary to all the worn-out stereotypes, enjoying the world God has made remains a fundamental principle of Reformed spirituality. Calvin symbolized this in his celebration of the sumptuous meal offered to the faithful in the Eucharist. God "admonishes us not to be

28. See Swimme, *Universe Is a Green Dragon*, 48ff., and Masson and McCarthy, *When Elephants Weep*, 91–92, 95–96, 112, 132.

29. Heller, *Ecology of Everyday Life*, 125.

30. Gould, "Unenchanted Evening," 14.

ungrateful for such lavish liberality, but rather to proclaim it with fitting praises and to celebrate it by giving thanks . . . We see that this sacred bread of the Lord's Supper is spiritual food, sweet and delicious . . . All the delights of the gospel are laid before us . . ." *Not* to taste and to savor this gift is the height of impiety.[31]

Embodied Attentiveness—*If God's Trinitarian nature delights in exquisite detail and simplicity alike, scattering beauty everywhere in creation, then our appreciation of the works of God should also engage us in meticulous study and sensuous fascination.*

A third way of perceiving the world, as informed by a Trinitarian Reformed theology, involves a practice of detailed, even scientific observation. Exercising curiosity as a conscientious student in the School of the Creatures heightens our ability to imagine the Trinity's incomparable beauty, even as God delights in our consequent appreciation of the intricacies of creation. Paying attention to the world (both its wonders and its problems) becomes a critical dimension of a contemplative life. We cannot enjoy (or seek to repair) what we do not know.

A Reformed doctrine of the Trinity points to the distinctive role of the Holy Spirit in attending to details, fostering differentiation and particularity through the whole of creation. "The Spirit is the principle of individuation," Moltmann says.[32] In creating and sustaining the world, God's Spirit attends to the intricate structure of DNA molecules, the exact pattern of Monarch butterfly wings, and the geometrical formation of crystals in underground caves. According to Calvin, "It is the Spirit who, every where diffused, sustains all things, causes them to grow, and quickens them in heaven and on earth . . . transfusing into all things his energy, and breathing into them essence, life and movement." Hence, "the beauty of the universe . . . owes its strength to the power of the Spirit."[33]

God's delight in details, numbering the lilies in the field, evokes our own attentiveness to the beauty (and absence of beauty) that marks the universe at every turn. The spiritual perception of the world demands a disciplined eye, a trained palate, a discriminating sense of smell, a

---

31. Calvin, *Institutes* (1536 edition), 1:136, 145–46, 148.

32. Moltmann, *God in Creation,* 100.

33. Calvin, *Institutes,* 1.13.14.

light touch, "a rectified musical ear" (as Jonathan Edwards would say). William Blake, that relentless celebrant of the holy imagination, argued that one can't be a Christian without also being an artist. Faith, for him, meant perceiving the world aesthetically, with a soul open to mystery. The Reformed tradition, given its contributions to the history of science, might also add that one can't be a Christian without being a *scientist*—without marveling at the elaborate and convoluted structure of the cosmos. This is how one encounters the Trinity as "a zestful, wondrous community of divine light, love, joy, mutuality, and verve."[34]

Reformed spirituality discloses a long tradition of serious meditative reflection on the mysteries of the universe. From Guillaume Du Bartas' sixteenth-century masterpiece on the first week of creation to Cotton Mather's extensive gathering of material for a "*Biblia Americana*" that he never published, studies of creation have flourished in the history of Calvinism. Du Bartas' hexaemeron in verse form provided the foundation of Milton's *Paradise Lost*. Mather's work was an effort to read the mysteries of God from the natural wonders of the American landscape, attending to the voices that speak God's praise from every hilltop and burrow in New England. Puritan writers continually urged the faithful to attend to the "school of desire" found among all the amazing creatures of the natural world.[35]

The thoroughness with which Christian saints have applied themselves to the study of natural phenomena through the centuries—perceiving this work as itself a spiritual exercise—is extraordinary. In the fourth century, Basil of Caesarea calculated the astonishing strength of hexagonal honeycomb cells designed by industrious bees and remarked on the discipline of cranes in flight, taking turns in leading their flock into the wind. So enamored by the lessons of the earth, he could say, "One grass, even one blade of grass is sufficient to occupy all your intelligence completely in the consideration of the art which produced it."[36]

Hugh of St. Victor eight centuries later would marvel at the crocodile's skill in chewing without moving its lower jaw, while Albert the

---

34. Plantinga, "Social Trinity and Tritheism," 28.

35. See *Divine Weeks and Works of Guillaume de Saluste Sieur Du Bartas*, 116. Cotton Mather's *Biblia Americana* is a massive six folio volume work located at the Massachusetts Historical Society. Thomas Taylor's *Meditations from the Creatures* is an example of the many Puritan works that draw spiritual lessons from the natural world.

36. Basil, *Hexaemeron*, 8.3 and 5.3, in *Saint Basil: Exegetic Homilies*, 124–25, 71.

Great—equally skilled as a scientist and theologian—devoted himself to sustained research on golden eagles. Over a six-year period, he regularly lowered himself down a cliff in a wicker basket to study their nesting behavior.[37] These spiritual writers knew that desire has to be fed by knowledge. Perception necessarily attends to details.

Richard Baxter spoke of those who were most skilled in the "gathering art" of attending to nature's details as the ones who were most characterized by a "spiritual sweetness."[38] Being well versed in the "book of nature" as well as the "book of Scripture" was a high priority in Puritan spirituality, seen in the number of Puritan scientists found in the Royal Society and in Jonathan Edwards's careful notes on his Massachusetts landscape. In Reformed thinking, cultivating a disciplined eye for nature's mysteries was a necessary means of discerning (and maintaining) God's grandeur throughout creation.

Shared Suffering—*If God's Trinitarian beauty is most apparent in the cross of Christ, then our understanding of suffering will have to be informed by God's own deep participation in its enduring mystery.*

A Trinitarian perception of the cosmos also has to reckon with what doesn't connect, with what disappoints rather than delights, revealing brokenness and disorder at every turn. It reaches beyond a shallow fascination with lovely things, so as to attend most carefully to where beauty has been disfigured or may require broader definition. It recognizes God's own participation in suffering, perceiving the world (as God does) from the underside of its pain.

In a world driven by longing, desire can be as dangerous as it is compelling. The desire of an African lion for a sickly gazelle, falling behind the rest of the herd, disturbs our human sensitivities. Violence in nature is difficult to accept, even when we recognize a beauty in the hunt and in the lion's providing for its young. On the other hand, the yearning of multi-national corporations for an endless increase in profits may strike us as shrewd and savvy, yet the hidden cost to the Third World poor can be horrendous. In each case—whether the apparent

37. See Hugh of St. Victor, "'Three Days of Invisible Light," 17–20; and Albertus Magnus, *On Animals*, 6.6.50. These and other examples are discussed in Schaefer, "Appreciating the Beauty of Earth," 23–52.

38. Baxter, *Saints Everlasting Rest*, 110–11, 168–69.

harshness of desire serves a larger vision of life or whether a desire distorted by sinful greed creates a demeaning poverty—God stands in solidarity with those who suffer. The death of the sickly gazelle and the hunger of children in Latin American barrios are both embraced by a crucified God who shares deeply in their agony.

The cross thus offers an opportunity for glimpsing God's wild beauty in all its paradoxical horror and awe. It shows how far the Trinity is willing to go in risking God's self to brokenness and loss for the sake of love.[39] In describing the difficult "beauty" of the cross, Edwards said that "infinite highness and infinite condescension" both met in Jesus' crucifixion. Here we find "all the spiritual beauty of his human nature, consisting in his meekness, lowliness, patience, heavenliness, love to God, love to men, condescension to the mean and vile, and compassion to the miserable."[40] In the suffering and death of Christ we discern the extent to which God embraces the most tragic consequences (at deep personal expense) for the sake of larger growth and ultimate wholeness. Christopher Southgate argues that "an evolving creation [inevitably struggling with pain] was the only way in which God could give rise to the sort of beauty, diversity, sentience, and sophistication of creatures that the biosphere now contains."[41]

The Reformed tradition, as a result, tries to hold in tension God's immense power witnessed in the awesome exigencies of a wild and wondrous world right alongside God's amazing vulnerability disclosed in the humility of Christ on the cross. This is never easy. It wrestles with the paradox that God creates a world of fierce splendor (where the timid have to tread lightly), while God simultaneously exposes God's self to its greatest threats, identifying with those most at risk.

This paradox demands that Christians develop a much more nuanced perception of human and natural suffering, avoiding simplistic analyses of a universe that can be baffling in its moral complexity. They dare not romanticize the "picturesque" image of a robin feeding live earthworms to its young, for example, while denigrating the

---

39. As Moltmann says, "The inexhaustible creative power of God in history always makes itself known first of all in the inexhaustibility of the power of his suffering." See *God in Creation*, 210.

40. Calvin, Commentary on John 13:31, CO 47:317; CNTC 5:68; Edwards, "The Excellency of Christ," YE 19:565–66; and *Religious Affections*, YE 2:258–59.

41. Southgate, *Groaning of Creation*, 16.

"monstrous" image of a grizzly bear attacking careless campers. God's presence must be owned in robin and worm alike, in the hungry bear and in the camper having left food in his tent. All are part of the natural order of a world where danger is ever-present—heightening awareness, stirring fear, nurturing courage and fostering community as a result. Given a God who shares in the sufferings of the world, how wild a universe can we envision?

The reality of the cross requires that Christians acknowledge death and suffering as part of the wild order of things—an aspect of the evolutionary process of advance and decline that inevitably characterizes God's continuing pursuit of the Kingdom. Paul Santmire admitted that such an idea cuts against the grain of traditional Christian theology.

> Nevertheless, it is possible to contend that both death and suffering belong in some sense to the world as created. Such modern theologians as Reinhold Niebuhr, Paul Althaus, and Karl Barth have argued persuasively in this vein. The theology of the Bible generally seems to move in the same direction, providing little support for the alternative view that physical death and suffering are the result of a cosmic fall.[42]

How, then, do we understand the inclusion of death and suffering—of predators and prey—within a universe where God's providence prevails? Unless our conception of God is wild and imaginative enough to embrace such a world, we end up with a theology of creation radically at odds with any of the biological realities we know. It would require our imagining an Eden where lions placidly grazed on grass, where deciduous trees never lost their leaves in the Fall, where decomposers (from maggots to bacteria) had no way of surviving in a pre-lapsarian world. Decay and dying is, and always has been, an integral part of biological (and, for that matter, inter-stellar) life. God thrives (and anguishes) in a world rich in ambiguity.

Biblical faith does not affirm a God who shrinks from the inevitability of suffering and death, but a God who—in sanctioning the process of birth and decay—nonetheless identifies (and grieves) with every death that occurs. God doesn't stand outside the process of change and risk, where pain recurs as an agonizing reality. God longs instead to see

---

42 Santmire, *Brother Earth*, 125. Violence inescapably characterizes what Karl Barth calls the "shadow side" of creation. Yet he says, "The great mystery is not violence, but beauty." *Church Dogmatics* III/3, 296–97.

death lose its sting, participating in its horror so as to make it transformative rather than merely destructive. This, finally, is the hope of the cross, anticipating a transformed world not yet fully realized.

Our romantic (and bloodless) fantasies of an idealized world, free of threats and unpleasantness, keep us from coming to terms with a God who exults in wildness even while identifying with those who are harmed by it. We cringe at images of killer whales attacking innocent penguins, preferring blithe images of nature as an idyllic paradise. We like to think of ourselves as "experiencing wilderness" on vacation at Disneyworld's "jungle safari." We prefer, in short, a world as small as the God we're able to imagine.

Hiking in the Maine woods last Fall, a friend of mine came upon a beautiful red fox in a forest clearing. She noticed the poor creature was bleeding at the mouth, assuming it had been hurt or attacked in some way. But her compassion quickly turned to awe as she noticed a dead rabbit at the fox's feet. The blood on its mouth wasn't its own. This fox was no helpless victim. It was a predator, gloating over its kill. Nature continually surprises us in such ways. Annie Dillard stubbornly refuses to let us forget it. God's world is as insistently wild as it is lovely.[43]

We can't afford to be naively romantic about suffering. Doing so keeps us from a critical consciousness of our own role and responsibilities in the world. On the one hand, we have to get over our squeamishness about the rough edges of a world given at times to a reckless beauty. Natural suffering is inherent in the world as presently marked by death and predation. On the other hand, as human beings instructed by God's revelation in the cross, we share a relationship with all who suffer, necessarily holding ourselves accountable for the pain we inflict on others. Distinguishing the ugliness and injustice for which we bear responsibility from the often harsh character of natural cycles is no easy task. It poses a theological and ethical quagmire for those with a God too small. Only in the shadow of the cross are we able to grasp the extent of God's own investment in the earth's ultimate healing.

43. I'm indebted to Quaker author Kathy Whitmire for this story. Annie Dillard reflects on creation's dark side in her books *Pilgrim at Tinker Creek* and *Holy the Firm*.

Justice as Bestowed Beauty—*If God is not content with merely celebrating beauty, but also bestowing it on others, then an ethical life will express itself through actions that seek to beautify the world, mending webs of interconnectedness where these have been broken.*

A Trinitarian perception of the world demands our acting (wherever possible) to alter structures of ugly injustice that mar the world's natural beauty. This enhances the cosmos as a mirror of God's glory, even as it imitates God's own beautifying activity as Holy Trinity. Edwards defined true virtue as a disposition (or habit of the heart) that recognizes and extends the beauty of God into ever new expressions of loveliness. As he understood it, the divine grandeur "is more fully exhibited in *bestowing* beauty than in receiving it."[44]

Beauty adds grace and largesse to the exercise of justice. It illumines and restores the original goodness of God's creative work. Indeed, beauty and justice are inseparable dimensions of a single truth. Justice, for example, will demand more than stopping sewage and toxic wastes from being dumped into a stream in an urban neighborhood. It requires that garbage be removed, the stream's banks replanted with trees and native plants, its waters restocked with fish. Only then will it mirror God's image in its beauty, invite children to play along its edges, and enhance the dignity of the larger community.

Beauty cultivates an eye for the correction of abuses. But it looks even more for possibilities that create a lasting sense of refinement and shared pride. Walter Rauschenbusch spoke out against labor conditions and "slave wages" at the turn of the twentieth century, not only because of the demeaning poverty they caused, but because of the "ugly and depressing" nature of the work itself, shorn of any beauty. "The mediaeval craftsman could rise to be an artist by working well at his craft," he observed. But "the modern factory hand is not likely to develop artistic gifts as he tends his machine."[45] As the Social Gospel theologian perceived it, a justice that fails to serve beauty remains incomplete.

44. Edwards, *Nature of True Virtue*, YE 8:544, 542; Delattre, "Religious Ethics Today," 70–71. Emphasis added.

45 Rauschenbusch, *Christianity and the Social Crisis*, 234. Rauschenbusch (1861–1918) served a Baptist church in the Hell's Kitchen area of New York City at the end of the nineteenth century.

Thus, he and John Ryan defended the importance of a "living wage," knowing that a mere subsistence income was never enough. A fair wage should also allow working-class families to include beauty and dignity in their lives. Calculations of economic justice have to embrace museums and music in a family's life, for example, providing for the expansion of mind and soul as well as body. These, too, are necessary ingredients of a just (and truly aesthetic) life.[46] Deconstructing oppressive human systems is only part of the work of justice. It requires as well a vision of winsome alternatives able to sustain new life. The "art" of social justice is not a work for dilettantes; it stretches the holy imagination in reconfiguring the blueprint of justice for the long-term.

Considering beauty as a factor in the shaping of moral judgments isn't anything new in discussions of environmental ethics. As early as the 1930s, Aldo Leopold's land ethic argued that the earth's grandeur provides legitimate grounds for its preservation. He offered this succinct moral maxim: "A thing is right when it tends to preserve the integrity, stability, and beauty of the biotic community. It is wrong when it tends otherwise."[47] If we take seriously the notion of the world is a theater of God's glory, a concern to identify, preserve, and restore creation's scarred beauty becomes a natural expression of a Reformed spirituality of desire.

A sharpened perception allows us, then, to identify when and where a broken creation can be reclaimed. An aesthetic sensitivity of this sort operates from the bottom up, not simply from the top down. Its call for justice, as a result, may differ radically from the new-found environmental concerns of First-World nations who have profited from years of endless expansion and subsequently expect other less-developed nations to limit themselves in the name of ecological responsibility. Environmental justice involves more than an elitist concern of middle-class Christians who, having had all their other needs met, are now able to preoccupy themselves with beauty.

How, then, do we make moral decisions that take into account all the relationships involved in maintaining a just and aesthetic world?

---

46. Monsignor John A. Ryan (1869–1945) was deeply influenced by Pope Leo XIII's social encyclical *Rerum Novarum* in the writing of his book *A Living Wage*.

47 Leopold, *Sand County Almanac*, 262. For a list of ethicists who use beauty as an argument for environmental action, see Schaefer, "Appreciating the Beauty of Earth," 23–24.

Edwards would say it requires the imaginative gift of a new spiritual sense—recognizing God's image in each of the threads that make up the web of the whole. Consider the decisions we make about the way we eat, for instance. Increasingly people are repelled by the process that brings factory-farmed chickens to their supermarkets. The birds spend their lives in small cages, pumped with hormones to create more meat and antibiotics to counteract the effects of standing continually in their own filth. Some shoppers become vegetarians as a result. Edwards himself was appalled by the excesses of the meat markets on the Boston waterfront. But is a vegetarian diet, with its greater sensitivity to animal life, intrinsically more moral?

Not necessarily, says Chaia Heller. Eating bananas may require as much ethical discernment as eating chicken. There are no easy ways of untangling the lines of moral responsibility that cross each other in the complex production of food.

> When we reveal the social context of banana production, we are confronted by a moral paradox: while the *content* of the banana (a form of non-sentient plant life) may represent a moral food choice, the *social relations* surrounding the agricultural production of a factory-farmed banana, may render such a food choice immoral.[48]

These larger "social relations" are, of course, a central concern in creating a just and harmonious society. In the case of the banana, these relationships involve the low wages paid to workers who harvest the fruit in Third World countries (who also lack health benefits and are often exposed to pesticides). They include the use of indigenous land to grow cheap crops for First World consumers when it could be used to cultivate food for local communities. They entail the buying of bananas shipped (by polluting airliners) from thousands of miles away when people could eat local (and seasonal) fruit native to their own region. How, then, do we measure justice as a means of fostering beauty? Only by attending carefully to the intricate threads that maintain the web of life around us. This doesn't mean we remain paralyzed by an endless consideration of conflicting moral claims, but it does mean we sensitize ourselves to the various relationships that constitute a moral (and beautiful) life.

48. Heller, *Ecology of Everyday Life*, 27.

Liturgical World-Making and Hope—*If God's desire in beautifying and restoring creation is a work still in process, then the whole earth lives in expectation, straining (along with God) toward a reality not yet fully realized. In worship (as liturgical action) we boldly proclaim and call into being the redeemed creation God envisions.*

Calvin's lively image of the world as a theater of God's glory points us to the overwhelming importance of worship as the foundation of Reformed theology and ethics. Beginning his *Institutes* with the wonders of creation, he viewed the entire earth as properly caught up in praise. "The stability of the world depends on the rejoicing of God in his works," he declared.[49] As Calvin saw it, the continued viability of creation rests upon the fact of its being actively celebrated. Ecological sustainability is rooted, he knew, in the power of liturgical action. "If on earth such praise of God does *not* come to pass. . . . then the whole order of nature will be thrown into confusion and creation will be annihilated."[50] At the core of Reformed spirituality is an exercise of imagination and hope that anticipates (and liturgically "performs") the new world God is continually bringing into being.

This way of perceiving creation as a dynamic, on-going event is indebted to the enthronement psalm tradition in the Hebrew Scriptures. In ritually inaugurating Yahweh as King of Creation on Rosh Hashanah each year, Israel celebrated the world God calls into being once again in that moment.[51] Such a view of the cosmos suggests the immediacy of a creation continually being made new as well as the precarity of a world dependent upon the invocation of God's sustaining presence. Jonathan Edwards knew that creation wasn't a one-time, static event, long ago completed, but a "present, remaining, continual act" of God's creative energy.[52] A perception of this sort approaches the world with a Buddhist sense of Beginner's Mind. The amazement of the wide-eyed child is its normative way of seeing.

Calvin urged the same kind of awareness. His metaphor of the world as theater emphasized the ritual value of "framing" one's perception of

49. Calvin's Commentary on Ps 104:31; CO 32:97; CTS VI:170.
50. Calvin's Commentary on Ps 115:17; CO 32:192. Emphasis added.
51. See Walter Brueggemann, *Israel's Praise*, 4–38.
52. Edwards, *Miscellanies*, #346; YE 13:418.

God's glory in the natural world. To view God's presence in creation as a performance, with all the immediacy of a theatrical experience, is to grasp its vitality and life. It further acknowledges the worshipping community's responsibility in celebrating God's works. The legendary "fourth wall" disappears as the spectators actively participate in the birth of a new world occurring on stage. They submit to its spell as an alternative reality takes shape before them.[53]

This dynamic conception of liturgy is central to Calvin's understanding of the Sabbath. The seventh day provides a stunning recreation of the entire world, a weekly rite of singing into being an astonishingly new universe. As a consequence, the Sabbath "opens creation for its true future," says Jürgen Moltmann. "On the Sabbath the redemption of the world is celebrated in anticipation."[54] Moreover, the celebration itself prompts the congregation to the action necessary for realizing the world now envisioned.

Ecological awareness (and justice), therefore, naturally emerge out of the doxology we share with the rest of creation. In Calvin's thinking, a persistent act of adoration, spanning all species, is what upholds the fragility of the universe.[55] Hence, the power of the cult to engender what it names—the capacity of ritual to summon what it celebrates—is a mystery full of ecological as well as liturgical significance. Tom Driver argues in *The Magic of Ritual* "that the life-threatening pollution of the earth's oceans, streams, and atmosphere is partly due to the neglect and decline of rituals that once regulated people's relation to their habitat."[56]

53. On the importance of liturgy in the Calvinist tradition, see Rice and Huffstutler, *Reformed Worship*; Old, *Worship: Reformed according to Scripture*; and Vischer, *Christian Worship in Reformed Churches Past and Present*.

54. Moltmann, *God in Creation*, 276. In speaking of how God's work in sustaining the world is celebrated in Sabbath praise, Calvin acknowledges that "if God should but withdraw his hand a little, all things would immediately perish and dissolve into nothing." Calvin's Commentary on Genesis 2:2, CO 23:31–32; CTS I:103.

55. He specifically included all species in the work of praise when he said, "It is evident that all creatures, from those in the heavens to those under the earth, are able to act as witnesses and messengers of God's glory . . . For the little birds that sing, sing of God; the beasts clamor for him; the elements dread him, the mountains echo him, the fountains and flowing waters cast their glances at him, and the grass and flowers laugh before him." John Calvin, Preface to the French translation of the New Testament by his cousin, Pierre Robert Olivetan, 1534). CO 9:795. Joseph Haroutunian's translation, in *Calvin: Commentaries*, 60.

56 Driver, *Magic of Ritual*, 32.

Consequently, the recovery of liturgical vitality in the Reformed tradition (and in other religious communities today) becomes more important than ever.

The church's ritual life not only sustains its work for justice but also grounds its hope for the long haul. We're able to make sense of the world's sufferings—all the unfulfilled desires of creatures who have never realized the beauty for which they were created—only as we anticipate the renewed cosmos that the liturgy calls forth. This eschatological hope for a world that finally discloses God's justice is central to a Reformed theology of creation.[57] It banks on the confidence that God is actively bringing a world-in-travail into the fulfillment of its ultimate redemption. Paul declares in Romans 8:19–23 that this is the hope the entire cosmos awaits with eager longing. This passage became a definitive text in Reformed reflections on the earth and its future and was prized by Jonathan Edwards at the height of the Great Awakening. He had a keen expectation of the coming kingdom, seeing the new creation to be growing out of the preserved (and enhanced) beauty of the world we already have.

Visions of a new heaven and earth filled his imagination, though he couldn't envisage another world any more lovely than this one. "Clothed in new garments, appearing in raiment of new life, glory and joy," Edwards's vision of a new creation incorporated the beauty of the original and the wonder of God's continuous creation alike.[58] *Creatio originalis*, *creatio continua*, and *creatio nova*: all three were, for him, joined in God's on-going work of bestowing beauty on a world tarnished by sin.

Thomas Berry reminds us that the "Great Work" of restoring creation—God's work as well as ours—will not be finished in a single lifetime. It requires pledging ourselves to a hope that demands unrelenting action. Someday we'll have to answer the questions that future generations will ask of us: "You knew there was a hole in the sky (in the ozone layer) and you did nothing? You watched 5,000-year-old arctic ice melt and dismissed concerns over global warming?" Our answers

---

57. Whether creatures in the coming Kingdom will be recapitulated only in the memory of the Trinity, restored as representative species, or re-created as individual creatures enabled at last to fulfill the desire for which they were created is still debated, as Christopher Southgate observes in *Groaning of Creation*.

58. Edwards, *Miscellanies*, #1296, "New Heavens and New Earth." YE 23:238.

will depend on the extent to which we have held ourselves accountable for sharing God's dream of restoring the earth. Hope doesn't exclude deliberate planning for ecological sustainability. It demands it.

Anticipating the day when "creation itself will be set free from its bondage to decay," we are sustained by the larger community of created beings who share that expectation with us. Calvin observed that we aren't alone in our longing. The "straining forward" (*epekteinomai*) of the saints to which Paul refers in Phil 3:13, isn't exclusively a human experience. "Paul joins all creatures to them as companions" so "that their courage may not fail in this race" (Rom 8:19).[59]

All these others—wheatfields, waterfalls, and wildebeests—stand on tiptoe along with us, awaiting God's promised renewal of the world. "Not that they are endowed with any [human] perception," Calvin hastened to add, "but they naturally long for the undamaged condition whence they have fallen." Aching desire for God is woven through the fabric of nature. "There is no element and no part of the world which, touched with the knowledge of its present misery, is not intent on the hope of the resurrection."[60]

This recognition of the wider "communion of saints," all participating in a shared beauty not yet fully realized, becomes the motivating force of a Reformed environmental ethic. What drives the sons and daughters of Calvin to moral action is not, finally, any utilitarian or anthropocentric concern about what serves human life alone, but what serves the greater glory (and beauty) of God—what drives us to the endless extension of that beauty throughout the biosphere.

Those who have drawn from the wells of a Reformed spirituality of desire will at the end of their lives want to echo the words of Mary Oliver in her poem "Death Comes." In looking back, Oliver hopes that she will lived her life as "a bride to amazement," having embraced the world completely.[61] A universe filled with astounding mystery, and their own experience of God, will have taught them by then that what their minds can't fully grasp their hearts can still love. Having been driven to radical amazement—and the work for justice that it evokes—they will have discovered wonder as their final response to a God who adorns the world with a reckless, exuberant beauty.

59. Calvin, *Institutes*, 3.25.2.
60. Calvin's Commentary on Rom 8:19–20; CO 49:151–52; CTS XIX:303.
61. Oliver, "When Death Comes," 10.

Bibliography

Albertus Magnus. *On Animals: A Medieval Summa Zoologica.* Translated by Kenneth F. Kitchell Jr. and Irven Michael Resnick. Baltimore: Johns Hopkins University Press, 1996.

Aquinas, Thomas. *Summa Theologica.* [**Pub. Info**]

Barth, Karl. *Church Dogmatics.* 13 vols. Translated by G. T. Thomson et al. Edinburgh: T. & T. Clark, 1960.

Basil. *Saint Basil: Exegetic Homilies.* Translated by Agness Clare Way. Washington, DC: Catholic University of America Press, 1963.

Baxter, Richard. *The Saints Everlasting Rest.* London: Epworth, 1962.

Benyus, Janine. *Biomimicry: Innovation Inspired by Nature.* New York: Morrow, 1997.

Berry, Thomas. *The Dream of the Earth.* San Francisco: Sierra Book Club, 1988.

Boff, Leonardo. *Trinity and Society.* Translated by Paul Burns. Maryknoll, NY: Orbis, 1988.

Brueggemann, Walter. *Israel's Praise: Doxology Against Idolatry and Ideology.* Philadelphia: Fortress, 1988.

Burke, Edmond. *On the Sublime.* Edited by J. T. Bolton. London: Routledge & Paul, 1958.

Calvin, John. *Calvin's Commentaries.* Grand Rapids: Baker, 2005.

———. *Corpus Reformatorum.* Brunswick: A. Schwetchke and Son [M. Bruhn], 1863–1900.

———. *Institutes of the Christian Religion.* Edited by John T. McNeill. Philadelphia: Westminster. 1960.

———. *Institutes* (1536 edition) In *The Selected Works of John Calvin, Ioannis Calvini Opera Selecta,* in five volumes, edited by Peter Barth, et al. Munich: Chr. Kaiser. 1926–1959.

Delattre, Roland. *Beauty and Sensibility in the Thought of Jonathan Edwards.* New Haven: Yale University Press, 1968.

———. "Religious Ethics Today: Jonathan Edwards, H. Richard Niebuhr, and Beyond." In *Edwards in Our Time: Jonathan Edwards and the Shaping of American Religion,* edited by Sang Hyun Lee and Allen C. Guelzo, 67–86. Grand Rapids: Eerdmans, 1999.

Dillard, Annie. *Holy the Firm.* New York: Harper & Row, 1977.

———. *Pilgrim at Tinker Creek.* New York: Harper & Row, 1974.

Driver, Tom F. *The Magic of Ritual.* San Francisco: HarperSanFrancisco, 1991.

Du Bartas, Guillaume de Saluste Sieur. *The Divine Weeks and Works of Guillaume de Saluste Sieur Du Bartas.* Translated by Josuah Sylvester. Oxford: Clarendon, 1979.

Edwards, Jonathan. "Religious Affections." In *The Works of Jonathan Edwards,* edited by John E. Smith. New Haven: Yale University Press, 1959.

Ferguson, Ronald. *Chasing the Wild Goose: The Iona Community.* London: Collins, 1988.

Gerrish, B. A. *Grace and Gratitude: The Eucharistic Theology of John Calvin.* Minneapolis: Fortress, 1993.

Gould, Stephen Jay. "Unenchanted Evening." *Natural History* 100 (1991) 4–9.

Harrison, Verna. "*Perichoresis* in the Greek Fathers." *St. Vladimir's Theological Quarterly* 35

(1991) 53–65.

Heller, Chaia. *Ecology of Everyday Life: Rethinking the Desire for Nature.* Montreal: Black Rose, 1999.

Hemenway, John, and John Todd. *Gaia's Garden: A Guide to Home-Scale Permaculture.* White River Junction, VT: Chelsea Green, 2001.

Hugh of St. Victor. "The Three Days of Invisible Light." In *Corpus Christianorum*, vol. 177: Book 7. Tournhout, Belgium: Brepols, 2002.

Lane, Belden C. "Spirituality as the Performance of Desire: Calvin on the World as a Theatre of God's Glory." *Spiritus* 1 (2001) 1–30.

Leopold, Aldo. *Sand County Almanic.* New York: Ballantine, 1970.

Masson, Jeffrey Moussaieff, and Susan McCarthy. *When Elephants Weep.* New York: Dell, 1995.

Miles, Margaret. "Theology, Anthropology, and the Human Body in Calvin's *Institutes of the Christian Religion." Harvard Theological Review* 74.3 (1981) 303–23.

Mollison, Bill, and Reny Mia Slay. *Introduction to Permaculture.* Tyalgum, New South Wales, Australia: Tagari, 1991.

Moltmann, Jürgen. *God in Creation: A New Theology of Creation and the Spirit of God.* Minneapolis: Fortress, 1993.

Old, Hughes Oliphant. *Worship: Reformed According to Scripture.* Louisville: Westminster John Knox, 2002.

Oliver, Mary. "When Death Comes." In *New and Selected Poems*, vol. 2. Boston: Beacon, 1993.

Plantinga, Cornelius. "Social Trinity and Tritheism." In *Trinity, Incarnation, and Atonement: Philosophical and Theological Essays*, edited by Ronald J. Feenstra and Cornelius Plantinga Jr. 21–47. Notre Dame, IN: University of Notre Dame Press, 1989.

Rauschenbusch, Walter. *Christianity and the Social Crisis.* New York: Harper Torchbooks, 1964.

Rice, Howard L., and James C. Huffstutler. *Reformed Worship.* Louisville: Geneva, 2001.

Ryan, John A. *A Living Wage.* New York: Macmillan, 1906.

Santmire, H. Paul. *Brother Earth: Nature, God and Ecology in a Time of Crisis.* New York: Thomas Nelson, 1970.

Schaefer, Jame. "Appreciating the Beauty of Earth." *Theological Studies* 62 (2001) 23–52.

Southgate, Christopher. *The Groaning of Creation: God, Evolution, and the Problem of Evil.* Louisville: Westminster John Knox, 2008.

Swimme, Brian. *The Universe is a Green Dragon.* Santa Fe: Bear, 1984.

Vischer, Lukas, editor. *Christian Worship in Reformed Churches Past and Present.* Grand Rapids: Eerdmans, 2003.

Wolfe, David W. *Tales From the Underground: A Natural History of Subterranean Life.* Cambridge: Perseus, 2001.

5

Orthodox Spirituality and Contemporary Ecology

John Cassian, Maximus the Confessor,
and Jürgen Moltmann in Conversation

Brock Bingaman

> Today we recognize that the subject of Christian spirituality is
> the human being as a whole: spirit, mind, and body; individual
> and social; culturally conditioned and ecologically intertwined
> with all of creation; economically and politically responsible.[1]

IN HIS REFLECTION ON THE TRINITARIAN ASPECTS OF CHRISTIAN SPIRI-
tuality, Mark McIntosh notes the renaissance in recent decades regarding the question of spirituality and creation.[2] While this renewed
interest in spirituality and creation has led to many important (re)
discoveries and transformed attitudes toward creation, some scholars
have noted the all too often shallow treatment of concomitant theological and spiritual themes. David Cunningham argues, "much of
this recent 'eco-theology' is composed of roughly 95 percent ecology,
with theological considerations entering the picture only in order to

---

1. Schneiders, "Study of Christian Spirituality," 17. Schneider's essay, which deals
with various approaches to the academic study of Christian spirituality, is quite helpful.
In view of her essay, the approach taken in this chapter combines elements of the historical, theological, and anthropological methodologies. Also informative is Williams'
reflection on methodologies in *On Christian Theology*, xii–xvi. His overall point, that
one often displays various modes of arguing and interpreting (including the *celebra-*
tory, *communicative*, and *critical*), is well taken and applied in this essay.

2. McIntosh, "Trinitarian Perspectives on Christian Spirituality," 177–89.

buttress a position that was already ecologically warranted."[3] In light of Cunningham's contention (which, I think, can be verified) this essay seeks a more balanced perspective in eco-theology or the conversation between Christian spirituality and ecology. In this chapter, therefore, I argue that John Cassian's (c. 360–345), Maximus the Confessor's (c. 580–662), and Jürgen Moltmann's (1926–) consonant notions of spirituality and ecology reinforce humanity's mandate to global stewardship. As the argument unfolds, I demonstrate how reading Cassian, Maximus, and Moltmann in conjunction sheds light on the growing interest in spiritual and ecological matters, theologically deepens the discussion, and illustrates the resourcefulness of Christian spirituality and theology in the contemporary milieu.[4] Accordingly, the various aspects of the chapter's argument will be considered as we explore the parallel, interrelated themes of eschatology, *theosis*, ethics, community, and ecumenism in each of these three authors.[5]

Eschatological Perspectives

First, we consider the notion that the eschatological perspectives of these theologians, which value and anticipate God's glory in the universe, provide a creation–esteeming worldview. Cassian portrays the monastic life in eschatological terms. His well-known *Conferences* serve as a map that sketches out how monks are to prepare in this life for the vision of God in the age to come. Cassian explains that the desired "goal" in life is "purity of heart," and the "end" is to enter the kingdom of God and behold the glory of God in the face of Christ.[6]

3. Cunningham, *These Three Are One*, 260–61. Regarding this surge of interest in the environment among Christians, Cunningham adds: "And even when a more theological approach has appeared, it often veers toward a vague pantheism. If God is understood as being 'in' the earth, or even as *being* the earth, then (it is assumed) Christians will be ethically inclined not to injure the earth, for they would thereby be injuring God, 261."

4. See also McIntosh, *Mystical Theology*, for examples of the issues within and resourcefulness of contemporary studies in Christian spirituality, particularly 18–30, 90–118.

5. For basic (and more detailed) information on each theologian, see: Stewart, *Cassian the Monk*; Chadwick, *John Cassian*; Thunberg, *Microcosm and Mediator*; Bauckhum, *The Theology of Jürgen Moltmann*.

6. Cassian *Conferences* 1.2–4 (hereafter, *Conf.*). Because the *Nicene and Post-Nicene Fathers* edition tends to be more available in many libraries, this is the version to which

While some might suggest that Cassian's spirituality is "other-worldly" or lacks earthly-grounding, this is, arguably, a misunderstanding of Cassian. While it is the kingdom of God or the (eschatological) end for which Cassian encourages monks to prepare, in the mean time, striving for purity of heart in everyday life leads to personal transformation. The persistent contemplation of God and the idea that one will see God in the consummation of the kingdom, according to Cassian, renews a person's earthly existence. And, in the true spirit of monasticism, human beings on the road of personal transformation demonstrate the high value of God's created order. This can be seen in Cassian's threefold schema of the spiritual life, a framework he picks up from the influential Christian ascetic, Evagrius Ponticus[7] (c. 345–399): *praktikos, physikos, theologikos*. In short, *praktikos* is the cultivation of the virtues, particularly through the activity of asceticism in pursuit of purifying the mind. *Physikos* is the contemplation of created things, when the purified mind begins to discern their inner structures. *Theologikos* is the goal, when contemplation ushers one into knowledge of and unity with God.[8] Building on this Evagrian schema, which is based to some extent on Paul's teaching regarding the perception of God in creation in Romans 1:20, Cassian urges contemplative pray-ers to "feed on the beauty and knowledge of God alone."[9] Thus, for Cassian, the spiritual life is on an eschatological trajectory, leading to the kingdom of God, and must be prepared for *now*. In his view, "every creature of God is good," and genuine contemplation of creation can lead to discerning the beauty of the invisible God within the visible world.[10]

I refer throughout this chapter, unless noted otherwise. I also recommend the more recent and complete translation in the Ancient Christian Writers series, *John Cassian: The Conferences*, by Ramsey.

7. For recent studies in Evagrius, see Harmless, *Mystics*, 135–57 and Konstantinovsky, *Evagrius Ponticus*.

8. For a concise yet informative look at the threefold schema in Evagrius, see Tugwell, "Evagrius and Macarius," 168–73.

9. Cassian *Conf.* 1.1.8.

10. Cassian *Conf.* 1.21.8. Evagrius, who is so influential for Cassian, speaks of natural creation as letters written to humanity by God. He also tells the story of St. Antony's encounter with a philosopher who marvels that the famous hermit lives without books. Antony replies, "My book, O philosopher is the nature of things that exist (*ton gegonoton*), and it is there whenever I want to read the words (*tous logous*) of God," Stewart, *Cassian the Monk*, 52.

In addition to Cassian, we find an eschatological orientation in the theology of Maximus, one that also highly values the glory of God in the cosmos. Related to this eschatological outlook is the primary role that christology plays in Maximus' theological vision. More specifically, it is the incarnation of Christ that often figures so prominently in his thinking. According to Maximus, the

> mystery of the Incarnation of the Word contains in itself the force and meaning of all the challenging puzzles and symbols of Scripture, as well as the significant content of all visible and intelligible creatures. Whoever understands the mystery of the Cross and the grave has grasped the essential content (*logos*) of all the things we have mentioned; and whoever, in addition, has been initiated into the mysterious meaning and power of the Resurrection knows the primordial (*proegoumenos*) purpose for which God created the universe.[11]

Notice how he links the incarnation with the meanings, principles, and purpose of all things. For Maximus, the understanding of Christ's incarnation, according to the Council of Chalcedon (451)[12] – the hypostatic union of his two natures – serves as God's paradigm, plan, and goal for humanity and the universe. Hans Urs von Balthasar posits that Maximus' "ontology and cosmology are extensions of his Christology, in that the synthesis of Christ's concrete person is not only God's final thought for the world but also his original plan."[13]

Furthermore, Maximus speaks of the connection between Christ's incarnation and God's goal for the created universe, a notion pregnant with meaning and positive implications for a creation-esteeming worldview. He writes:

> Here is the great and hidden mystery. This is the blessed end, the goal, for whose sake everything was created. This was the divine purpose that lay before the beginning of all things . . . With this goal in mind, God called the natures of things into existence. This is the limit toward which providence and all the things it protects are moving, where creatures realize their reen-

11. Maximus, quoted in Balthasar, *Cosmic Liturgy*, 278.

12. See Meyendorff, *Byzantine Theology*, for helpful analyses of the Council of Chalcedon, 32ff., 151ff.

13. Balthasar, *Cosmic Liturgy*, 207. Moreover, Thunberg asserts that for Maximus "the Incarnation in its proper and historical sense can be directly related to the constitution and meaning of the cosmos," *Man and the Cosmos*, 76.

try into God. This is the mystery spanning all the ages, revealing the supremely infinite and infinitely inconceivable plan of
God, which exists in all its greatness before all the age . . . For
Christ's sake, or for the sake of the mystery of Christ, all the ages
and all the beings they contain took their beginning and their
end in Christ. For that synthesis was already conceived before
all ages: the synthesis of limit and the unlimited, of measure
and the immeasurable, of circumcision and the uncircumcised,
of the Creator with the creature, of rest with movement – that
synthesis which, in these last days, has become visible in Christ,
bringing the plan of God to its fulfillment through itself.[14]

In passages like this, Maximus states clearly that Christ's incarnation
embodies the eschatological goal for the entire universe. God's great
and mysterious plan is to bring creation into union with Godself based
on the union between the divine and human natures in the incarnation
of the Word. As Andrew Louth explains, the union between Creator
and creature is described in terms of a "Chalcedonian logic."[15] That is,
according to Maximus, the reunification of God and creation does not
result in the creature's dissolution or absorption into God. Rather, the
union between God and creation, like Christ's hypostatic union, means
that they are joined in an "unmixed" and "unchanged" manner.

Regarding the high view of creation that stems from his incar-
nationally based thinking, von Balthasar argues that Maximus "is the
most world-affirming thinker of all the Greek Fathers; in his basically
positive attitude toward nature he goes beyond Gregory of Nyssa."[16]
Therefore, in Maximus the intertwined threads of eschatology, God's
glorious plan for creation, and Christ's synthesizing incarnation lead
to a reverent attitude toward a universe on its way to reentry into God.

We find ideas that accord with the eschatological and world-
affirming perspectives of Cassian and Maximus in Moltmann's theological project. In his six systematic "contributions,"[17] Moltmann

14. Maximus, quoted in Balthasar, *Cosmic Liturgy*, 272.

15. Louth explains how Maximus works out a consistent "Chalcedonian logic,"
based on his fondness of the four Chalcedonian adverbs: *asynchtos, atreptos, adiairetos,
achoristos*. These terms, emphasizing that the two natures in Christ undergo no confusion, no change, no division, and no separation, are applied by Maximus to safeguard
the integrity of the natural, *Maximus the Confessor*, 49–51.

16. Balthasar, *Cosmic Liturgy*, 61.

17. Moltmann, *Trinity and the Kingdom*; *God in Creation*; *Way of Jesus Christ*; *Spirit
of Life*; *Coming of God*; and *Experiences in Theology*.

explicates a "social doctrine of the Trinity"[18] and an "ecological doctrine of creation." In *God in Creation*, Moltmann intends to present an emphatically Christian doctrine of creation, one that is "messianic," that is, formed by the person, proclamation, and history of Jesus the Messiah. Moltmann's doctrine of creation is "a view of the world in the light of Jesus the Messiah," one shaped by the perspective of messianic time which has begun with Christ and which he defines. Moreover, it is directed "towards the liberation of men and women, peace with nature, and the redemption of the community of human beings and nature from negative powers, and from the forces of death."[19] This messianic doctrine of creation "therefore sees creation together with its future— the future for which it was made and in which it will be perfected." Moltmann suggests, in line with ancient Christian teaching, that "the future of creation" pictured as "the kingdom of glory" provides a symbol of cosmic hope. This cosmic hope indicates that creation in the beginning is an open creation, and that its consummation will be to become the home and dwelling place of God's glory. Consequently, human beings already experience the indwelling presence of God through the Spirit in history, even if this indwelling is only partial and provisional. This promissory indwelling is the basis of hope that in the kingdom of glory, the triune God will dwell wholly and eternally in creation, allowing all God's creatures to participate in the fullness of divine life.[20]

The realization of this hope means that the poor and alienated find their "home" in the world. It also means "being at home in existence," so that the relationships between God, human beings, and nature lose their tension and are resolved into peace and rest. For, if "the creative God himself dwells in his creation, then he is making it his own home, 'on earth as it is in heaven.'" Thus, all created beings then "find in nearness to him the inexhaustible wellspring of their life, and for their part find home and rest in God."[21] Moltmann's reflection on the Trinity and

18. There are various opinions on Moltmann's social doctrine of the Trinity. Some of the particularly insightful reflections on Moltmann's social doctrine of the Trinity (including negative critiques, calls for clarification, and responses to criticism) are found in: Ayres, *Nicaea and its Legacy*, 384–429; McIntosh, *Divine Teaching*, 125–27; McDougall, *Pilgrimage of Love*, 119; and Moltmann's attempts to clarify his views, *God in Creation*, 241.

19. Moltmann, *God in Creation*, 5.

20. Ibid.

21. Ibid.

creation entwines various themes, using them to shed further light on the others. That is, Moltmann explores these interrelated ideas – the messianic, the liberation of creation, the future of an open creation, the indwelling of God, and creaturely participation in God – in ways that disclose the eschatological trajectory of creation. For Moltmann, as with Maximus, the idea that creation is indwelt by the transcendent God and is on its course to reunification with God, engenders deep respect for creation and resists exploitive practices.

Theosis: The Divinization of Humanity and the Cosmos

In this section, my aim is to show how the aforementioned eschatological perspective is expressed by the Orthodox in terms of *theosis*, the divinization of humanity and the cosmos.[22] Linked to his eschatologically oriented teaching on the spiritual life, in his exposition of the Lord's Prayer Cassian voices the biblical teaching that the "will of God is the salvation of all people" (cf. 1 Tim 2:4). He explains that when "we say then, 'Thy will be done as in heaven so on earth,' we pray in other words for this; viz., that as those who are in heaven, so also may all those who dwell on earth be saved, O Father, by the knowledge of Thee."[23] In light of this teaching, and of the prominence of Evagrius' influence on Cassian, one might find it surprising that Cassian does not develop the important Orthodox doctrine of *theosis*. Certainly, similar elements are found in Cassian: the longing for the salvation of all people, for heaven and earth to be united, for people to gaze contemplatively on the glory of God now in preparation for seeing God in the heavenly kingdom, and for believers to be transformed into the image of Christ while still living on earth.

Additionally, in one section from *Conference* 10, Cassian reflects on the prayer of Jesus found in John 17. In these reflections, we find concepts that suggest a doctrine of *theosis*, even though the specific language of deification is not found, at least as it is in Maximus and Moltmann.[24] For example, Cassian explains that the prayer that Jesus

22. One of the foundational biblical texts for the doctrine of *theosis* is 2 Pet 1:4, which speaks of believers partaking of the divine nature through the promises of God. For a thorough treatment of the doctrine, see Russell, *Doctrine of Deification*.

23. Cassian *Conf.* 1.9.20.

24. Ladner's elucidation on the various concepts of reform, renewal, and the recov-

prayed for his disciples (for their maturity in love and their unity, Jn 17:26, 21) is fulfilled "when every love, every desire, every effort, every undertaking, every thought of ours, everything that we live, that we speak, that we breathe, *will be God*." Then, that unity which the Father has with the Son will carry over into our lives, so that just as God loves us with a pure and indissoluble love, "we too may be *joined to him* with a perpetual and inseparable love and [be] so *united with him* that whatever we breathe . . . understand . . . [and] speak, *may be God*."[25] When we come to Maximus' and Moltmann's treatments of *theosis*, we will find some of these same basic ideas about the transformation of human thinking and being, unification with God and one another, and the primary role that love plays in the whole process.

Columba Stewart offers a number of helpful insights in his discussion of "seeing and knowing Christ" in Cassian's theology. First, Stewart points out that for Cassian "pure prayer" means to "see" God in the glorified Christ, to have one's spiritual senses awakened as one contemplates the divine nature in Christ. To illustrate, Stewart cites Cassian: "I see the ineffable illumination, I see the unexplainable brilliance, I see the splendor unbearable for human weakness and beyond what mortal eyes can bear, the majesty of God shining in unimaginable light."[26]

Stewart indicates that, according to Cassian's teaching, there are two kinds of contemplation of Jesus, both of which depend on the measure of one's purity of heart and character of life. Some are able to see the humble and fleshly Jesus among the common people in towns and villages (i.e., those who are still at the "practical" stage of the spiritual life). Others, who are advancing in purity of heart and experiencing freedom from earthly encumbrances, are enabled to ascend the high mountain of solitude, where they see the glorified Jesus of the Transfiguration. Stewart explains that in this vision of the glorified Jesus, where one beholds the glory of his face and the image of his

---

ery of humanity's likeness to God, is very helpful, especially when looking at different figures from the Christian East and West alongside one another, *Idea of Reform*, 98ff., 194ff.

25. *Conf.* 10.7 [italics mine]: from McGinn, *Essential Writings of Christian Mysticism*, 95–96.

26. Cassian, quoted in Stewart, *Cassian the Monk*, 95–96.

splendor, the believer is granted a glimpse of that future beatific vision that is promised to the saints, when "God is all in all" (1 Cor 15:28).[27]

Noting the interesting parallels between Cassian's exegesis of the Transfiguration and that of Origen, Stewart highlights Cassian's insistence that "seers" of Christ grow in their ability to ascend the mountain and see him in his divine glory.[28] This image of Christ being transfigured before his disciples on Mt. Tabor, and the graced ability to increasingly see him, is key for a number of Orthodox theologians and their teaching on *theosis*, including Maximus.[29] For these theologians the story of Christ's transfiguration, in which the divine glory rests upon and radiates from him, serves as a living illustration of how the glory and energies of God transform the followers of Jesus as they gaze upon him and grow in his likeness.

Finally, Stewart explains Cassian's teaching on how the life and ministry of Jesus is a model for approaching God with a pure heart. But, in Cassian's estimation, this is not enough. Simply following Jesus' instructions regarding prayer or his example of praying in solitude, which are necessary and commendable activities, is not the complete picture of life in God through Christ. Stewart says, "Cassian wants to move his readers beyond imitation of the earthly life of Jesus to real participation in the glorified Christ." For Cassian, "imitation of Christ is the way to recover the full image and likeness of God in the perfection of love." Then, "one is able to climb the mountain to see Christ transfigured."[30] Therefore, while Cassian articulates these interrelated themes (of seeing God in the glorified Jesus, previewing the beatific vision through contemplating Christ as his disciples did on Mt. Tabor, and moving beyond imitation of Christ to participation in his glory) in different terms than Maximus, one can discern the congruency. For both theologians, the transfiguration of humanity through participation in the divine glory, and the eschatological promise of God being all in all are crucial dynamics and recurring motifs.

Where Cassian seems to give only glimpses of the doctrine of *theosis*, or more accurately, uses different language and concepts, Maximus displays a thoroughly nuanced vision of the deification of

27. Stewart, *Cassian the Monk*, 96.

28. Ibid.

29. See Ware, *Orthodox Church*, 69, 226; cf. Maximus, *Writings*, 146.

30. Stewart, *Cassian the Monk*, 96–97.

humanity and the cosmos.[31] Again, as noted earlier, Christ's incarnation (in Chalcedonian terms) provides the paradigm for the way divinization plays out. Von Balthasar, quoting Maximus, posits that the Confessor "can never have enough of praising 'all the different syntheses between diverse creatures that are realized through Christ.'" After "Christ brought his historic work of salvation to completion for our sakes and ascended along with the body he had assumed," writes Maximus, "he united heaven and earth through himself, connected sensible creation with the intellectual, and so revealed the unity of creation in the very polarity of its elements." The five great cosmic syntheses, as Maximus states, that lead to this unity begin with the notion that Christ "unites man and woman . . . unites the earth by abolishing the division between the earthly paradise and the rest of the inhabited globe . . . unites earth and heaven . . . unites sensible and intelligible things . . . and ultimately—in an ineffable way—unites created and uncreated nature."[32] For Maximus, the incarnation of the Word affirms the goodness of creation by his entry into it. The synthesis that occurred in his incarnation, therefore, is that which brings about all the other cosmic syntheses.

While limited space does not allow us to fully develop Maximus' doctrine of *theosis* and how he deals ultimately with the "restoration" of the cosmos in Christ, suffice it to say that Christ's own person prefigures the unification of the world with God. Everything in Maximus' theological reflection is aimed at this synthesis between God and the world. "With this step, [Maximus] fulfills the passionate longing of the whole patristic tradition, especially that of Alexandria, for divinization."[33] Interestingly, what distinguishes him from his interlocutors is that he

---

31. Classic and more recent scholarship on *theosis* can be found in: M. Lot-Borrodine, *La Deification*; Lossky, *Vision of God*; Ladner, *Idea of Reform*, 96ff.; Russell, *Doctrine of Deification*.

32. Balthasar, *Cosmic Liturgy*, 273–75. In doing this, Balthasar asserts that Maximus "has built the Alexandrian doctrine of divinization into his own theory of syntheses by removing its Neoplatonic and spiritualist sting. In the form in which he presents it, there is not the slightest danger of pantheism." It is true that Scotus Erigena "must have built his own system directly on texts such as this. But the pantheistic tones that he added to it through his theory of four natures are not present in Maximus." Thus, the "East's instinct for divinization is held in check here by the Chalcedonian term 'unconfused' (*asugkutos*)," 275. See also Lossky's informative discussion of the five cosmic syntheses, *Orthodox Theology*, 74–75.

33. Balthasar, *Cosmic Liturgy*, 343.

refuses to go "on the record" by proclaiming a universal restoration [*apokatastasis*] in a direct way, as Origen and Gregory of Nyssa did.[34]

In terms accordant with Maximus, Moltmann delineates his eschatological perspective.[35] One example is when Moltmann explains that *God in Creation* is an "ecological doctrine." He says that one sense of this is intended to highlight the ecological crisis of our time, while the deeper sense references the symbolism of "home" and "indwelling." Noting the Greek derivation of the word "ecology," and its definition as "the doctrine of the house," Moltmann asks what the Christian doctrine of creation might have to do with a doctrine of the house. He suggests that if we see only a Creator and the Creator's work then there is no connection. But if we think about the Creator, his creation, and the goal of that creation in trinitarian terms, then the Creator, through his Spirit, *dwells in* the whole of creation and in every individual created being, since the Spirit holds them together and keeps them alive. Thus, Moltmann explains that the inner secret of creation is *God's rest*. If we ask about creation's goal and future, we ultimately arrive at the transformative indwelling of the triune God in his creation, which through that indwelling becomes a new heaven and a new earth (Rev 21), and at God's eternal Sabbath, in which the whole creation will find rest, bliss, and ultimate fulfillment.[36]

Another brief example of Moltmann's consonance with the Orthodox notion of *theosis* is evidenced when he says: "The patristic church's doctrine of physical redemption was more comprehensive in its cosmological dimensions. Today it must be transformed into an ecological doctrine of redemption." It "could then be in a position to redeem the modern world from its deadly limitations and conflicts." Moreover, when we neglect to consider the cosmic dimensions of Christ's death and resurrection (Col 1:20), our understanding of sin and death remains anthropocentric. For "Christ's resurrection from the

---

34. Maximus takes the notion of *apokatastasis*—the doctrine of the abolition of hell, something viewed as heretical by the Orthodox and Catholic Churches since Origen— and develops and broadens its meaning. Still, in the end, Maximus opts to not go on record for his final thoughts on universal restoration. Rather, he says, "The hidden, better meaning, however, must be reserved for those who have a better understanding of mysteries. We must 'honor it by silence'" (Balthasar, *Cosmic Liturgy*, 356ff.).

35. See Bauckham, *God Will Be All in All*, for a fine collection of essays on various aspects of Moltmann's eschatological perspective.

36. Moltmann, *God in Creation*, xiv.

dead is not merely the endorsement of his death for the salvation of sinners; it is also the beginning of the transfiguration of the body and of the earth."[37] Therefore, as Moltmann suggests, critically retrieving ancient soteriological concepts like *theosis* is important for constructing ecologically sound theology, theology that articulates the cosmic scope of God's saving activity in Christ through the Spirit.

It should be pointed out, however, that Moltmann's discussion of *theosis* is multivalent. More specifically, it seems that Moltmann holds contradictory or conflicting opinions about the doctrine of *theosis*. On one hand, Moltmann demonstrates deep appreciation for the cosmic, all embracing emphasis of the doctrine of *theosis* and the way this corrects the tendency in Reformed theology (his own tradition) that often focuses on more anthropocentric categories like justification, sanctification, and glorification. Further, through ongoing dialogue with Orthodox teaching on *theosis*—such as Athanasius' axiom regarding God becoming human so that humans can become God, or Gregory of Nyssa's meditations on the cosmic link between Christ's resurrection, the new creation, and the transfiguration of all things, or Maximus' insistence that deification includes the whole person, body and soul—Moltmann speaks about deification in glowing terms. Moreover, he utilizes *theosis* to counter modern, atomistic thinking that divides God and creation, humanity and nature, and body and soul, in his attempt to encourage more unitive, holistic, and cosmic theologizing.[38] On the other hand, Moltmann offers a critique of *theosis*, especially its tendency towards "spiritualizing the cosmos," that suggests an element of docetism, rather than portraying "a new creation."[39] At other times, Moltmann simply recounts certain developments in the doctrine without speaking in favor of or against it. For example, in his discussion of cosmological christology, he explains the growth of the ideas of participation in and correspondence to the divine glory, and how the "Fathers of the church saw this all-embracing goal of salvation as 'the deification of the human being' and 'the deification of creation.'"[40] Here he references Dimitru Staniloae: "The world, as the work of God's love,

37. Moltmann, *Coming of God*, 92, 93.

38. For a few examples where Moltmann employs the doctrine of *theosis*, see *Coming of God*, 92ff.; *Spirit of Life*, 299ff.

39. Moltmann, *Coming of God*, 272–74.

40. Moltmann, *Way of Jesus Christ*, 47.

is destined to be deified."[41] Moltmann's conversation with Orthodoxy on *theosis*, while oscillating between different opinions of it, might be viewed as a paradigm of critical, creative, and appreciative engagement. Through this discussion of *theosis*, Moltmann illustrates some of the ways that theological and spiritual reflection might lead to a more comprehensive, ecologically inclusive understanding of salvation.

Stewarding Life and the Environment

Having reflected on the eschatological perspectives on God's glory in creation, and the notion of the transfiguration of humanity and the cosmos, I want to consider how this outlook on universal *theosis* formulates a spirituality that encourages responsible stewardship of life, resources, and the environment. For Cassian, two things in particular are worth noting. First, in unfolding his teaching on preparing to see God in the kingdom and on the transformative effects of the contemplative life, Cassian speaks of "fasting, diligence in reading, works of mercy, justice, piety, and kindness." He also quotes Matt 25:34, 35, where Jesus speaks of rewarding those who give food to the hungry and drink to the thirsty.[42] According to Cassian, the truly spiritual person, someone who is being transformed by God's Spirit, is the person who both prayerfully worships God *and* serves fellow humans. A second thing worth noting briefly is Cassian's maxim: "extremes meet" (*akrotetes isotetes*).[43] Cassian instructs his readers to avoid the extremes of gluttony and excessive abstinence, both of which lead to injury. He says that living in due moderation is the *via media*. The ethical implications of Cassian's teaching on social justice, works of mercy, and moderation speak directly to many important issues in today's global and ecological milieu. Cassian's teaching on moderation, as simple as it might seem, holds incredible potential for individuals and communities (and nations, for that matter) seeking to live more responsibly in relation to the environment. Evidence for this is found in particular early monastic communities, where living, eating, and drinking in moderation illustrated a kind

---

41. Ibid., 253.

42. Cassian *Conf.* 1.1.9.

43. Cassian *Conf.* 2.16.

of harmony between human beings and the environment, a respect for the earth and its many gifts that sustain life.[44]

As noted earlier, Maximus is known as the most world-affirming of the Greek Fathers. This is seen in his teaching on *theosis* and his conviction that Christ's incarnation, life, death, and resurrection guarantee the recapitulation of humanity and the cosmos. In light of this, it is not surprising when he speaks so forthrightly about the goodness of created things and the imperative for their proper use. To illustrate, he explains that "it is not food which is evil but gluttony, not the begetting of children but fornication, not possessions but greed, not reputation but vainglory." Further, "if this is so, there is nothing evil in creatures except misuse, which stems from the mind's negligence in its natural cultivation."[45] I am underscoring three things here: first, countering all Gnostic errors, Maximus asserts the goodness of creatures and material things. Second, Maximus says that it is only the misuse of things that is evil. Finally, Maximus indicates that misuse arises from improper thinking. So, what is it that we can glean from Maximus here? In short, Maximus' teaching on *theosis*, linked with his notion of the goodness of creatures and the proper use of things, offers us a healthy alternative to the modern approach of objectifying and exploiting creation. Developing an ethic based on Cassian's "moderation axiom" and Maximus' world-affirming viewpoint could lead us to fresh perspectives regarding our stewardship of life, resources, and the environment.

Moltmann adds further brush strokes to the picture. He asserts that according to the Christian interpretation, creation "is a trinitarian process: the Father creates through the Son in the Holy Spirit. The created world is therefore created 'by God,' formed 'through God' and exists 'in God.'" He cites the Orthodox theologian Basil:

> Behold in the creation of these beings the Father as the preceding cause, the Son as the One who createth, and the Spirit as the perfecter; so that the ministering spirits have their beginning in

44. For example, see Burton-Christie, *Word in the Desert*, 213–35; and "Nature," 478–95. Interestingly, one also finds this kind of thinking and living among the various Native American traditions. Recent research demonstrates the importance of Native American teaching on moderation, the value of reciprocity, and the balance and tempering of human life on the planet. Native American theologians have a great deal to add to this conversation. For a creative and bracing example of this, see the groundbreaking work by Kidwell et al., *Native American Theology*, especially 32–51.

45 Maximus, *Writings*, 62.

the will of the Father, are brought into being through the efficacy of the Son, and are perfected through the aid of the Spirit.[46]

The implications of this Trinitarian view of creation are manifold. One
consequence, according to Moltmann, is that "we have to understand
every created reality in terms of [divine] energy, grasping it as the realized potentiality of the divine Spirit." It is through the energies and
potentialities of the Spirit that the Creator is present within creation.
The Creator does not merely confront it in his transcendence, but enters
into it, so that he is also immanent within it.[47]

Further, Moltmann reasons that if the Holy Spirit is "poured out"
on the whole creation, then the Spirit creates "the community of all created things with God and with each other, making it that fellowship of
creation in which all created things communicate with one another and
with God, each in its own way."[48] In line with the previous discussion
of Cassian and Maximus, this means that we have to discover new ways
of thinking about creation, moving beyond modern thinking which, in
Moltmann's estimation, has "developed by way of an objectifying, analytical, particularizing and reductionalistic approach."[49] A new world
view emerges if we experience and understand creation as the work of
the triune God, the God who exists in community and relationship,
the God who indwells and brings humanity and creation to the fullness of its deified potentialities. Moltmann explains that this view of
"life as communication in communion" will shape different aspects of
life. First, on what Moltmann calls the legal and political level, we will
understand that such a worldview facilitates "a covenant with nature,"
in which the rights of human beings and the rights of the earth are
respected and balanced out. Nature is no longer viewed as unclaimed
property. Second, on the medical level, this symbiotic understanding of
life is to be defined as "the psychosomatic totality" of the human being
who stands over against him/herself. The body, therefore, is no longer
to be seen as something that we possess. Third, on what Moltmann calls
the religious level, the vision of humanity and nature is to be interpreted

46. Basil, quoted in Moltmann, *God in Creation*, 9.

47. Moltmann, *God in Creation*, 2–4.

48. Ibid., 11.

49. Ibid., 9.

as "a community of creation." Thus, creation is not viewed as the world that human beings are supposed to "subdue."[50]

Related to this is Moltmann's attempt to revise misunderstandings of the image of God in human beings and the commission to "rule" over creation (Gen 1:26–27). In his consideration of the *imago Dei* and the misguided interpretation of Gen 1:26–27 as license to dominate and exploit nature, Moltmann argues that human beings are commissioned to function as a "justice of the peace." As those made in the image of the triune God, who live within the community of all creation, human beings are to serve as God's representatives on earth, manifesting divine love for all of God's creatures.[51]

It is, therefore, by implementing the insights of thinkers like Cassian, Maximus, and Moltmann that we will be better equipped to formulate a spirituality for the proper stewardship of life and resources on our planet. Each of these is an important part of an ecologically responsible vision of stewardship: Cassian's teaching on contemplation, social justice, and moderation, Maximus' teaching on *theosis* which encourages a respectful attitude toward creation, and Moltmann's Trinitarian and pneumatological vision of a community of all creation. Bringing together these various ideas and practices can help transform our understanding of living properly in our world.

Communal Embodiment and Implementation

Having explored some of the ways that Cassian, Maximus, and Moltmann encourage responsible stewardship of life, we turn now to consider how this ethical vision is embodied and implemented within communities of interrelated persons. All three of these theologians are committed to the notion of communities which flesh out an ethic that values other people and God's creation. Cassian devotes his entire *Conference* 16 to

50. Moltmann, *God in Creation*, 2–4, 9, 11. See Johnson, *She Who Is*, 71ff., for her reflections on human stewardship, community, and a holistic understanding of human being. Here, and in other places, she references Moltmann.

51. Moltmann, *God in Creation*, 224. In his reconsideration of theological anthropology, Moltmann explores human beings as *imago Dei* (the original designation), *imago Christi* (the messianic calling), and *gloria Dei* (the eschatological glorification). His reflections hold many valuable insights regarding the role of human beings in creation 215–43. See also Kidwell et al., *Native American Theology*, for an interesting critique of the idea of stewardship in Christian theology, 47ff.

friendship. He repeats the theme of valuing hospitality over personal discipline four times in the *Conferences*.[52] Further, Cassian highlights the importance of love in the life of the monk. He explains that if a monk is "inflamed with true and perfect love of our Lord," increasing numbers will be attracted to him and should not be turned away but welcomed kindly.[53] Additionally, in *Conference* 16 Cassian reinforces the notion of human partnership in the monastic quest, explaining that it is not a solo endeavor or even something worked out between two monks. Rather, it is the cooperative effort of persons living in community, committed to friendship and chastity, and devoted to the supreme value of love for God and neighbor.[54]

Maximus resonates with Cassian on the primacy of love for God and neighbor. He devotes his entire *Four Hundred Chapters on Love* to the theme. He asserts that the wise person is a flowing source of good, someone who loves all people, who becomes the revelation in the world of God's hidden love. Moreover, love for God and the world are not two distinct loves but two dimensions of the one, indivisible love. By this love, the total synthesis of humankind comes to realization in a single identity, in which every individual exchanges his/her own being with wider humanity, and all with God.[55] Again, Maximus' ability to take a theme, like the virtue of love, and cast it in cosmic and universal dimensions is helpful. Love is not an individual affair, nor something worked out between oneself and God or two people. Rather, Maximus posits that "if someone loves God, [he/she] cannot avoid loving all people."[56]

52. Cassian *Conf.*, 2.26, 17.21–24, 21.14, 24.20; cf. Stewart, *Cassian the Monk*, 44, where he explains that the practice of hospitality is a strong theme in the Egyptian desert tradition of the *Apophthegmata*.

53. Cassian *Conf.*, 24.19.1.

54. cf. Stewart, *Cassian the Monk*, 74–75, for his discussion on "Solitude and Encounter," where he spells this out in more detail. Also worth noting is Cassian's example of selfless love in the life of a woman who served widows in the church in *Conf.* 3.18.14. Cassian tells of how she overcomes the meanness of an elder woman through humility, gentleness, and kindness, virtues that are needed today if we are to live peaceably with one another.

55. See Maximus, in Balthasar, *Cosmic Liturgy*, 340. Regarding the centrality of love in Maximus' theological vision, see Thunberg, *Microcosm*, 309ff.

56. Maximus, *Centuries on Love* I, 13; PG 90, 964B; cf. Ware, *Orthodox Way*, where he reflects on the relationship between love for all people, living lives of compassion and service, liberating the oppressed, and how the doctrine of the Trinity can inspire such living, 39ff.

For it is by love that all things were created, and by love all things are brought together and find rest in God.[57]

Furthermore, Maximus' teaching on the church and its liturgical engagement with God and creation is fecund, offering rich and relevant themes for contemporary spiritual theology and ecology. In his work *The Church's Mystagogy*, a mystical interpretation of the church and its liturgy, we find several elements in his understanding of the Christian community that inform spiritual and ecological interests. One is the way that Maximus transplants Evagrian spirituality into an ecclesial context. Put succinctly, Maximus takes up the threefold Evagrian schema of the spiritual life (*praktike*, *phusike*, and *theologike*), correlates it to the human person, and roots it in his vision of the church as the cosmic body of Christ. Accordingly, in Maximus' understanding, the first stage (*praktike*) is linked to the believer's body and the church's nave, where one observes the commandments in moral wisdom and ascetic activity. The second stage (*phusike*) is connected to the believer's soul and the church's sanctuary, in which one engages in natural contemplation. The third stage (*theologike*) is seen in relation to the believer's mind and the church's altar, where union between Creator and creature takes place as signified and realized in the Incarnation and in the celebration of the Eucharist.[58]

In these dense, multifaceted meditations, where the church symbolizes humanity and humanity symbolizes the church, Maximus interweaves elements of Evagrian spirituality, anthropology, ecclesiology, and the liturgy. Like Matryoshka (Russian nesting dolls) that fit inside one another, Maximus' vision of the cosmic Christ opens up his vision of the church, the human person, and the realization of the human vocation through spiritual growth and union with God. For Maximus, Christians are seen as individuals who realize their created purpose by functioning as "little churches" in which the rhythms of the universal church's liturgy are embodied and manifested.

In addition to transplanting Evagrian spirituality into an ecclesial context, Maximus portrays the church's vocation to function as

---

57. See Maximus, *Ambiguum 7*, in Blowers, *On the Cosmic Mystery of Jesus Christ*, 47.

58. See Dragas, "Church in St. Maximus's Mystagogy," 385–403, for an exposition of these and other related elements, as well as an overall analysis of the structure of the *Mystagogy*.

God's living icon in the world, a community of individuals who mediate Christ's reconciling activity to all creation. The general problem
Maximus addresses in the *Mystagogy* is how the divine image is restored
to us, after having been snatched away by the devil through deception
and disobedience. This restoration of the divine image through spiritual
growth in the context of Christian community is, as we have seen, central to Maximus' teaching on *theosis*.[59]

While Maximus is adamant that God is ultimately beyond all affirmation and negation as the unknowable and inaccessible One, he
also suggests that the church, as the image that reflects its archetype,
functions as God's living icon in the world so that, in some sense, the
invisible, transcendent God becomes visible through the worshipping
community. Furthermore, as God's living image in the world, believers
actually cooperate with God in the reunification of all things with their
Maker.

According to Maximus, the church's calling to function as God's
living icon in the world is rooted in his Trinitarian-christocentric vision. That is, Maximus describes this unifying work in Trinitarian terms
so that the Christian community is the place where divine freedom
and love unifies humanity without erasing their differences. Moreover,
Maximus carefully applies elements of Chalcedonian Christology—with
its emphasis on the "unchanged" and "unmixed" natures of Christ—in
order to express how those who participate and "converge" in God's life
do so without forfeiting their differences.

In his synthesizing approach—in which he brings together the
above threads of Evagrian spirituality transplanted into ecclesiology, the church's vocation as God's icon in the world, and Trinitarian
and christologically grounded thinking—Maximus says that in order
for the work of the evil one to be overcome and to realize the deification of human beings, we must transcend our own particular, fragmented existence, and be joined to God and one another in faithful
and universal union. As McIntosh explains in his consideration of the
Mystagogy, Maximus portrays the church as the "ongoing communal
event of Christ's reconciling activity."[60] Accordingly, the Body of Christ,
as the image of God in the world reflecting its divine archetype, builds

59. See Sherwood's pioneering work in Maximus regarding the role of the church as
an agent of deification, *St. Maximus the Confessor*, 73–77.

60. McIntosh, *Discernment*, 252ff.

a new communal structure in which divisions are overcome as they are brought into the very depths of the Trinitarian life. This new communal structure in which a divided humanity and cosmos are reconciled in Christ does not entail homogeneous conformity. Rather, this reconciliation and reunification means that all the features of men, women, and children who are distinct from one another in many ways, are brought together into a united whole that respects the integrity of each particular creature.

Weaving these various themes together in a meditation on Gal. 3:28, Maximus says:

> For numerous and of almost infinite number are the men, women, and children who are distinct from one another and vastly different by birth and appearance, by nationality and language, by customs and age, by opinions and skills, by manners and habits, by pursuits and studies, and still again by reputation, fortune, characteristics, and connections: All are born into the Church and through it are reborn and recreated in the Spirit. To all in equal measure it gives and bestows form and designation, to be Christ's and to carry his name. The purpose of this is so that the creations and products of the one God be in no way strangers and enemies to one another by having no reason or center for which they might show each other any peaceful sentiment or identity, and not run the risk of having their being separated from God to dissolve into nonbeing. Thus, as has been said, the holy Church of God is an image of God because it realizes the same union of the faithful with God. As different as they are by language, places, and customs, they are made one by it through faith.[61]

Hence, in this text Maximus describes how the church, as Christ's body, is graced to image and carry out the reintegration of all believing humanity into a glorious whole. As the human body has many diverse parts, but is brought together into an organic whole, so the church brings together all peoples into oneness with the Holy Trinity and with one another.

McIntosh reinforces this point when he says that the divine power and activity in which the church cooperates with God is Trinitarian.[62] The church is the place where God's unifying activity is made visible

---

61. Maximus, *Mystagogy*, 187–88.

62. McIntosh, *Discernment*, 252–53.

in the world. The triune God is seen in this activity that causes every creature to "converge in each other by the singular force of their relationship to him."[63] Through their mutual relationship to God, creatures are freed from their divisive interactions with one another, placing them in a new communion with each other. Maximus explains:

> This reality [the new relation to one another through their communion with God] abolishes and dims all their particular relations considered according to each one's nature, but not by dissolving or destroying them or putting an end to their existence. Rather it does so by transcending them and revealing them, as the whole reveals its part.[64]

Maximus utilizes language and concepts forged in Trinitarian and christological formulations in order to describe the church's role as an agent of deification, a community that brings human beings together in a way that mirrors the inner Trinitarian relations. Through this distinction between nature and one's particular mode of existence, Maximus conveys how creatures can move beyond the divisive and limiting interactions at play in the world into liberating and uniting relations to one another.

As McIntosh explains, "God's activity is precisely to *release* the creatures from 'their particular relations considered to each one's nature,'" so that creatures "discover God bringing about relationships among them based not necessarily on the self-preserving instincts of *nature* but based on the development of *persons* whose identities are given in God."[65] In other words, as creatures are drawn out of themselves in response to the self-giving of God in Christ, they rediscover their own identities and those of their neighbors in the light of God's unifying love. "This sets up a divine pattern of life subverting the world's structures," asserts McIntosh, "a heavenly pattern in which a completely new mode of relation and personal identity can come to birth in the matrix of the divine unifying power."[66]

As Maximus' meditation on the church proceeds, he develops the rich metaphor of the church functioning as God's living icon in the world. It is, as I have already noted, the "holy Church of God" that

---

63. Maximus, *Writings*, 186.
64. Ibid.
65. McIntosh, *Discernment*, 253.
66. Ibid.

"works for us the same effects of God" by realizing the union of the faithful with God. "As different as they are by language, places, and customs, they are made one by [the church] through faith." God "realizes this union among the natures of things," Maximus says, weaving together the many threads, "without confusing them but in lessening and bringing together their distinction . . . in a relationship and union with himself as cause, principle, and end."[67] Therefore, Maximus offers a rich vision of community, one in which individuals transcend their own particular, fragmented existence, being united to God and one another, and empowered to function as God's image in the world.

Moltmann discusses themes similar to Cassian and Maximus. As noted earlier, he encourages his readers to re-think and re-form theology in light of the Spirit being outpoured on the whole creation and, therefore, creating "the community of all created things with God and with each other."[68] According to Moltmann, this perspective, with its emphasis on the Spirit's presence in creation, is our best hope for avoiding ecological disaster and nuclear annihilation. He asserts that "we have only one realistic alternative to universal annihilation: the non-violent, peaceful, ecological world-wide community in solidarity." Moreover, Moltmann seeks to promote cooperation between theology and the sciences, in an effort to develop "*a community* of scientific and theological insights." For it "is only in our common recognition of the danger of universal ecological and nuclear catastrophes, and only in our common search for a world capable of surviving, that we shall also then be able to put forward the particular contribution of the Christian traditions and the hope of the Christian faith."[69]

In addition to reformulating a pneumatological vision of creation and encouraging cooperation between theology and the sciences, Moltmann also argues that a transition from the modern mechanistic, patriarchal world view to an ecological perspective will liberate not only the environment but also the relational world of women and men. He says, "This means that this ecological world view is bound up with new egalitarian forms of society, in which patriarchal rule is ended and

---

67. Maximus, *Writings*, 188.

68. Moltmann, *God in Creation*, 13.

69. Moltmann, *God in Creation*, 12, 13. In his *Method in Theology* Lonergan also calls for cooperation between theology and the sciences, and sets forth a whole method for a theology that mediates within its cultural matrix.

co-operative communities are built up."[70] Therefore, the re-imagining of theology in pneumatological and ecological terms plays an important part in helping us avoid ecological and nuclear threats of disaster, encouraging cooperation between theologians and scientists, and seeking transformative liberation in the world of relations between women and men.

Ecumenical and Interdisciplinary Dialogue

This final section exemplifies briefly how these three authors work in an ecumenical fashion—bridging the worlds of East and West, and setting promising trajectories for interreligious and interdisciplinary dialogue regarding contemporary ecology. Cassian is an ecumenical figure, someone who bridges East and West, through his writings, life, and travels. As a disciple of Evagrius and ardent follower and supporter of John Chrysostom, Cassian moved from Bethlehem to Egypt to Constantinople, then to Rome, Gaul, and Marseilles, where he founded two monasteries, one for men and the other for women. Though usually not recognized adequately, Cassian's contribution to the Western tradition through Benedict and Gregory is evident.[71] Bonafice Ramsey, a specialist in Cassian studies, says that the influence of Cassian's writings might be expressed to be in inverse proportion to the obscurity of his life. Ramsey notes that, in addition to influencing Benedict and Gregory, Cassian also inspired Rhabanus Maurus (d. 856), Rupert of Deutz (d. 1129), and Thomas Aquinas (d. 1274), who cites him over a dozen times in the section on moral theology in his *Summa Theologiae*.[72] Further, Cassian is the only Latin Father to be included in *The Philokalia*, the treasured Orthodox compendium of spirituality.[73] He could, perhaps, be viewed as a living conduit through which the spirituality of the Eastern desert made its way into the Western world.

70. Moltmann, *God in Creation*, 320.

71. See Stewart, *Cassian the Monk*, 116ff., where he highlights Cassian's integrative work, that was "continued by theological heirs such as Maximus the Confessor and Symeon the New Theologian," and "was vitally important for the development of eastern Christian spirituality."

72. Ramsey, *John Cassian: The Conferences*, 7. Ramsey adds, "It would not be an exaggeration to refer to the author of *The Conferences* as one of the great, albeit less well known, preceptors of the West," 7.

73. See *Philokalia*, vol. 1, 72–108.

Like Cassian, Maximus is a bridge between East and West. He stands as an example, as Jaroslav Pelikan explains, of a bi-lingual theologian, someone able to speak the language of spirituality and theology with equal fluency, bringing together the traditions of Rome and Constantinople in his remarkable synthesis. More than that, Maximus reaches inside and opens up a host of intellectual worlds that appeared to have lost contact, bringing light from each one to illuminate the others, leading to new connections and surprising similarities and relationships. Maximus unites these worlds in his own approach to theology, as a contemplative biblical theologian, a philosopher trained in Aristotelian thought, a mystic in the Neoplatonic tradition of Gregory of Nyssa and Pseudo-Dionysius, a devout monk of the Evagrian tradition, and a man of the church who gave his life for the orthodox christology of Chalcedon and for a church centered in Rome.[74]

Moltmann follows in the same vein, as someone committed to bringing different spheres of thought together through ecumenism, interreligious dialogue, and interdisciplinary collaboration. Examples of this are found in his engagement of Ernst Bloch's Marxist philosophy of hope, the Jewish theology of Franz Rosenweig and Abraham Heschel, Gestalt psychology, theologies of disability, and environmental science. Moreover, in his approach to theology and spirituality, he follows what he calls an "ecumenical method," drawing from Protestant and Catholic sources, entering into discussion with theologians from both sides, looking for common points of interest while acknowledging the differences, and encouraging mutual exploration and understanding.[75] Moltmann also engages in dialogue between the churches of the East and West, something illustrated by his deep friendship and ongoing conversation with Orthodox theologian Dumitru Staniloae. In his dialogue with the Eastern churches, Moltmann discovered the rich creation wisdom preserved in Orthodox theology, something that, in his opinion, was often pushed aside and lost in the West, largely because of modern developments in science, technology, and industry. Emblematic of his

---

74. Balthasar, *Cosmic Liturgy*, 57.

75. See Bauckham, *Theology of Jürgen Moltmann*, 1–3, for further information regarding the different spheres Moltmann attempts to bring together in his theology. Also, Moltmann's autobiography, *Broad Place*, outlines the numerous influences on his theology, as well as the various circles in which he has moved. These include his dialogue with James Cone and Black theology, Latino/a theology, Feminist theology, Asian theological movements, and Pentecostal/Charismatic theology.

ecumenical method, and his appreciation for the many ancient concepts in various Christian communities, Moltmann asserts that it "is the earliest traditions of Christian theology which frequently offer the most pregnant ideas for the revolution in our attitude to nature which is so vitally necessary today."[76] Hopefully, we have been able to see examples of this critical appropriation of fertile ideas within these various traditions, concepts that can help transform our understanding of the relationship between spirituality and ecology, and therefore, our thinking about and living in this beautiful world.

Concluding Remarks

In conclusion, I have attempted to demonstrate how a correlative reading of Cassian, Maximus, and Moltmann reinforces humanity's mandate to environmental stewardship. I have sought, moreover, to show how reading these three authors in conjunction sheds light on the burgeoning interest in ecological matters, and illustrates the resourcefulness of Christian spirituality and theology. By appropriating these congruent elements—eschatology, *theosis*, ethics, community, and ecumenism—the church and wider humanity can catalyze the ecological mission through extensive collaboration. While I have only been able to touch briefly on these consonant notions, my aim is to encourage further exploration into how the relationship between spirituality and ecology might lead to new discoveries, perspectives, and responsible action.

Bibliography

Ayres, Lewis. *Nicaea and its Legacy: An Approach to Fourth-Century Trinitarian Theology*. New York: Oxford, 2004.
Balthasar, Hans Urs von. *Cosmic Liturgy: The Universe according to Maximus the Confessor*. San Francisco: Ignatius, 2003.
Bauckham, Richard. *God Will Be All in All: The Eschatology of Jürgen Moltmann*. Minneapolis: Fortress, 2001.
———. *The Theology of Jürgen Moltmann*. Edinburgh: T. & T. Clark, 1995.
Blowers, Paul. *On the Cosmic Mystery of Jesus Christ: St. Maximus the Confessor*. Crestwood, NY: St. Vladimir's Seminary, 2003.

76. Moltmann, *God in Creation*, xv. For other instances of Moltmann's engagement of these early traditions, see Constas, "Eschatology and Christology," 191–99.

Burton-Christie, Douglas. "Nature." In *The Blackwell Companion to Christian Spirituality*, edited by Arthur Holder, 478–95. Oxford: Blackwell, 2005.

———. *The Word in the Desert*. New York: Oxford, 1992.

Chadwick, Owen. *John Cassian: A Study in Primitive Monasticism*. Cambridge: Cambridge University Press, 1968.

Constas, Nicholas. Constas, "Eschatology and Christology: Moltmann and the Greek Fathers." In *God's Life in Trinity*, 191–99. Minneapolis: Fortress, 2006.

Cunningham, David. *These Three Are One: The Practice of Trinitarian Theology. Challenges in Contemporary Theology*. Oxford: Blackwell, 2003.

Dragas, George. "The Church in St. Maximus's Mystagogy: The Problem and the Orthodox Perspective." *Theology* 1 (1985) 385–403.

Gibson, Edgar C. S. (transl.) *John Cassian: The Conferences*. In *Nicene and Post-Nicene Fathers*, Second Series, vol. 11. Peabody: Hendrickson, 2004.

Harmless, William. *Mystics*. New York: Oxford, 2008.

Johnson, Elizabeth. *She Who Is: The Mystery of God in Feminist Discourse*. New York: Crossroad, 1992.

Kidwell, Clara Sue, et al. *A Native American Theology*. Maryknoll: Orbis, 2001.

Konstantinovsky, Julia. *Evagrius Ponticus*. Surrey: Ashgate, 2009.

Ladner, Gerhart. *The Idea of Reform: Its Impact on Christian Thought and Action in the Age of the Fathers*. New York: Harper & Row, 1967.

Lonergan, Bernard. *Method in Theology*. Toronto: University of Toronto, 2003.

Lossky, Vladimir. *Orthodox Theology: An Introduction*. Crestwood: St. Vladimir's Seminary Press, 1978.

Louth, Andrew. *Maximus the Confessor*. New York: Routledge, 2006.

Maximus the Confessor. *Selected Writings*. Translated by George Berthold. New York: Paulist, 1985.

McDougall, Joy Ann. *Pilgrimage of Love*. New York: Oxford, 2005.

McGinn, Bernard. *The Essential Writings of Christian Mysticism*. New York: Random, 2006.

McIntosh, Mark. *Discernment and Truth*. New York: Crossroad, 2004.

———. *Divine Teaching*. London: Blackwell, 2008.

. *Mystical Theology*. Oxford: Blackwell, 1998.

———. "Trinitarian Perspectives on Christian Spirituality." In *The Blackwell Companion to Christian Spirituality*, edited by Arthur Holder, 177–89. Oxford: Blackwell, 2005.

Meyendorff, John. *Byzantine Theology*. New York: Fordham, 1979.

Moltmann, Jürgen. *A Broad Place: An Autobiography*. Translated by Margaret Kohl. Minneapolis: Fortress, 2008.

———. *The Coming of God: A Christian Eschatology*. Translated by Margaret Kohl. Minneapolis: Fortress, 2004.

———. *Experiences in Theology: Ways and Forms of Christian Theology*. Translated by Margaret Kohl. Minneapolis: Fortress, 2000.

———. *God in Creation: A New Theology of Creation and the Spirit of God*. Minneapolis: Fortress, 1993.

———. *The Spirit of Life: A Universal Affirmation*. Translated by Margaret Kohl. Minneapolis: Fortress, 1992.

———. *The Trinity and the Kingdom: The Doctrine of God*. Translated by Margaret Kohl. Minneapolis: Fortress, 1981.

————. *The Way of Jesus Christ: Christology in Messianic Dimensions*. Translated by Margaret Kohl. Minneapolis: Fortress, 1990.

Palmer, G. E. H., et al. *The Philokalia: The Complete Text*. 2 vols. Boston: Faber, 1981.

Ramsey, Bonafice, translator. *John Cassian: The Conferences*. Mahwah: Newman, 1997.

Russell, Norman. *The Doctrine of Deification in the Greek Patristic Tradition*. New York: Oxford University Press, 2006.

Schneiders, Sandra M. "The Study of Christian Spirituality." In *The Blackwell Companion to Christian Spirituality*, edited by Arthur Holder, 15–33. Oxford: Blackwell, 2005.

Sherwood, Polycarp. *St. Maximus the Confessor: The Ascetic Life, The Four Centuries on Charity*. Mahwah: Newman, 1955.

Stewart, Columba. *Cassian the Monk*. New York: Oxford, 1998.

Thunberg, Lars. *Man and the Cosmos: The Vision of St. Maximus the Confessor*. Crestwood: St. Vladimir's Seminary, 1997.

————. *Microcosm and Mediator: The Theological Anthropology of Maximus the Confessor*. Chicago: Open Court, 1995.

Tugwell, Simon. "Evagrius and Macarius." In *The Study of Spirituality*, edited by Cheslyn Jones et al., 168–73. Oxford: Oxford, 1986.

Ware, Timothy. *The Orthodox Church*. London: Penguin, 1997.

Williams, Rowan. *On Christian Theology*. Challenges in Contemporary Theology. Oxford: Blackwell, 2000.

6

Contemplation in the Vibrant Universe

The Natural Context of Christian Spirituality

Robert John Russell

The Cosmic Metaphor

NEAR THE ENDING OF HER AUTOBIOGRAPHY, ST. TERESA OF JESUS DEscribes God through an exquisite metaphor:

> Let us suppose the Godhead to be a most brilliant diamond, much larger than the whole world . . . and that all our actions are seen in that diamond, which is of such dimensions as to include everything, because nothing can be beyond it.[1]

In contemplation Christians are led to explore the inward mystery of existence. Yet Teresa's metaphor directs the contemplative attention outwards as well as into the limitless reaches of God's creation, the universe. With all its vast splendor, the universe is our home. Our history is written out of its nature. We have made stardust our flesh, made our name out of genes, and those of us who are Christians are called to follow a covenant with our God which extends to all of creation. Everything, from the atoms in our palm to the farthest galaxies whose light caresses the lenses of our telescope, exists and evolves within the Godhead. God "includes everything" and infinitely transcends it. Surely then, the inward and the outward journeys blend as two spiraling paths, each leading in its own way towards the source and destiny of our lives.

---

1. Teresa of Avila, *Life,* 412.

Thus, I would like to use this metaphor to expand our spiritual journey outward into the universe. Like Beatrice to Dante, I will ask contemporary science—cosmology, quantum physics, and evolutionary biology—to be our guide. If it is true of a diamond that each facet reflects a glimmer of its central illumination, it is even more the case that as one contemplates the multiple facets of our cosmic diamond through the light of science, these reflections will seem to mingle, blend, and converge on a single, central illumination, the divine Life in which all dwell.

The spiritual journey leads not only outward into the universe. It leads outward into the world, where the people of the Word are called to bear witness to the redemptive power of God with us. Thus what I hope to show is that the convergence of inner and outward paths brings about insights that benefit both our Christian pilgrimage and the world we are called to love and to serve. In my own faith journey, convictions about the presence of God in my life and a *moral imperative* about the future of our endangered global community drive me to seek this convergence. So this essay is a reflection of my own journey and an invitation to others to share in the exploration of inward Light and cosmic Logos.

Spirituality: The God Within is the God Throughout

Christian spirituality centers on knowing God through contemplation. Prayer itself is a form of service and Christian discipleship. The interior path demands hard work and a lifetime commitment. I want to a suggest that spiritual insights, gained and developed through prayer, can be expanded, illustrated and transformed by viewing them in the context of all of God's creation as understood by contemporary natural science, particularly physics and biology.

This suggestion, in turn, is based on both a theological and a philosophical premise. My *theological* premise is that the God known through Christian faith and encountered in prayer is the creator of the world—the cosmos. God continues to create through and with the world's intricate, evolving and exquisite processes, by which we ourselves emerge, find life, and undergo change. Finally, we are an unending part of this divine creativity. Therefore it seems worth considering whether the insights of Christian spirituality can converge and mingle creatively with our growing scientific knowledge of creation. If so, this convergence could deepen and enrich our spiritual journey even while the journey remains focused on the interior life.

Of course, our new scientific self-knowledge may throw a critical light on our choices about the human future in an ecological context, and thereby challenge and alter our spiritual journey. Our understanding of the universe has changed enormously since the founding of the great Christian spiritual traditions—from a static, earth-centered cosmos to a dynamic, expanding universe of unimaginable complexity; and from an understanding of life on earth as fixed in separate, unfaltering species to an account of life which is now irrevocably cast in evolutionary terms.

Thus the need for a new, fruitful interaction between science and spirituality is urgent. Indeed, Pope John Paul II, in a message on the Church and the scientific community, spoke out boldly on the potential benefits of a new interaction between science and religion: "Science can purify religion from error and superstition; religion can purify science from idolatry and false absolutes. Each can draw the other into a wider world, a world in which both can flourish."[2] In this document, John Paul II underscored the need for theologians to draw on the discoveries of science, and for scientists to recognize the broad context of human culture as they go about their work. Rather than isolated forces or, worse yet, enemies, the religious and scientific communities are beginning to discover a new form of unity within diversity. "We need each other to be what we must be, what we are called to be."[3]

My *philosophical* premise is basic to modern epistemology: knowledge of things is conditioned by the knower, by the personal, socio-political, and historical contexts in which it comes about. I wish to suggest that the broadest possible context for our human knowing, including spiritual insight at its apex, is the context of *nature*, the evolutionary cosmological context in which we emerge and live.[4]

2. Russell et al., *Physics, Philosophy, and Theology*, 13.

3. Ibid., 14.

4. I think it is wonderfully appropriate that the Logo for the Bicentennial of Carmel in America, 1990, depicted a rectangle framing the entire design. According to the description of the Logo, the purpose of the rectangle is "to give an impression of this-world stability and balance and to tie Carmel securely to ordinary human life, to this material universe and the humanity that peoples it." It is to this "material universe and the humanity that peoples it" that I dedicate this essay, for this is the living context of our spirituality, a universe fifteen billion years old now peopled in at least one fragile,

Moral Imperative: From Resource to Partner

This same philosophical premise leads me to the second conviction of my presentation: There is a moral imperative in our attempt at convergence. The future of humanity depends more and more on the linkage between our self-understanding and our understanding of the entire sweep of evolving nature. If humanity is to solve some of the global disasters caused by technology in the service of greed, injustice and militarism, it must re-conceive nature not as artifact of a distant God, not as an indifferent resource at our disposal, not as a mere stage on which human experience and human history is played out, but as a fragile web of ecological integrity out of which all life, including human life, arises and on which all life depends.

We must discover the *intrinsic* values of nature and not just the *instrumental* value of nature for us. We must discover a new vision of nature in which humanity, having the interior vision of God as its crowning jewel, is a crucial, but not a dominating, part. We must discover a new vision of nature in which we are not lords but servants, not the center of the universe but a determining partner with all life in shaping the universal future. It is my conviction that Christian spirituality can contribute a vital component of that vision.

An Overview

In this essay I will consider five perspectives on nature, five facets of the diamond St. Teresa spoke of, drawn from contemporary physics, cosmology and biology. These are: the origin of the universe; the quantum world; the origin of life on earth; the ecological web; the far future of the universe.

From each I draw certain key insights about the relation between human nature and the creation as a whole. I hope to show how these insights can illustrate and expand our understanding of God's relation to human nature discovered through the practice of Christian spirituality.

To set up the imagery for each facet in the diamond I suggest a new composite symbol drawn from *two* sources: the traditional images of St. John of the Cross which so infused the cosmology of his age: earth,

---

fragrant corner, with teaming terrestrial life and human culture.

water, air and fire; and contemporary science as it lays bare to us the challenging new vistas and mysteries of a universe of epic proportions and ever-evolving, inter-connected species of life.

I will focus on nature as understood by science in relation to Christian spirituality. The goal is to prepare for the extended task of envisioning better ways to care for the earth as Christian stewards, shepherds, and friends.

First Facet:

The Origins of the Universe-The Cosmos as Mystery

FIRST SYMBOL: COSMIC FIRE

Imagine a clear summer's night, lying on a grassy meadow gazing up into the dark sky above. If it is "good seeing" there will be several thousand stars in the sky, along with the broad mottled-white streak of the Milky Way. The entire night sky seems to rotate ever so slowly about an axis lying near the North Star. The earth is still.

Yet it is, of course, the earth that is moving, the sky fixed. (How counter-intuitive nature is! Should we be confident in the motif, "seeing is believing"? The mystical way of knowing is needed, since it may be closer to the way things "really are" than that given to ordinary sense perception!) And if you were to watch the sky night after night, you might notice that a couple of the stars move relative to the rest of the constellations — sometimes eastward, sometimes westward. These "wandering stars" troubled the ancient Greek astronomers so much that a series of increasingly complicated models were constructed to explain their motion.

By the time of Aristotle, 56 spheres were needed to accommodate the motion of these "planets"; later Ptolemy employed his famous system of equinoxes and deferents to more closely approximate their erratic movement. Both systems manifested an aesthetic criterion as well, for they resolved the irregular motion into circular motion (of complex combinations). Yet by the sixteenth century, increasingly careful data on planetary motion forced the revamping of the entire cosmological system. With the Copernican revolution and its culmination in the aesthetic simplicity of Keplerian elliptical orbits and the mathematical elegance of Newtonian gravitational mechanics, our modern heliocentric model of the solar system emerged.[5]

Return now to that starry night sky. We now know that all the visible stars at night are part of our own galaxy of over one hundred billion stars. Indeed what we call the Milky Way is just the region in the sky where we are looking through the galactic plane, and the density of stars gives the appearance of a continuous flow. The rest of the stars we see are part of the galaxy, appearing like a veil as we look outward perpendicular to the galactic plane.

Now imagine it's a winter's eve. Looking carefully at the region near the constellation Pegasus you spot a small smudge of light. It's not unlike other such objects you might see, many in or near the Milky Way. Yet this one is not part of our galaxy but another entire galaxy, the Great Spiral Galaxy in Andromeda. It lies over 1.5 million light years away from us; the light we see began its journey long before *homo sapiens* emerged on planet earth!

To look further we need a telescope. Astronomers have invented not only increasingly large optical telescopes, but now use radio, infrared, x-ray, and other complicated telescopic instruments both ground-based and in Earth orbit. With these instruments they have made staggering discoveries about the universe this century.

We now know that our galaxy, Andromeda, and about eighteen other galaxies form what is called our Local Group. This cluster of galaxies, in turn, is part of a Supercluster, approximately 75 million light years in diameter. The Virgo cluster, another member of our Supercluster, is much richer than our Local Group, containing thousands of member galaxies. Most of the space in the Supercluster is empty. However, recent evidence suggests that the distribution of clusters and superclusters form enormous strings and filaments in space.

But the most remarkable discovery of this century, first reported by Edwin Hubble in 1929 and now confirmed for much greater scales, is that these superclusters are moving apart from each other with speeds proportional to their separation distance. We have discovered the expanding universe!

A voyage outward into space is also a voyage backwards in time. As we look further and further outward into space, past the clusters and

5. The Greeks, of course, were the first to speculate about a heliocentric model of the universe. See the writings of Aristarchus in the third century, BC.

superclusters to the realm of the quasars, we are moving backwards in time. How far back can we go?

Using theories by Albert Einstein and contemporary cosmologists, we are led unalterably to an event which is "off the map," the beginning of time ("t=0"), the origin of the universe some fifteen billion years ago. As we approach this event temperatures soar, the universe shrinks to below the size of an atom, densities climb exponentially, and the laws of physics as we know them begin to fail us. Using scientific methods, we simply cannot describe, let alone explain, the "uncaused moment" where it seemingly all began. "T=0" lies at the boundary of science and metaphysics, a signature of the mystery of nature found at the heart of nature and yet transcending nature. According to Big Bang theory, our universe was born out of an indescribable explosion of matter, light and geometry, of a fire that burns *as* nature herself.[6]

I am reminded here of John of the Cross's eloquent verses about Creation:

> 'Thanks to You, Almighty Father,
> 'The Son made answer to the Sire,
> 'To the wife that You shall give
> Me I shall give My lustrous fire,
> That by its brightness she may witness
> How infinite My Father's worth
> And how My being from Your being
> In every way derived its birth.'[7]

And so I propose as our first symbol that we take fire from St. John and express it in truly universal proportions: the universe as Cosmic Fire.

---

6. The "t=0" scenario raises exceedingly difficult and controversial research questions both for scientists and for philosophers and theologians seeking to interpret responsibly the meaning and significance of current cosmology. Future scientific theories may indeed explain this event in terms of a prior universe (perhaps an oscillating universe, etc.), the use of quantum gravity, or some other means, but within the standard Hot Big Bang model, even with inflation taken into consideration, the problem of "t=0" remains. My task here is to suggest some of the insights one can take from the standard model, where the "t=0" problem was first discovered, and which has received the most attention in interdisciplinary studies. For further reading, see articles by Arthur Peacocke and Ian Barbour in Peters, *Cosmos as Creation*, and articles by Sallie McFague, Bill Stoeger, Ted Peters, John Leslie, Frank Tipler, Ernan McMullin, Norris Clarke, and Chris Isham in Russell et al., *Physics, Philsophy, and Theology*.

7. John of the Cross, *Poems*, 57.

In contemplating nature as cosmic fire one can discover that all of reality is contingent, fragile, consuming and persisting. Nature is utterly dependent on something which goes beyond it for its very existence; it flickers, wavers, ignites and extends again and again to its source, ever beyond reach. At the very heart of science lies a mystery which transcends science, a mystery as to the sheer existence of all that is. We now know beyond any ancient knowing that ours is indeed a universe of vast, unimaginable beauty, of searching, unfathomable complexity, of reachless, overwhelming size and unending yet unrepeatable history, of staggering future and limitless complexity—and yet a universe whose sheer existence in the face of non-being cries out for an explanation, for a power which can ground it and give it reality. And this truly is God.

We also learn that as creatures of atoms and molecules, our history extends back to the beginnings of the universe and forward into the misty horizon of the universe's far future. Our dependence is cosmic: we depend on the universe for our atoms and molecules, our bones and genes, our primate heritage and our transcending vision. Not only are we linked to the universe as a whole, in a deeper sense we *are* the universe as it expresses itself in conscious speech. We are the universe, a complex new geometry of hydrogen and oxygen, carbon and nitrogen, whose properties includes temperature, texture, and now—astonishingly—thought and moral deliberation.

We also know that many other forms of *intelligence* exist in our universe: ants, dolphins and chimpanzees—perhaps machine intelligence and extra-terrestrial species. Do these share awareness and even self-awareness, the marks of *homo sapiens*? Do they reflect an aspect of the Biblical claim about being created in the image of God? The discovery of other life and intelligence in the universe would have the greatest possible effect, that of humility, against what can become a dogmatic anthropocentrism underlying our spiritual journey to God.

Perhaps it is best, then, to acknowledge with humble gratitude that we humans do indeed, in our own way, participate in and manifest the universal mystery of existence, of finitude, which even at the level of the universe itself is the kind of being which cannot carry within itself its own explanation, the kind of being which points beyond to the great mystery of Being Itself, the ground and goal of all being, the "God who made heaven and earth."

And so we return to the start of our exploration on cosmology, with our primary discovery of the creatureliness of the universe itself. The universal contingency of nature, including as it must human nature as part of the natural order, reflects the great contemplative insight that God alone is God, worthy of our adoration and service. Nothing in nature is God's rival, not even the cosmic whole of nature herself. The universe in all its history and splendor is a single, seamless, global creation of the living God, both encountered in the interior journey and recognized as the only ultimate source of all there is, from atom to galaxy. And in its unbroken contingency the universe speaks of God the transcendent, the eternal source of existence, the ground of the universal mystery of being, the God who creates Cosmic Fire.

Second Facet:

The Heart of Matter-The Quantam World

SECOND SYMBOL: NATURE AS GOSSAMER EARTH

Let us shift our attention from the large-scale structure of the universe to the small-scale structure of matter. In a strange inversion, physicists are finding that they must probe matter with larger and larger accelerators and higher and higher energies in order to discover the structure and processes of matter at smaller and smaller scales. While an ordinary sewing needle can extract a splinter from your finger, it takes a three-mile long linear accelerator such as at Stanford University to reach down to the atoms and sub-atomic particles contained in that splinter. Here we enter the world of "quantum physics," where nature seems modular, discrete, chaotic rather than continuous and predictable.

A striking question emerges, as we move down-scale from needles and splinters to complex organic molecules, to simple molecules, to atoms, to atomic nuclei, and on to today's "fundamental particles," to quarks and gluons: is there a limit, a bottom rung, or does the descent continue forever? (Nature is again so counter-intuitive! Is our being open to infinite depth like a swimmer in the deepest ocean, or is nature just what it appears to be: rocks, trees, water, flesh? The mystical insight is needed here too, for it speaks to us of the depth of all experience.)

Here too we find a question lying at the frontiers of science, philosophy and theology, like those in cosmology.

Every possible answer seems to tease out further questions at the edges of science. If there is a bottom rung, why does it exist and exist in the way it does? If there is no bottom rung, what grounds the infinite series of layers, the "onion without a core"? As science probes to deeper and deeper levels of matter, it raises once again the fundamentally spiritual question of the mystery of existence and existence's Ground of Being.

Still the most striking fact about nature at the microscopic level is that chance rules the day. While rocks seem solid and passive, and oceans break endlessly on the shore, their atoms undergo millions of collisions per second and the elementary particles annihilate and create new particles in an endless seething swarming bonfire. A billion atoms make up a grain of uranium. All are identical, yet only one decays spontaneously. Why? "It's just chance." No theory has yet been advanced which can predict which atom will decay, though the facts have been known for almost a century! Many are convinced that no theory *ever could* make such a prediction; that ordinary cause and effect explanations are at a dead end here.[8]

This kind of chance, quantum chance, is not like ordinary chance, the chance of the roulette wheel or the insurance tables. It is not so much a process of chance undoing structure and order (like entropy in which things always seem to run down) as it is chance itself building the orderly structures of the world. Order is like *embodied chance*, the expression of multiple random events. Chance at the quantum

8. These issues are far from being settled. Many physicists and philosophers persist in wrestling with the meaning of quantum chance. Is nature truly subject to pure chance, where even the idea of continuous motion through space and time is up for grabs and classical ideas like cause and effect flounder on the rocks of quantum theory? Though quantum theory works to extraordinary precision (with errors of less than one part in a hundred million billion billion), isn't it at least possible that a better theory will come along and do away with chance, replacing it with a homey, causal picture? The jury is out so far, but meanwhile a few preliminary results can be taken as generally agreed upon. It is these which I presuppose in what follows. For further reading, see Polkinghorne, *Science and Providence,* and articles by Polkinghorne and Russell in Russell, et al., *Physics, Philosophy, and Theology.* For an introduction to the competing interpretations of chance written for non-specialists, see Herbert, *Quantum Reality.* More technical writings include those of Max Jammer and Ernan McMullin.

level underlies the order and structure of matter we find at the macroscopic level.

What then *is* nature like at the subatomic level? Amidst the continuing debate over quantum chance there is a growing opinion that if quantum chance is as non-classical as it appears, then nature at the quantum level is fundamentally *non-local*. Distant events which seem entirely independent in most respects can also appear to be inter-related, in a sense, connected as though part of the same system. Two particles, once joined but now separated to very large distances, act in tandem, as though still forming a single system. Matter at the sub-atomic level is like a finely spun gossamer, a delicate global veil, a sparkling and spontaneous arrangement of chaotic order.

And so quantum physics depicts nature filled with counter-intuitive mystery. Particles act like waves, jumping instead of moving continuously, tunneling through barriers, acting in groups as though somehow connected, and when once bonded, forever correlated. Chance, which acts to reshape structure in *our* experience, is now the very *structure of structure*, that which gives structure its shape. Gossamer earth is a fine-structured veil formed out of atoms and quarks, while cosmic fire shapes the universe as a whole—a universe whose final explanation transcends its own nature.

In contemplating the universe of atoms and particles, I am led to discover that the God that is known in prayer is ever at work in the on-going process of creating and re-creating the world of nature and human experience. This God creates order and structure and relationships out of chaos. This is not a God against chaos, nor as many claim does chaos make God's creative action impossible. This is a God who fashions chaos into sublime form. The quantum facet in the jewel of creation reflects the meticulous care of One who works all things spontaneous, random, in flux, at sea, into a gossamer-like universal whole of surpassing beauty. This is the ever immanent God, birthing and mothering her universe within her womb. This is the loving God whose ongoing, continuous creation reflects the inter-connected handiwork of the seamstress, the pre-verbal recognition of parent and child, the intimate touch of lover and beloved. This is the God who as Creator produces the intricate interwoven cosmos, as Compassion takes up into the divine being the groaning of all creatures, and as Wisdom knits and heals the raveled garment of nature.

And so to bring the first two facets together, from the reaches of cosmic fire to the depths of gossamer earth: God is both transcendent and immanent, the divine source beyond and the acting power within each particle and process of nature.

Third Facet:

The Origins of Life-Nature as a Tree with Many Branches

THIRD SYMBOL: LIVING WATER

As a scientist I accept the Darwinian theory of evolution as the best current explanation of life on earth. Does this force me into conflict with my faith as a Christian?

Admittedly it raises many questions. Those who take the Bible literally would say that conflict is inevitable. I do not. Short of giving a detailed account of how I work through the tangle of issues between faith and evolution, a task not appropriate here,[9] let me simply say that I, like many contemporary theologians, accept a form of evolutionary theism: evolution is the way in which God is producing life on earth. Knowledge of evolution is then basic to a clearer understanding of how God acts in the natural world.

The evolutionary sweep is staggering, like a tree with many branches, a meandering river forking constantly in a shifting environment. It is a blue, green, brown, and red journey littered with the discarded products of countless opportunities and remorseless dead-ends, a seemingly purposeless journey marked by a receding future horizon toward which even today we move. But evolution's mysteries and destinies escape us, blurred by the inter-mediate mist.

---

9. In general there are three approaches one can take to any of these faith and science issues: conflict, in which one seeks to disprove and replace the other (e.g., scientific materialism or "creation science"); divorce, where they are kept in watertight compartments with no possibility of conflict—or mutual illumination (faith versus fact, reason versus revelation, nature versus God); or interaction and mutual modification (such as espoused by Pope John Paul II). A prerequisite for the latter position is that one rejects the literalism of both religious fundamentalism (with regard to both Scripture and Magisterium) and reductionist scientism, two of the strongest voices in our culture. Clearly if we are to be heard in contemporary secular culture, the task for those of us who speak for the Church against *both* literalist extremes is to give a creative account of our Christian faith and spirituality in fruitful relation to science and technology.

We now know that the earliest life on earth arose over three billion years ago. Six hundred million years ago, the first vertebrates (fish) appeared; later came the first amphibians and then the reptiles. The first mammals differentiated from reptiles about two hundred million years ago. Seventy million years ago the primates appeared. This line split some Twenty-five million years ago, one line leading to the great apes (such as chimpanzees) and the other to our human ancestors.

Two million years ago, *homo habilis* was the first tool maker, to be followed one million years ago by *homo erectus*. Finally about two to three hundred thousand years ago, *homo sapiens* appeared. By forty thousand years ago human culture was emerging with the proliferation of types of tools; ten thousand years ago we began to domesticate plants and animals.

Yet with all the ages gone by, all the species which have risen and fallen, we see enormous continuity between all living things. The biological basis of all life on earth consists of the same six elements and the same twenty amino acids. The DNA codes which carry the secret for the growth of all life is written in the same molecular alphabet. The fetal development of primates reflects the evolutionary history of fish and amphibian. We carry the primordial salty ocean in our veins and in our tears, the flame of oxygen in our lungs, the incessant clamoring sensations and responses in our nervous system, the pulsing throb of life in our hearts.

What does this tells us for our spiritual journey? Contemplation on the origins of life leads to the discovery that as creatures of flesh and bone, cellular community, amino acid and encoded DNA, we are of a piece with the entire sweep of life on earth, whose history and continuity traces back over billions of years. The common thread and simple beauty of all life on earth displays the care and detail of a divine creative presence, God at work knitting, striding, defending, crafting, jealously guarding, caring for all creatures "great and small." It is not a matter of design in the full-blown teleological sense, for Darwinian evolution has done away with that forever. But what is left conveys a more subtle sense of presence and pattern, seen most clearly from the eyes of faith.

I am reminded again of the Poems of John of the Cross, particularly his Songs between the soul and the bridegroom where he writes about divine design:

Question to all Creatures
O thickets, densely trammelled,
Which my love's hand has sown along the height:
O field of green, enamelled
With blossoms, tell me right
If he has passed across you in his flight.

Reply of the Creatures
Diffusing showers of grace
In haste among these groves his path he took,
And only with his face,
Glancing around the place,
Has clothed them in his beauty with a look.[10]

The universal continuity of life with life reflects the contemplative insight that those who grow closer to God in prayer bring to God the common voice of all living beings, the weavings of the spider and the song of the canary, the undulations of the sea horse and the curiosity of the chimp, the hopes of all mortal flesh on earth. To discover how much we are an intimate part of all life on earth is to understand more deeply how God's love for us is a sign of God's love for every creature, and that discovery brings a great spiritual joy, that all things are special to God for all things are God's own creation. God's Spirit is present through the Word in the evolutionary process. Theologian Sallie McFague, for example, envisions God as the Mother of the world, the world as the body of God, for nature suggests the love of a parent which cares for us while yet releasing us into the freedom of separate life and future.[11]

We also must face the reality of death as integral to life, and the grim fact that on the savannah, death most often is violent death. Life is a dynamic process of struggle, devouring itself and through this devouring, producing itself and its progeny. It is a process of eating, of predator and prey, and it is a process of speciation. Life entails death: new species evolve through the extinction of the old. To study evolution is to learn that evil casts a shadow over the heart of life, that horror, pain and suffering are not only human atrocities but are somehow a part of nature "red in tooth and claw."

This universal struggle for life, this endless battle against death, underscores the contemplative insight that the passion of Jesus on the

10. John of the Cross, *Poems*, 15.
11. McFague, *Models of God*, 97–123.

Cross, poured out for us, and expands to all living creatures as they too groan for liberation, healing, and hope. The Gospel must be released from the limiting boundaries of mere human experience. Its power is that the full scope of nature is implicated by it. It must be allowed to thrust out beyond the reaches of human community and human misery to embrace all of life, to extend to all those creatures who suffer and die the promise of salvation, of liberation, and of life everlasting beyond the grave.

The *message* of the cross is given to humanity and human history, but the *power* of the cross goes beyond any anthropocentric straitjacket to bring healing grace to all of nature, to all God's creatures "great and small." As New Testament theologian Gerd Theissen has suggested, we are called to challenge the great sweep of nature's cruel competition and to rescue the weak, the disenfranchised, the forgotten, the dying through the power of a cross in which God took on the suffering of terrestrial flesh.[12]

Finally, we know that all life is made of water, and that all land creatures on earth carry the ocean in their veins. This knowledge resonates beautifully with the contemplative insight about life in the Spirit. To awaken to God with us is to be water come alive with Spirit, water reaching out to drink from that Living Water which Jesus gives daily. It is to carry Living Water in our earthly bodies as we journey from primordial sea to that final, joyful shore. And so the symbol of Living Water offers a profound interpretation of the evolutionary insight that we are of a piece with all life on earth and with the very water of the earth itself.

Fourth Facet:

The Ecological Web-Humanity as Steward and Co-Creator

FOURTH SYMBOL: FRAGILE AIR

It is both a fact and a sublime symbol that air is the invisible ocean binding us together as it envelops our planet. Air binds us to each other and it binds us to the past, linking us to generations gone by. With every breath we take we breath in some of the same air breathed by Teresa of

---

12. Theissen, *Biblical Faith*.

Jesus, John of the Cross, even by Jesus himself. Air is the common medium of all breathing life on earth, the ocean in which we now live, even as the sea is the ocean from which we came. We are truly amphibious creatures, linked to our past and to each other with the air and water of which we are made.

Yet air is vulnerable, and our air is increasingly polluted by the excesses of human greed and unbridled power. With every breath we take we literally breathe in the wages of sin, our individual and corporate pollution, and unless we reverse the abuse we will surely bequeath our pollution to 'the seventh generation' to come. They too will breathe the air of Teresa and John, and with it, our breath and our sins, the spoliation of a fragile ecosystem.

With the air there are many other problems in the growing crises between human need and environmental sustainability. Here I can only touch on this vast subject. Clearly the conflict has many dimensions: between human material needs, distributive justice and personal fulfillment; between first, second and third world voices; between present and future generations; between seeing the ecosphere as a resource to be used or abused or conserved; between growth and no-growth scenarios; and ultimately between human and environmental priorities.

Ian Barbour has argued that there is a high level of correspondence between our attitudes toward nature and our attitudes toward technology.[13] Those who advocate the right to dominate nature tend to see technology as an instrument of human liberation; often those who urge unity with nature see technology as a threat; finally those who seek a role of stewardship of nature may view technology as a value-neutral instrument the responsible use of which rests with us.

Shaping the debate is the growing realization of how truly finite our resources are, including fossil fuels, and how exponential population growth will inevitably outrace any conceivable linear increase in resource exploration. Driving the debate is the increased reality of environmental destruction: to the ozone layer, via the greenhouse effect, the massive loss of species and rain forest, the global effects of air, land and water pollution. What can the Church's response be to the mounting crisis?

It is ironical that Carl Sagan, who was no particular friend of Christianity, was one of the strongest voices for the very concerns which

13. Barbour, *Technology, Environment, and Human Values.*

Christians must hold. In an eloquent chapter in his book, *Cosmos*, Sagan asks this question: "Who speaks for earth?"[14] I am convinced that Christians, in unity with all those of other faiths and even with those who have discarded religion (or have supposed themselves to have), must answer: we all speak for Earth.

In particular, though, I charge the Church to own this claim: We Christians must speak for Earth, if we want our Christian voice to *deserve* a hearing in the secular and the interreligious world today. We must speak for Earth, if we want there *to be a Church*, at least a Church worth serving, *tomorrow*. We must speak for Earth, if we want there to be a *world* tomorrow in which to worship God. We must speak for the Fragile Air, our home and habitat, our ever-enveloping source.

And we have the spiritual roots out of which to speak, if we only choose to listen and follow. For dominion (Gen 1:27) should never license domination. History is an articulation of nature and not a performance on the stage of nature. And nature is a divine creation for whose stewardship we are held responsible. The roots of valid stewardship lie in the witness of Genesis, the Psalms, the wrestlings of Job, the eschatological vision of Paul for the groaning of all creatures, and in the spirituality of St. Benedict, St. Francis, St. Teresa, and St. John.

Thus Christians can join with those of Eastern and Native American religions who speak for unity with nature, with those in the ecological communities who call us to walk gently on this gentle planet, with all those who seek distributive *and* ecological justice, the sustaining and integrity of creation, the rights of future generations and the intrinsic values of nature.

Theologians like Phil Hefner go beyond stewardship and speak of our being created co-creators.[15] Stewards we are, but with the new technologies of life and its alteration, are we not being challenged to take something of evolution into our own hands? Can this be thematized theologically as cocreators with God, but *created* co-creators, still utterly dependent on God to work through us?

As we contemplate the ecological web of life, we learn that all species are inter-dependent, that the future of human life depends on an intricate relationship of give and take with all of nature, and that the only way to envision a *human* future is to envision a future for *all of*

14. Sagan, *Cosmos*, 320.

15. Hefner, "Evolution of the Created Co-Creator," 211–33.

life together. Certainly the highest object of contemplation, the only subject worthy of full attention, is God. Yet as witnessed by tradition and discovered through personal experience, this God is the source of that very ecological web through which we have emerged in time. Our duty is to the sustaining of that web out of gratitude for life itself and the God who is author of life, the God encountered in prayer. Surely in the splendid silence of spiritual quiet we can hear the multiple voices embodied genetically in us, the generations which have gone before us—both human and pre-human. Their voices filter through us, reaching to the divine presence and crying out "You are our God, our Creator."

We are not just *in* the ecological web, in a sense *we are the web.* In praying to God the *whole* fabric of nature prays a silent but real prayer. When even the tiniest creature falls, God knows and is present. Surely there are many non-human voices articulating the joy of being, the travail of living, and a hope, however muted, for life beyond death, which God hears and cherishes. Surely every facet of the great web of life is a facet reflecting the creative power and compassionate presence of God. If we have a special role in preserving the environment it is one calling for the strictest humility in the face of an infinite diversity of creatures, all of whom God creates, loves, and preserves for the future which alone God ultimately determines. It is in contemplation of a God so loving, that we are called in daily prayers.

To understand prayer as giving expression to the prayers of all creation is to realize that the contemplation is a form of service in a universal scope. One may pray in solitude, and in prayer leave behind thought of all earthly concerns, but it is *precisely as one does so* that a clearer voice is given to the *whole creation recapitulated through evolution and gestation in us.* For we do not leave behind, but we internalize and take with us on our journey, all that made us who and what we are. Each cell of our body recapitulates in its genes and living structures the entire history of life on earth. "Blessed be the tie that binds."

Out of contemplating the role of humankind in nature, a call is born to be ever mindful of one's responsibilities as God's stewards of nature. We must become a humble partner of the divine creation in nature's ongoing evolution of which we are both a product and an instrument, struggling to envision the future for all creatures.

Fifth Facet:

The Prospects for the Future-Nature as Longing

Fifth Symbol: ?

What symbol is appropriate for the far future, the future of all life in the universe, the future of the universe itself, the universal creation of God? In this paper I used fire, earth, water and air, the four classical elements which figure in Christian spirituality. What fifth element can symbolize the universe as a whole and its ultimate destiny?

Let me leave my answer aside for a moment and turn to the cosmological scenario for the far future. This essay began by exploring the Hot Big Bang in which the universe began fifteen billion years ago. As it turns out, there are two versions of the Big Bang. Although both have the same scenario for the past, their predictions for the far future are radically different.

First, if the universe is closed and finite in size, it will keep expanding for another 100 billion years or so, and then recollapse, ending in an event of infinite temperatures and densities and vanishing size very much like its beginning. Second, if the universe is open, it will expand forever, cooling as it goes until it is essentially at a temperature of absolute zero. So "freeze or fry" is the verdict for the future of the universe according to standard scientific cosmology.

Both would seem to present serious challenges to Christian faith. In either case, biological life as we know it will one day expire. Not only will the earth die in the nova of our sun some five billion years from now. Even if terrestrial life were to expand beyond the solar system and spread out to the stars, it will eventually be faced with universal unending cold or searing heat. Biological life seems doomed in the future, no matter what happens to the universe. Moreover the universe itself seems destined to a future of tragic meaninglessness: unending lifeless expansion or recollapse and extinction.

What then for Christian faith in the God who will be with us to the end of time, in the Christ who will come again, in the Resurrection of the dead and eternal life? What hope is there for those who labor in the vineyards of social justice and personal discipleship when they raise their eyes beyond the narrow horizons of human history to gaze at the beckoning stars beyond?

The professional theologian faces a similar problem. Eschatology, long thought to be a mere appendage to Christian systematics, is now seen by a growing number of theologians as *the* central Christian doctrine. But how can one tackle eschatology in light of science? Of course eschatology must focus on the present and the near future, but what about the final grounds for hope that anchors all our present struggle and gives a theoretical framework for understanding the longterm mission of the Church?

It is striking that this problem surfaces, not only among Christian theologians (indeed only occasionally there; for the most part, theologians ignore scientific issues like this!), but recently among those who have little interest in formal religion. Some take a dim view of the far future. Nobel laureate, physicist Steven Weinberg, writes at the close of his excellent book on scientific cosmology, "The more the universe seems comprehensible, the more it also seems pointless."[16] On the other hand, Freeman Dyson, Frank Tipler and John Barrow, have suggested scientific scenarios in which life continues into the far future and eschatology is given a peculiar, scientific flare (Dyson 1988; Barrow and Tipler 1986; Tipler in Russell, Stoeger, and Coyne, 1988).

Where Christian theology has tackled the problem, it has done so with limited results. For all the beauty, insight, and care of Teilhard's great vision, his scope was in many ways cripplingly limited to the earth. The noosphere was a terrestrial phenomena, the Omega point, the culmination of terrestrial evolution. But the earth will be gone someday, and as aeons roll on the verdant period of the stars and planets, the greening of the galaxy, will be forgotten, a springtime's dream lost to summer's relentless blaze or the growing shadow of an icy fall.

What then can be said about the coming of the Lord in light of twentieth century cosmology? How can salvation, resurrection, paradise, and all those other symbols at the heart of Christian life and faith be understood? Do they mean being somehow spiritually 'snatched to safety' from this failing universe, leaving behind a world of hollow shells, a cosmos of broken skeletons, a universe of countless forgotten dreams and failed evolutionary strategies? In my opinion it is more faithful to the Judeo-Christian vision to hope that God's victory includes and takes up within it all that is and all that will ever be, indeed the very universal creation of God.

16. Weinberg, *First Three Minutes,* 154.

Yet this surely is one of the toughest theological issues today, especially for those trying to relate the intelligibility of faith to scientific knowledge of the universe. I must be honest and acknowledge that, compared with efforts to relate the doctrine of creation to contemporary science, the problems of Resurrection and eschatology loom as unyielding, massive hurdles. There are a few scattered attempts at making sense out of it all but for the most part the task of theology as *fides quaerens intellectum* seems stymied by the challenge of the cosmic future.

And so today I can only offer some very slight suggestions regarding our spiritual journey along this fifth facet. The first suggestion is this: to contemplate the far future from a Biblical perspective, knowing that all life on earth will cease when the sun supernovas, is to realize that the province of life must be expanded from the environs of the earth to the universal horizon of the cosmos. If life is to have enduring meaning and fulfillment it must somehow expand into the cosmos. Teilhard de Chardin spoke of the Omega point of all terrestrial life. Such a vision must now be seen in more than terrestrial perspective; it must eventually include all forms of life in the universe, even non-biological forms which might lie in our future. For the universe, not just this planet, is our final home and the domain of God's continuous creation and redemption.

Yet it is extremely hard to think through what a cosmic perspective means. Will life continue forever in the expanding universe? Will it become increasing isolated as it explores stars and galaxies? What is the real goal of life and the far future? It is precisely our inability to conceptualize our hope for the far future which leads to my second suggestion, for our inability leads to a posture of trust in the mysterious providence of God. For only God can bring to fulfillment such an overwhelming task. The horizon of the future must lie in *God's* hand, for it extends vastly beyond the horizons of our planet to include *all* the reachless depths of the cosmic ocean beyond. Such a realization can bring a deepened humility towards life and its God. The cosmic proportions of the challenge to life's final hope leads to a greater understanding of the spiritual insight that *only God* can bring about a final, universal victory.

Thirdly, I suggest that we all will be made even more grateful to God if we can in some as yet unknown way be instruments of the divine peace which is *cosmological* in scope, for truly such a peace passes all our understanding. And those who struggle for justice and liberation can be encouraged by the conviction that God holds in caring hands even the far future in which our destinies eventually lie, so that their sacrifice is not in vein.

To contemplate the unknown future for life is thus to bring to God the hopes of all creation—hopes that the struggles, the dreams, the victories, and the joy of all that lives, not only on earth but throughout the universe, may come at last into the divine mansion of unending love. To surrender one's knowing in the face of the dark unknown is to realize that only God can save all that is. To stand at the foot of the Cross and let one's voice be that of the thief who asked to be remembered even as death loomed inevitable is to gain the spiritual insight that Jesus was speaking for all of creation when he said "today you will be with me in paradise."

And so what symbol can stand for the future, the future which will remember and recapitulate all that still lies ahead of us in space and time? I believe that convergence is the clue, convergence of nature and spirit, of saving grace completing creating grace. And so the symbol I chose is the diamond of St. Teresa, the very diamond of which each previous symbol is a facet, for this diamond includes all of creation in her myriad facets even as they point towards the apex. The diamond of Teresa brings together all parts of creation into a single whole, a whole whose apex represents the Universal Omega Point, the unknown far future of the universe, the eschatological summit, in which all will be in immediate communion with God, and God will truly be "all in all." Rather than being a frightening future, the symbol of the diamond tells us that we can, in fact, trust the future, for the apex of the diamond guarantees the coherence of the facets, and the diamond itself represents the merging of creation with its divine source.

Conclusion

In contemplating God one discovers that this God is at work in an evolving world of cosmic proportions. The God who creates within us that splendid creature, the human soul, so powerfully envisioned by Teresa as the Interior Castle, is the same God whose reach is from the tiniest atoms to the most distant stars, whose diamond-like frame encloses the expanse of the universe filled with countless galaxies, and whose joy is in being present as Creator and Redeemer to each fragile creature in the immensity of space and the fathomless depths of time. This is truly the God who is known in prayer and faith as the God "in whom we live and move and have our being." It is this God who creates the Interior Castle as a cherished and unique part of the intricate tapestry of life in this astonishing and infinitely complex evolving universe. It is this God who calls us all to discover the complexity and interdependence of all creation for it is this which God is ever at work creating the *natural* context of human spirituality.

This truly is a God of cosmic fire, gossamer earth, living water, fragile air, all the facets of creation which will at last form the apex of the diamond, the Universal Omega Point. It is into the care of *this* God that I would place the human, indeed the cosmic, future. And it is to this God that the spiritual pilgrim journeys through contemplation in the vibrant universe.

Bibliography

Barbour, Ian. *Technology, Environment and Human Values.* New York: Praeger, 1980.

Barrow, John, and Frank Tipler. *The Anthropic Cosmological Principle.* Oxford: Clarendon, 1986.

Dyson, Freeman. *Infinite in All Directions.* New York: Harper & Row, 1988.

Hefner, Philip. "The Evolution of the Created Co-Creator." In *Cosmos as Creation,* edited by Ted Peters, 211–33. Nashville: Abingdon, 1989.

Herbert, Nick. *Quantam Reality: Beyond the New Physics.* Garden City, NY: Anchor/Doubleday, 1985.

John of the Cross. *Poems of St. John of the Cross.* Translated by Roy Campbell. New York: Grosset & Dunlap, 1967.

McFague, Sallie. *Models of God: Theology for an Ecological, Nuclear Age.* Philadelphia: Fortress, 1987.

Polkinghorne, John. *Science and Providence: God's Interaction with the World.* Boston: New Science Library—Shambala, 1989.

Peters, Ted, editor. *Cosmos as Creation: Theology and Science in Consonance.* Nashville: Abingdon, 1989.

Russell, Robert, et al., editors. *Physics, Philosophy and Theology: A Common Quest for Understanding.* Vatican City State: Vatican Observatory, 1988.

Sagan, Carl. *Cosmos.* New York: Random House, 1980.

Teresa of Avila. *The Life of St. Teresa of Jesus.* Translated by David Lewis. London: Thomas Baker, 1932.

Theissen, Gerd. *Biblical Faith: An Evolutionary Approach.* Philadelphia: Fortress, 1985.

Weinberg, Steven. *The First Three Minutes: A Modern View of the Origin of the Universe.* New York: Basic, 1977.

7

Practicing Christian Spiritual Discernment in Light of Natural Science

Nancy S. Wiens

WHAT CAR SHALL I BUY? WHERE SHALL WE GO ON VACATION? SHALL I take this job offer? What food shall we buy this week? Shall we order take out? How many children shall we have? Paper or plastic? Many questions from our daily experiences look different when seen with an ecological consciousness. Such varied voices shape our choices and decisions in every moment. These questions share a common theme: they all relate to Christian ecological spirituality. More precisely, they relate to the ancient Christian practice of spiritual discernment in light of the natural sciences.

This essay explores the ways that discernment, reformulated by the natural sciences, can help persons of Christian faith to engage such questions. My understanding of discernment begins with the assumption that God is present and active in our experiences all the time. God continuously manifests creativity, invites transformation, and inspires a fulfillment of God's hopes for the world. Given this ongoing divine self-revelation, discernment explores all lived experiences with an eye toward sifting and weighing their nuances, seeking to notice and align with God's movements. The practice of discernment, then, seeks to notice God in daily life so that a person can draw closer to and collaborate with God. This essay considers how discernment might become more vital and useful through the insights of four natural sciences—physical cosmology, evolutionary biology, quantum physics, and neuroscience. With science's insights, I show how God and human beings act simultaneously in discernment, where God

148

dynamically reveals through Nature without intervening in its regularities or infringing on human freedom.

A reformulated notion of discernment is important for at least two reasons. First, there is a significant increase in people's awareness of spiritual experiences in their daily lives. Popular book sales on spirituality and academic studies alike attest to the vast array of spiritual experiences and the spiritualities that emerge from them, not only in religious communities, but also in the workplace.[1] Yet with all these experiences, how do we determine what among them is life-giving and what direction to follow based on them? *How do we make sense of the encounters?* Experiences are ambiguous; they can be construed widely. Christian spiritual discernment offers an orienting clarity and wisdom as well as encouragement for faithful response, helping us grow closer to God and act according to our values.

A second reason to reform discernment via science's insights comes from a growing awareness of ecological issues and the scientific accounts of them. As humans become more aware of our considerable impact on nature, discerning God's specific invitations to revise our corporate lifestyles and personal habits can support the development of a sustainable relationship with nature. Toward that end, this reformulation of discernment uses science to focus on the human discerner *as* Nature, as well as discerning experiences of God *in* nature.[2] From the perspective of physical cosmology and evolutionary biology, the human person who discerns is part of the totality of the 13.7 billion-year old universe. Seeing humans as Nature shifts the questions we discern, the options we perceive, and how we perceive. Seeing humans this way offers a vivid departure from ancient understandings of discernment. Further, this reformulation of discernment draws on quantum physics to explore the ways God might interact with this evolving universe without intervening in its regularities. That is, this reformulation takes seriously both the laws of nature that describe the universe's orderliness, such as gravity and cell reproduction, and the genuine openness of its systems. The openness points to phenomena, such as dynamics in

1. See Wuthnow, *After Heaven;* and Dreyer and Burrows, "Preface," in *Minding the Spirit.*

2. I distinguish linguistically between the notion of *n*ature as the nonhuman universe and *N*ature that includes humanity within the universe. Using the same word underscores the radical continuity among everything in the universe, while the letter case depicts *n*ature as a subset of *N*ature. Thus, *n*ature + humanity = *N*ature.

the human brain that neuroscience explores, where we might point to God's activity in spiritual experiences of discernment.[3]

In order to reformulate discernment with the insights of natural science, I make five main movements. First, for context I clarify my use of 'experience' as it relates to Christian ecological spirituality. Second, I offer a brief description of discernment as a spiritual practice and some of its core elements. Third, I explore the value of including natural science in discernment. Fourth, I unpack the specific science necessary to reformulate notions of how God and humans act together in discernment. Finally, I summarize the changes in discernment when it is reformulated by scientific insights. In the end, I hope to show how valuable the Christian practice of discernment can be in light of the urgency of ecological needs and how it might empower a faithful response to God's creative, transforming, and inspiring initiative in the world.

The Context of Experience

Christian ecological spirituality focuses on people's lived experiences, both as the experiences relate to ecological issues and as they engage the ongoing Christian story of divine creativity, transformation, and inspiration. A definition of experience is far from self-evident. When a person encounters something, she perceives and interprets it in layers that *create or construct* an experience. That is, "experience" is not an uninterpreted reality, shared alike by all. Rather, with amazing speed our faculties of perception take in an encounter from the varied arenas of our lives. The data is compared and contrasted with pre-existing data and interpretations. The digested outcome is what we call an experience of something. Experience, then, is formed at the complex intersection of our perceiving faculties (cognitive intellectual claims, affective imaginative knowing, and kinesthetic awareness) as we notice all the arenas of our lives (our interior self, ourselves within relationships, in systems and structures, in relationship with nature, and as the human part of Nature). What we think, feel, imagine, intuit, and physically sense in

---

3. Importantly, the terms "activity" or "action" attributed to God are done so *analogically*, acknowledging the severe limitation in using words to describe everything related to God. Yet, the term suggests that God truly engages the energy and matter of Nature such that a genuine effect results.

these various arenas of life layer together to form an experience.[4] Thus, each experience is a constructed understanding of an encounter or event, shaped both by personal distinctiveness and by cultural factors. Among all these influential factors in constructing an experience, this essay explores one in particular: cognitive intellectual claims. Our intellectual claims, doctrines, or thoughts about *God's divine action* and *our human action* play an influential role in constructing an experience of God and thus of discernment. This cognitive dimension, as it interacts with the other dimensions, is the place in discernment where the cognitive claims from science apply most fully.

Turning to lived experiences that relate to ecology, humans have ongoing experiences that influence and are influenced by nature. Cars, vacations, jobs, food, children, and consumption all bear directly on the Nature that we are as human beings and the nature that surrounds us. The interdependence of the universe ensures such an enduring feedback loop, thus our ecological experiences abound. We have countless opportunities to make choices about how we impact nature every day. This is one hidden source of hope in the ecological challenges we currently face: we are deeply empowered to make a difference.

Looking at these ecological experiences through the lens of Christianity's unfolding story of divine action can both create meaning and shape our future experiences and choices. The doctrines and practices that make up Christianity can help to evaluate and make sense of these experiences in nature. They also can help us reform our identity as human beings, helping us to see ourselves as the human face of Nature. Attentiveness helps us to participate in God's

Discernment as a Spiritual Practice

Given the importance of attending to and participating with God's activity in our ecological experiences, I turn to focus on discernment. A broad description of the spiritual practice of discernment will provide basics for connecting later with natural science. Most generally, God gifts humans with the potential for spiritual discernment. The actualization of this potential involves a practice of sifting through daily experiences to notice and align oneself with God. Used by a particu-

4. See Liebert, "Role of Practice in the Study of Christian Spirituality," 32–49; and Childs, "Experience," 388.

lar person, a community, or people on behalf of an institution or an eco-system in nature, it seeks to distinguish the call of the Holy Spirit from other divergent influences.[5] At its simplest, Christian spiritual discernment presumes a doctrine of revelation, namely that God reveals Godself in the universe in comprehensible ways. Simultaneously, it holds that these communications are not transparent, and thus they need careful deciphering.[6] Centrally, discernment is for the purpose of growing closer to God.[7] Such growth involves an interior freedom to respond faithfully to God's invitation and thus join with God's actions in the world.[8] In this way, attending to spiritual experiences is also for the purpose of collaborating with the movements of the Holy Spirit; thus, Christian discernment has an inherent trajectory toward justice.

Because Christian spiritual discernment is practiced in a milieu of beliefs, habits, and worldviews based on varied ways of knowing, there is no single formula for the discernment process. It is not a ready-made program where entering abstract data will yield a computed and reliable answer or decision. The varied ways people personally and communally receive divine illumination as well as the diverse ways they are susceptible to being deceived and misled mean there is no monolithic process

---

5. For ease of language only, I tend to speak of a person, though the corporate and institutional applications of discernment are rich and play key roles in modifying human-nature relationships toward sustainability. Further, discernment about nature and eco-systems lies at the center of expanding the "love of neighbor" to include Nature as neighbor.

6. John Hick writes about this paradoxical situation, called epistemic distance, regarding the necessary atmosphere for moral growth. See Hick, *Evil and the God of Love*, 280–91. Theologian and physicist Robert John Russell extends Hick's analysis in his work in science and theology around the necessary conditions for both discernment and scientific exploration of nature. See Russell, "Natural Sciences," 327–28.

7. Ignatius of Loyola's ancient language sharpens the meaning of this growth. "In every good election insofar as it depends on us, the eye of our intention ought to be single. It ought to focus only on the purpose for which I was created, to praise God our Lord and to save my soul." *Spiritual Exercises*, [169]. The convention for citing Ignatius's writing in his *Spiritual Exercises* uses brackets to delineate the standard paragraph numbering.

8. Ignatius speaks of the essential character of this interior freedom in discernment in this way, "Normally, discernment confers on a soul that special sensitivity to diverse interior 'motions,' to such a degree that the election, to be sound and good, takes for granted that 'I keep myself like the needle of a balanced scale, ready to turn toward what I shall feel to be for the glory and praise of God.'" *Spiritual Exercises*, [179].

that is uniform for all.[9] Instead, discernment is about following the dynamic movements of the Holy Spirit. It is a process, not an outcome.

Still, broad distinguishable movements form the ancient practice of discernment. Centuries of Christian spiritual formation reveal patterns in the spiritual process of discriminating. Certain historic figures, such as the Desert Fathers and Mothers, Ignatius of Loyola, and Jonathan Edwards, discovered and explored these patterns, experimenting with them in their diverse cultural contexts. From their many insights, I focus here on the important role that intentions play and a general flow of movements that shape a discernment process.

Human Intention Intermingling with God's Grace

Discernment is like a dance between God and humans where both parties are needed. Each one's actions are necessary but not sufficient. I further explore God's role later, but for now, I simply call it grace. Regarding the human role, our intention is our contribution to collaboration with God. Intention acts like a traveler's compass point, directing one's movement along an ever-changing landscape. Intention involves purposeful choice in a way that self-consciously shapes activity and grounds a person in present time and space.[10]

Three overarching intentions impact the movements of a discernment process: loyalty, noticing, and aligning. As cumulative intentions, they progressively hone one's attention and responsiveness to God's calling. They add to one another and correlate with the movements or elements in a discernment process.

Through the discernment process, God's grace intermingles with each intention, manifesting attendant inner dispositions or felt senses: freedom, clarity and wisdom, and courage. The dynamic is human intention + divine grace → disposition. The attendant pairings:

---

9. Au, "Holistic Discernment," 17.

10. In this way, intention relates closely with contemplation, as Walter Burghardt defines it: "a long, loving look at the real." Burghardt, "Contemplation: A Long Loving Look at the Real," 15. This 'here and now' grounding of intention differs markedly from 'good intentions,' which often simply project into the future a desired effect, regardless of current reality.

Intention	+ divine grace →	Disposition
loyalty		freedom
noticing		clarity and wisdom
aligning		courage

The human part of the discernment process begins, then, with a person's initial intention or desire to choose God and intimate relationship with God above all else.[11] While this intention can be worded in a wide variety of ways to mirror one's spirituality, it reflects an utmost *loyalty* to and dependence upon the divine.[12] When this first intention intermingles with God's grace, it yields an inner disposition of *freedom* in the discerner—both freedom *from* attachment to a particular outcome and freedom to choose God's vision—once it is recognized. This disposition of freedom, called spiritual indifference, offers an initial orientation point to be renewed throughout the discernment process.

The second intention in discernment is to *notice* the movements of the Holy Spirit in a given situation. Noticing the movements of the Holy Spirit implicitly includes discriminating them from other influences, internal and external to the discerner. Noticing, touched by grace, evokes a disposition of *clarity and wisdom*. Clarity arises through practice in sifting and weighing when a pattern of inner and outer plumb lines or points of reference develop. Integrating inner senses and outer traditions, plumb lines form through the blend of unique, individual experiences and those of the community of faith, both contemporary and as witnessed to in scripture and tradition. These plumb lines, then, assist in coming to a relative certitude, without reaching absolute certainty,

11. That humans have the capacity to choose or have free will is a necessary claim of this essay that I do not explore here but merely adopt from philosophical claims about human agency.

12. This language grounds it squarely in biblical roots. The shape of loyalty in the Christian tradition comes from Jesus' naming of the two greatest commandments, the first of which draws on the *Shema*. The deuteronomic tradition, ultimately shaped by the *Shema*, springs from the Hebrew *'ahav*, meaning loyalty love. "Hear, O Israel, the Lord is our God, the Lord alone. You shall love (*'ahav*) the Lord our God with all your heart, with all your soul, and with all your might." See Bascom, "Adaptable for Translation," 166–83. Further the *Shema's* "semantically concentric phrases form a climactic parallelism to reinforce absolute singularity of personal devotion to God." Janzen, " Claim of the Shema," 246. Second, in the Matthean tradition, this loyalty to God has an equally important expression in the world: loving one's neighbor. Thus, one cannot love God without loving neighbor. See Davies and Allison Jr., " Gospel According to Saint Matthew," 243.

about God's calling in a particular situation. Inherent in the relative certitude is a blend of insight and humility that the biblical tradition calls wisdom.[13] In this second part of discernment, then, one notices a particular movement and then sifts and weighs it in comparison with other movements until, with God's grace, a clarity and wisdom about its nature emerges. In this way, clarity and wisdom deepen with practice, using the plumb lines to discover movements' distinctions and nuances.[14] The third intention follows: to align oneself with God's particular invitation once it is clear. Here divine grace and human practice woven together foster *courage*. The courage to follow the invitation of God, perhaps against a familiar path, a community's expectations, or a structure's constraints, develops from an overriding, core belief in God's ultimate vision for the world. Such a vision in the Judeo-Christian tradition was invited by the Law, championed by the prophets, embodied by Jesus, and is continuously empowered by the Holy Spirit. Thus, the courage to respond to God draws upon one's personal and/or communal history with God. Trust in this overarching hope mirrors one's ultimate loyalty to God, instilling courage to move from noticing the Spirit's movements to aligning with a specific, divine invitation.

Common Elements of Discernment

Given these dynamics of intention and grace, some common elements of discernment form a pattern.[15] While they have a particular order, in practice they loop back over each other, as changes occur in both the discerner and the situation under discernment.[16] Notice the way the three intentions build on each other in the movements.

13. The large body of wisdom literature in the Hebrew testament denotes rich characteristics of wisdom, primarily the humble orientation of one's life toward God. In particular, see Proverbs 1 and 8.

14. This deepening clarity and wisdom in order to discover movements' distinctions and nuances describe the process Ignatius of Loyola has carefully articulated in his "Rules for Discernment," *Spiritual Exercises*, [313–70]. The role of wisdom in discernment deserves greater research, especially in relationship to biblical spirituality. In particular, see James 3:13–18 with its reliance upon the wisdom tradition and its list of the fruit of wisdom, closely akin to the fruit of the Spirit in Gal 5:22–29.

15. This description draws on Elizabeth Liebert's work in various traditions, including Ignatian, Quaker, and social systems theory.

16. Ignatius, of all the historical figures in Christian spiritual discernment, most clearly outlines his understanding of these movements. They appear in his notes [178–83]. I have noted the cross references to his work in the parentheses.

1. *Open to a Free Inner Disposition* of spiritual indifference. Begin with the freeing intention first and foremost to follow God's call in one's being and doing. Praise of God is the highest value; all else follows that. Release all attachments to the outcome, or in Ignatius's language, release all disordered affections. Continue to renew a desire for this grace of freedom throughout the process (Ignatius [179 and 184].) Intention of loyalty to God.

2. *Name the Question for Discernment.* Formulate a specific matter to be discerned based on where the person notices the Spirit already moving through one's desires and longings. The question itself is already a beckoning gift from the Holy; what is the question that God is longing to answer? A "yes or no" question is easiest but not always possible. Discernment is an appropriate spiritual practice for a morally neutral or positive matter (Ignatius [170–174]). Intentions of loyalty to God and noticing.

3. *Gathering Data.* Gather appropriate data about options and related consequences, as they are known. Use all one's faculties to gather data: thought, feeling, imagination, felt-sense, and intuition (Ignatius: focused on reason, [end of 180 and 181], and on imagination [185, 186, 187]). Intentions of loyalty to God and noticing.

4. *Pray and Reflect.* Allow the foreground of prayer to be one's presence with God and the details and data of the question to become background. Notice what God is like in this prayer. What is Jesus' demeanor? What is the quality of the Spirit's movement? (Ignatius beginning of [180]). Intentions of loyalty to God and noticing.

5. *Make a Tentative Decision.* Come to a tentative decision by considering this question: returning to the freedom of spiritual indifference and given the data and what I have noticed in the prayer, how do I join with what God is already doing? What potential from the Spirit am I called to actualize? (Ignatius [182]). Intentions of loyalty to God, noticing, and aligning.

6. *Bring Tentative Decision to God for Confirmation* and test it against familiar plumb lines from one's prior discernments and the tradition. For example, would this action manifest the fruit of the Spirit (Gal 5:22)? Would it fit with biblical witness to God's

grace and justice? (Ignatius [183, 188, and 316]). Intentions of loyalty to God, noticing, and aligning.

7. *Enact the Decision* with an attentive eye toward the confirming touchstones above. Is there sustainable energy to continue enacting this decision? Does the freedom from earlier continue? In living out the decision, what is the quality of the alignment with God's desires? Is it akin to the experience in the prayer and reflection time? Intentions of loyalty to God, noticing, and aligning.

8. *Evaluate the Discerned Decision* at the end of this process and some time later after enacting the decision. Notice the way the current situation relates to the touchstones, looking for the fruit of the Spirit manifesting from one's decision. Attune to what new direction or discernment now comes into view. Intentions of loyalty to God and noticing.

These common elements may come in different order, or one may entail much more time than another. For example, in the data gathering time, attachments to certain options or resistance to others can emerge, returning the discerner to the first step of seeking utmost loyalty to God and spiritual indifference. Or, sometimes the process of distinguishing the Spirit's voice from the other voices that influence a person calls for accessing alternative ways of knowing. One's commonly used faculties may need to be supplemented by non-dominant faculties. For example, exploring intuitive knowing alongside reason may loosen up default patterns of listening and attending and, thus, heighten an awareness of the Spirit.

In the end, discernment is never finished because one continues to look for confirmation or disconfirmation, places where one had congruence with God or was at odds. While those learnings helpfully facilitate the next discernment process, discernment remains a dynamic practice because the situation of discernment, both within the person and in the world, continues to change. Further, while a person's spiritual practice and learnings facilitates the process, the dynamic movements of the Spirit make every discernment practice new, and growth with God continues.

Value of Including Natural Science in Christian Spiritual Discernment

The natural sciences contribute greatly to an exploration of spiritual experiences in general and to spiritual discernment in particular. I focus on three areas of science's contribution: the value of interdisciplinary dialogue partners, updating discernment via contemporary understandings of Nature, and providing viable and robust ways to address the double challenge of simultaneous divine-human action, which stands at the crux of discernment.

Interdisciplinary Dialogue Partners

All too often, narrow strands of science and theology are pitted against each other, producing conflict and entrenched positions. At other times, those who acknowledge the complexities and nuances in both fields avoid a conflict approach by suggesting that the two address separate, unrelated topics. That approach yields a great loss of insight in both disciplines. Alternatively the contemporary dialogue between science and theology focuses on a constructive relationship between the two, where each one's measurement criteria, or methodologies, are respected and research propels the formation of further knowledge in both disciplines.[17] With dialogue, the practical fruit for Christian spirituality[18] is that people often experience freedom from splitting their "heads and hearts." That is, they can have an intelligible *and* passionate faith. They can value cognitive claims about God *and* appreciate additional ways of

17. For a thorough exposition of numerous paths of interaction between science and theology, see Russell, *Cosmology from Alpha to Omega*, 20–23. The interaction depends upon a critical realist philosophy of knowledge. Biochemist and theologian Christopher Southgate defines critical realism as, "a philosophical view of science and/ or theology that asserts that our knowledge of the world refers to the-way-things-really-are, but in a partial fashion which will necessarily be revised as that knowledge develops." Southgate, "Glossary s.v. Critical Realism." This philosophical stance argues that cognitive claims in *both* science and religion are possible because they point to how the universe genuinely is, though not exhaustively or completely. That cognitive claims are intelligible in *both* fields is crucial for their mutual interaction.

18.. Important nuances exist between the science-theology dialogue and the science-spirituality dialogue that surpass the focus of this essay but are addressed in depth in Wiens, *Discernment and Nature*.

knowing God through affect, image, intuition, and kinesthetic sensation, all the while embracing the ultimate Mystery of God.[19]

A vibrant, interdisciplinary dialogue between science and spirituality can lend its keen insights to discernment, with its focus on noticing God and of faithfully responding. Specifically, science makes instructive claims about the universe in which we describe these ecological and spiritual experiences happening and about the human beings who have these experiences. Most simply, on one hand, science describes and analyzes the characteristics and dynamics of the natural world. On the other, Christian spirituality describes and analyzes people's lived experiences of God's activity and presence, as revealed in that same natural world. Holding the two together, Christian spirituality then enters into dialogue with science, in part, to evaluate if its own cognitive claims about human experience of divine action mesh with science's descriptions of the universe.[20] How we describe the character of the universe shapes what we can cogently say about experiences of divine action. Intelligible *and* passionate faith is not a given. It requires purposeful evaluation and integration of all that makes up our beliefs.

Updating the Milieu of Discernment

A second major contribution of science to Christian spirituality and discernment is the significantly different perspective it offers on the milieu of discernment than the Christian tradition has most often taken. In much of Christian history, discernment incorporated theological understandings of Nature that conflict with contemporary science. Those notions of discernment emphasize a God-human relationship where a person is to discover God's will, as though it is a predetermined and fixed, external plan. In that view, nature may be ignored as the irrelevant backdrop to divine-human communication. The theological goal of escaping this physical world and this human body for an immaterial, heavenly realm of souls easily extends from this understanding of

19. For a detailed exploration of the crucial role that cognitive claims play in discernment, please see Wiens, *Discernment and Nature*.

20. Importantly, the dialogue is two-way. Christian spirituality can also make constructive contributions to natural science by impacting the philosophical assumptions, imagination, analogies/metaphors, and models that scientists, who are open to the cognitive claims of Christian spirituality, might use in their scientific research programs. See Wiens, *Discernment and Nature*.

nature. Or with this fixed divine will, nature may be considered but in a scientifically unsophisticated way that sanitizes the death and decay out of nature's dynamics. These two theological approaches to nature involve a number of misunderstandings: 1) Nature as superfluous to God's communication; 2) Nature as unrelated to humanity; 3) Nature as a sentimentally romanticized, idyllic, and static entity.

Today, discernment can benefit from contemporary science's instructive insights. On the first misunderstanding, neuroscience explores the material stuff of Nature in the brain, for example, neural synapses that stimulate sensate knowing or intuitions or feelings or ideas. I adopt the philosophical interpretations of neuroscience that there is no physical substance called the 'mind' separate from the body to which God can transmit divine intentions. Rather, it is through the complex make up of the brain and the emotional, mental, and spiritual faculties, which register in the body, that God's self-revelation to humanity occurs.[21] Similarly, there is no physical substance called "soul" or "spirit" separate from the body with which the Holy Spirit can surreptitiously and directly communicate divine will. *In pondering how Nature is indispensable to God's communication, discernment takes neuroscience seriously, claiming that the Spirit communicates through the physical matter and energy of Nature.*[22]

Second, the misunderstanding that Nature is unrelated to humanity reflects a worldview more familiar to our Christian ancestors, with their geocentric and anthropocentric perspectives. It falls away when physical cosmology and evolutionary biology describe humans as both in continuity with Nature, emerging through a long evolutionary process, *and* in discontinuity with nature, with particular capacities for free choice. Physical cosmology paints the expansive and spectacular history

---

21. Philosophy plays a significant role in the dialogue between science and theology but exceeds the scope of this essay. A key point becomes clear in noting the difference between mind/soul/spirit, as nouns, and mental/spiritual, as adjectives, to describe human faculties or capacities. The philosophical positions of emergentist monism and non-reductive physicalism both fit in this use of science with discernment. Philip Clayton and Nancey Murphy offer nuanced reasons for their respective philosophical choices. See Clayton, "Neuroscience, the Person, and God," in Russell et al., *Neuroscience and the Person*, 211; and Murphy, "Supervenience and the Downward Efficacy of the Mental," in Russell et al., *Neuroscience and the Person*, 147.

22. See Peacocke, "Sound of Sheer Silence," in Russell et al., *Neuroscience and the Person*, 216.

of this ancient, expanding universe.[23] According to physicist and theologian Ian Barbour, "We can no longer assume the static universe of the Middle Ages, in which the basic forms of all beings were thought to be unchanging. Coming-to-be is a continuing process throughout time, and it continues today. Nature in all its forms must be viewed historically. Here astrophysics adds its testimony to that of evolutionary biology and other fields of science [showing that] genuine novelty appears in cosmic history."[24] Contemporary physical cosmology indicates that this universe has an unrepeatable history—unidirectionally formed through formation of plasma, galaxies, first- and second-generation stars, planets, and life. The biological pre-conditions for the possibility of life are built into the physics of universe; although it is widespread now, life arrived late in the process, especially human life.

Humans are inextricably linked to the cosmos. Addressing the cosmic context for the uniqueness of human development, Barbour says, "The greatest complexity has apparently been achieved in the middle range of size, not at atomic or galactic dimensions. There are a thousand billion synapses in a human brain; the number of possible ways of connecting them is greater than the number of atoms in the universe. There is a high level of organization and a greater richness of experience in a human being than in a thousand lifeless galaxies. It is human beings, after all, that reach out to understand that cosmic immensity."[25] Describing humanity as Nature, British biochemist and natural theologian Arthur Peacocke describes humans as the discontinuity-within-continuity of Nature.[26] Sallie McFague uses the image of humans as middle grounders depicting us as the conscious ones between the extremes of galaxies and quarks.[27] *Drawing on each of these images, discernment claims that the human-divine communication occurs as part of Nature.*

---

23. It is difficult to over emphasize that cosmic evolution is a necessary precursor to the evolution of humanity. Like our ancestors shifting their notion of the world from being flat to spherical, the shift to knowing ourselves as part of Nature can stretch us. On the other hand, once it is integrated into our self-identity, it becomes second nature. These huge lengths of time stretch beyond the concepts that shape most discernment. Yet, who a human is here and now and what she experiences and chooses draws directly from this long arrow of time.

24. Barbour, "Creation and Cosmology," 143.

25. Ibid., 147.

26. Peacocke, *Theology for a Scientific Age*, 74.

27. McFague, *Body of God*.

On the third misunderstanding of Nature as a sentimentally romanticized, idyllic, and static, it dissolves as biology shows that the characteristics of life—emergence, growth, pain, death, and decay—are inherent features of one another. They give Nature its distinctive, differentiated, yet interdependent shape. There is no emergence or growth without pain, death, and decay.[28] *Positing God's presence in each of these dynamics of Nature, discernment claims realistic notions of Nature as central to a deepening relationship with God.*

Thus, confounding any notion of a fixed, idyllic stage on which God plays out a static plan with humanity, insights from physical cosmology, evolutionary biology, and the neurosciences point to the unfolding complexity of Nature's 13.7 billion year history. Countering an emaciated exchange, which is beneath the capabilities of God and humanity, these scientific insights enable the vivid claim that God dynamically reveals in and through the medium of Nature to a participating human, who is both part of Nature and distinct from nature.

Double Challenge of Simultaneous Divine-Human Interaction

Finally and most specifically, the value of including science in Christian spirituality and discernment enlightens the crux of the issue in discernment: *the intersection of divine and human activity.* Discernment implicitly comes to this intersection when it claims that God reveals Godself to humans in such a way that people can decipher the revelation and then freely act upon it. This claim involves a double challenge: how do we speak intelligibly about divine action in the world, given contemporary science *and* how do we describe simultaneous action by two actors as dissimilar as God and humans?

This particular experience of simultaneous action is called spiritual indifference: standing neutral before all the various options in a decision. When a person is spiritually indifferent, she chooses connection with God over anything else, including any outcome or decision. Far from not caring, she cares so much about the outcome of a situation that she seeks to be neutral, awaiting God's guidance so that she can follow. In most cases, humans cannot just "get neutral," however. Here, the central role of intention returns to the fore. We can intend to have

28. For a profound look at the theological implications of these characteristics in Nature, see Southgate, *Groaning of Creation*.

utmost loyalty to God and then await the gift of God's grace. Spiritual indifference emerges when a person's loyalty to God intermingles with grace. It is in such an experience of spiritual indifference that the double challenge is most clear: how do we depict intelligible divine action, or grace, concurrent with purposeful human action, or intention?

First, developing intelligible notions about God's actions in the world is crucial. At the center of the problem, many contemporary people believe they face a choice between either a God who *intervenes* in the world to make things happen, on one hand, or a God who *cannot act* in particular situations, on the other.[29] Neither of these understandings of God is sufficient if a person wants to take seriously the insights of contemporary science as well as the Christian claims of a living God. Thus, when God's action is thought of in ways that are *not* coherent with other beliefs, it can evoke an experience of cognitive dissonance. It can yield a split in "head and heart," disintegrating the ways that we make meaning.

Three general patterns of cognitive dissonance arise with this split. Among those who lean toward science, the dissonance may be: "The universe is governed by reliable laws. God could only act by intervening in them, and I am not interested in that kind of whimsical God." Among those who choose to focus on God's power, it might sound like: "I don't care *how* God can heal someone, I just want it to happen." Finally, for those who habitually dismiss the grate of cognitive dissonance in the name of honoring mystery, this routine can evacuate the role for intellectual knowing in matters of faith.[30] Don Saliers speaks of the common temptation toward this tendency. "The recovery of personal and experiential dimensions of religious faith often brings with it an anti-doctrinal bias. Many who claim extraordinary experiences say that personal transformation and encounter with God have little to do with doctrines or theology. Lines are drawn between experience

29. This false choice stems from the inheritance of seventeenth-century Newtonian mechanism and eighteenth-century Laplacian philosophical determinism that portray all of nature as a causally closed, impersonal mechanism. Instead, this essay describes a third option in section 3, called non-interventionist, objective, special, divine action. See also Russell, *Cosmology from Alpha to Omega*, 113–14.

30. My intention to explore cogent divine action in no way suggests that the intellect offers superior or complete ways of knowing God. Ultimately, the Mystery we call God can never be comprehended fully. But there are less inadequate ways of describing God's presence and activity in the world that more fully support people's faithful, daily living.

and doctrine, between feeling and thinking, between emotion and thought."[31] Far too commonplace is the dissonance from, "Leaving your mind at the church door."

Conversely, given the interpretive place of cognitive claims in both creating and discerning experiences, insightful doctrines can *support* the process of understanding spiritual encounters with the Mystery called God. Thus, in dealing with the first aspect of the double challenge, I embrace natural science's insights to develop intelligible claims about God's activity in the world, as section 4.2 describes.

The second part of the double challenge confronts simplistic notions of cause and effect. Simplistic approaches presume *either* God *or* a person acts sufficiently to cause an outcome. A teeter-totter, zero-sum game image arises. But these contrastive approaches confound the experience of *simultaneous* divine-human action where human intention to by loyal to God *intermingles* with divine grace to yield inner freedom. Spiritual indifference's very nature is the synergistic experience that Origen (c. 185–253) described in his analogy of a sailboat where humans are the captain and God is the wind in the sails.[32] While inherently unequal, there is genuinely shared power, and both partners are needed for a safe journey. The early Church's use of *synergia* communicates this participatory model of partnership, envisioning genuine collaboration between humans and the Holy Spirit. While much of this aspect of the double challenge relies on philosophical assumptions about causation, particular scientific insights are useful in making those assumptions coherent, as the next section explores.

Though science is not historically an obvious partner in Christian spirituality, the value of its contributions is difficult to overestimate. With this interdisciplinary dialogue, science's descriptions of Nature update discernment and illumine its core. Simultaneous divine and human agency becomes more comprehensible, and thus discernment is more useful in today's culture, which is shaped by an increasing awareness of spiritual experiences. It is to these more detailed descriptions of Nature from three specific sciences that I now turn.

31. Saliers, *Soul in Paraphrase,* 2.
32. See Bondi, *To Love as God Loves,* 35.

Specific Contributions from Natural Science

Thorough investigation of a science-spirituality dialogue about discernment raises critical questions and nuances that warrant in-depth description and analysis.[33] In this briefer context, I use two questions to narrow the focus, asking what specific scientific insights are necessary to: 1) describe the humans who discern; and 2) describe God's actions in the world intelligibly, without intervention, such that joint divine-human agency can be proposed as a meaningful description of spiritual indifference.

Human Nature: Spiritual Anthropology

Humans who discern do so as part of the long scope of cosmological time. Evolutionary biology and neuroscience build upon the descriptions of physical cosmology, as they describe this species that can sift and weigh. The physical conditions of the universe, which helped to give rise to humanity, include a biological richness that has unfolded over the past 4.5 billion years when the earth and rest of the solar system formed. The possibilities for life emerged about 3.5–3.9 billion years ago, when bacterial life became well developed on earth in millions of species.[34] Human beings emerged relatively late—perhaps 100,000 years ago, only two-thousandth of one percent of the earth's total age. Contemporary human beings are probably the legacy of the earlier 3–4 hominid species that lived concurrently on the African continent and overlapped with Neanderthals until about 28,000 years ago.[35]

Through this biological history, evolution reveals nature as a dynamic process of becoming, always changing and developing, and radically temporal in character. Such a dynamic cosmos is incomplete, marked by endless potentials, some of which become actualized through the creatively unpredictable, evolutionary process, and some of which are permanently omitted by particular developments, like extinctions.[36]

33. The modes of rationality that the two disciplines share in common, which inform vigorous methodological standards, as well as the expansive role that philosophy plays in bridging the two disciplines, reveal a fertile setting for extensive mutual dialogue. See Wiens, *Discernment and Nature.*

34. Hammond, "Current Magnitude of Biodiversity," 113–38.

35. Ayala, "Evolution of Life," 56–57.

36. Barbour, *Religion and Science,* 237.

For discernment, one significant aspect of this dynamism is its focus on the very next step, not on some future possibility, because the future is constantly emerging.

However, amid this biological dynamism and unpredictability, dependable regularities exist as well. Often called the laws of nature, these regularities provide stable structures, processes, and interrelationships that shape the universe's workings. Far from being rigid, the regularities in the universe allow novelty to emerge through chance variations in organisms and unpredictable changes in the environment. The chance actualization of potentials in law-like Nature, then, yields novel forms of life—like human beings—that emerge within the cosmos. It is in the interplay between regularities and dynamism, or law and chance, that the potential for genuine newness exists.

In the 1970s, Arthur Peacocke advanced the discussion of law and chance past a conflictual model to explain how they work together to stimulate evolution.

> During the last decade it has become increasingly apparent that it is chance operating within a law like framework that is the basis of the inherent creativity of the natural order, its ability to generate new forms, patterns, and organizations of matter and energy. If all were governed by rigid law, a repetitive and uncreative order would prevail: if chance alone ruled, no forms, patterns or organizations would persist long enough for them to have any identity or real existence, and the universe could never be a cosmos and susceptible to rational inquiry. It is the combination of the two that makes possible an ordered universe capable of developing within itself new modes of existence. *The interplay of chance and law is creative.*[37]

On all levels of this evolutionary system, relatively simple laws, principles, and relationships undergo chance alterations. Thus, all of life is predisposed, constrained, or conditioned by genes and the environment, *and* it is open to novelty, which emerges through the long, continual movements of evolution.

As it relates to discernment, law and novelty interact in Nature to produce humans who have not only free choice but also the ability to actualize the potential for discernment. In the interplay, both the choice and the potential are constrained by the regularities of genes and the

---

37. Peacocke, *Theology for a Scientific Age*, 65 (italics in the original).

environment, including relationships and culture.[38] *Positing that this evolutionary interplay is the way God creates Nature, discernment claims the emergence of a species with choice and the potential to discern as a reflection of divine action.*[39]

Neuroscience further describes the humans who discern. Recall the philosophical assumption that humans are not a duality of body and mind or soul. Rather, we are a psychosomatic unity with emotional, mental, and spiritual faculties that register in the body, and it is through that physical matter of Nature that God communicates with humanity. Given that, we can use neuroscience to explore humanity's complex nervous system, which influences the human role of intention in discernment.

Neuroscience research about the human brain's complexity continues to explode. Current estimates point to "some 100 billion neurons, each connect[ing] with hundreds or thousands of other neurons through synaptic junctions (perhaps 100 trillion of them)."[40] The human brain in the overall cosmic structure reaffirms Barbour's earlier comment that the greatest complexity in the universe has happened at the middle range of cosmic size—the human being. Within this neurological complexity, some philosophers want to locate the capacity for human choice.

38. Importantly for discernment, these predispositions are contrasted with any causally closed idea of being predetermined. The philosophical notion of determinism undercuts theological notions of human dependence upon God, biological theories of predispositions, and indeterministic interpretations of quantum theories. "Though a fascinating and long-debated theory, determinism raises serious difficulties regarding the nature of human knowledge and its bearing on our understanding of morality. For example, if one adheres to the idea of determinism and believes that one's life is simply the mechanical and unchangeable outplay of forces beyond one's control, then how does this affect one's relationship to the world and other people [and God who has dealt this fixed hand]. Does adherence to determinism not lead one into a sense of meaninglessness and impotence regarding one's fate and actions? Does determinism not also lead one into the belief that whatever one does is morally acceptable, by virtue of the fact that whatever one does is already pre-determined, and therefore, meant to be? . . . Here, determinism fails to take into account human freedom and choice . . . In essence, the acceptance of determinism makes one into a mere thing, a mechanical and non-autonomous entity without the power to deliberate or change one's direction in life." Russell, *Theology and Science*.

39. Notably, this claim does not attempt to describe *how* God acts in Nature but merely to describe where those actions become manifest. The *how* of divine action remains a mystery.

40. Barbour, *Religion and Science*, 258.

Of the many mental processes that impact discernment, I focus here on the specific area of attention formation.[41] Most broadly, the nervous system helps a person perceive environmental stimuli and respond appropriately through sensory input, integration, and motor output. Within the stimuli perceiving process, what we colloquially call, "paying attention" happens by inhibiting extraneous stimuli. For example, attention deficit disorder and autism reflect the nervous system's difficulty with screening stimuli. More routinely, driving in fog and rain involves screening more stimuli than temperate conditions. Some people close their eyes in prayer to draw their attention toward God. Neurologically, attention involves both interacting areas of the brain as well as biochemical processes: 1) an inhibitory function in areas of the brain where neurological conflicts are managed, such as competing stimuli; 2) certain chemicals, like chloride, which is a negative ion, flow between the neurons and can help inhibit the firing of the synapses, which commonly follows sensory input.[42] For example, one way to inhibit the firing of a neuron is to increase the presence of a certain kind of neurotransmitter called gamma-aminobutyric acid (GABA). When GABA neurotransmitters are high, the firing of the neurons that stimulate an experience diminishes. Many anti-anxiety drugs, for example, use this approach to interrupt the stimulus of anxiety.[43] Practitioners of highly focused attention, like athletes, surgeons, and spiritual contemplatives, have learned how to use this stimuli perceiving and screening process effectively.

This neurological process of attention formation, or eliminating distracting input, illumines discernment's focus on intention and

41. While central to discernment, the process of learning, especially in Long Term Potentiation, reaches beyond this essay's focus. Among the other factors in mental processing, neuroscience theory on decision-making would seem to be centrally pertinent to discernment. However, the experience of spiritual indifference is so early in the decision-making process and involves different neurological processes, that decision-making theory is not the focus of my limited application of neuroscience. However, it certainly points to intersections between neuroscience and spiritual discernment that are worth future exploration. One particularly interesting book on the neuroscience of decision-making also addresses free will. See Montague, *Why Choose This Book*; and Glimcher, *Decisions, Uncertainty, and the Brain*. I am indebted to the insights of computer scientist, Mark Graves for helping me make these links between neuroscience and discernment.

42. Graves, "Memory, Trauma, and Healing."

43. See LeDoux, *Synaptic Self,* 286.

spiritual indifference. Honing attention to follow God alone is primary in spiritual indifference. Hypothesizing God's activity at the neurobiological level of inhibiting competing stimuli, discernment claims that God supports the actualization of attention and neutrality that contribute to spiritual indifference.[44] That is, as a person practices attending to God, the Spirit's grace could act in, with, and through the ions or neurotransmitters to diminish one's focus on anything other than God or even to break prior allegiances to something other than God.

In sum, building on physical cosmology's insights, evolutionary biology and neuroscience suggest that from the interplay of regularity and dynamism in Nature, the human who discerns emerges in Nature with a capacity to choose and pay attention in ways that facilitate the discernment of God's communication. To explore the hypotheses about God's attendant role in discernment, or what I have been calling grace, I turn to one final science.

Grace or Divine Action

As I describe discernment, it rests on the notion that God acts generally in the universe all the time, holding it in existence, and specially in particular situations, revealing God's desire for a specific circumstance. Such claims are fraught with complexity for scientists and philosophers as well as theologians and spirituality scholars. In recent decades, many scholars in those fields have focused on how to address that complexity in cogent and pertinent ways.[45]

Amid the ongoing research into how science and philosophy can speak to such discernment claims, I adopt an approach to special divine action that focuses on quantum theory and interpretation.[46] In essence,

44. When hypothesizing a model of God's activity in the human neuroprocesses of becoming spiritual indifferent, the simpler the neurological process the better, per Occam's razor. For example, the mechanisms involved in affecting attention through GABA transmission are much simpler than the complex processes of gene signaling, transcription, translation, and transport required for long-term learning or memory formation.

45. For example, see the Vatican Observatory/Center for Theology and Natural Sciences series of five volumes, culminating in Robert John Russell et al., eds., *Scientific Perspectives on Divine Action*.

46. The analogical nature of the mediated theory I utilize and the nuances of its alternative to gaps or joints in the universe as well as the numerous scientific, philosophical, and theological underpinnings are crucial details beyond the scope of this essay but can be found in Wiens, *Discernment and Nature*. In the science-theology literature, this

this approach claims that God *creates* Nature's structure, including humanity, without enough influences, or sufficient causes, in its natural processes to produce a consistently, predictable outcome. That is, it is not determined. Therefore, while Nature has intrinsic causal properties, it also is *inherently open* to God's direct causal influence in the outcomes of those processes. This approach addresses both Nature and God: Nature's causal properties are necessary but not sufficient; God creates the universe in such a way that God can be an influential contributor while respecting the defining characteristics of Nature. In terms of discernment, it interprets the science such that God can participate alongside a person who actively seeks to discern God's call.

Perhaps a brief interpretation of a biblical story can illustrate this idea of necessary but insufficient causes in discernment. Jesus' ministry clearly demonstrated his proclivity toward healing the various infirmities of people around him. But on one occasion, a Gentile woman from Syrophoenicia sought healing for her daughter, and Jesus denied it. When she persisted in seeking even a crumb of his mercy, he responded to her faithfulness, "Let it be done for you as you wish" (Matt 15:21–28). In the denial, Jesus' ability to heal seems to be necessary but not sufficient, because he is not open to his ministry extending to people of her nationality. Subsequently, God's movement through the mother's persistent faithfulness actualizes Jesus' inclusive vocation.

This approach to divine action depends upon a philosophical interpretation of quantum theory that describes Nature as genuinely open and undetermined. The science of quantum physics uses probabilistic equations, reflecting an imprecision in the science: that is, it cannot conclusively say whether quantum events have causally sufficient preceding conditions. Philosophical interpretations of this uncertainty vary. For some scholars, the imprecision is due to a current limitation on human knowledge, merely an epistemic situation that will be resolved with more explanatory science in the future.[47] For others, including myself, the imprecision is because it is truly not knowable; Nature is genuinely unfixed, pointing to an ontological characteristic.[48] Either interpretation of the science is legitimate.

---

mediated theory is called non-interventionist, objective, special divine action.

47. Bohm, *Quantum Theory*.

48. In 1927, Werner Heisenberg concluded that the inability to measure accurately and simultaneously reflects an indeterministic property of nature, not just a human ex-

For Christian spirituality, the attraction of describing Nature as genuinely open lies in the potential for cogently depicting God's activity, while honoring Nature's authentic identity. Nature is not a puppet of God, and God is not a hamstrung bystander. Seeing Nature as undetermined fits beautifully with spiritual experiences of synergistic collaboration, where God and humans partner together. It allows for a robust theory of divine action in experiences such as spiritual indifference, where humans intend to follow God first and foremost *simultaneous* with God's actualizing of their freedom to do so. Thomas Tracy underscores this attraction as he writes about science's search for causal openness in complex levels of Nature, such as the human brain. "The obvious place to look [for this openness] is in the lives of rational moral agents. The idea of responsive and personal relationship with God is deeply rooted in the theistic faiths, and this suggests that the mental (i.e., emotional, rational/reflective, moral, spiritual) life of persons will be one of the loci of divine action."[49] Applying Tracy's comments to discernment, the openness in mental/spiritual capacities, such as human intention and the attention formation process, describes a rich domain for divine activity in discernment.[50]

Concluding Implications

As people's awareness of spiritual experiences heightens and concern about ecological matters rise, practices that point to their natural intersection are increasingly valuable. Christian spiritual discernment is one of those rich and timely practices. When scientific insights shape discernment's notions of spiritual anthropology and divine action, the whole enterprise of discernment is transformed and made relevant to today's spiritual needs.

1. *Open to a Free Inner Disposition.* One's inner disposition/attitude shifts when one becomes conscious of one's place in the whole universe; responsibility is put in order or balanced, freeing one from over- or under-responsibility; a sense of mystery

---

perimental limitation. This conclusion became known as the Heisenberg Uncertainty Principle or Copenhagen interpretation.

49. Tracy, "Special Divine Action and the Laws of Nature," 277.

50. The science for this kind of indeterminism being manifest at higher-levels remains to be explored.

grows in learning the science, altering our identity and thus our questions (#2 below); horizons of meaning shift to include the universe from simply personal or social contexts; disciplines of attention lengthen in the altered time-frames of the universe.[51]

2. *Name the Question for Discernment.* Our questions change as our self-identities change; issues that render anthropocentric gains at the expense of the rest of nature may be weeded out all together, following Ignatius's guidance to discern only that which is morally neutral or good. Simultaneously, new sets of matters for discernment appear when the universe is the horizon of meaning. For example, how will my vocation reflect my responsibilities in Nature and my particular gifts within it? How does being part of the species with free choice influence how I respond to warring policies? How does being part of the species with self-consciousness influence the use of my time?

3. *Gather Data.* The cognitive claims of the science-religion dialogue have a specific influence on discernment, producing intellectual data and illumining consequences in an intelligible way. The data of ecological interconnections, evolutionary history, unrepeatability of species, or quantum indeterminacies, for example, can significantly shape the options one sees for a discerned decision as well as how one notices God's movements. Human experience of mystery grows the more we see ourselves as Nature, influencing our entire horizon of knowing.

4. *Pray and Reflect.* Knowing that indeterminacy is one description of the quantum world allows one's intellect to embrace the knowledge that God can come alongside a person to fulfill the possibilities already inherent in a situation. Prayer and reflection then become ways of noticing what God is already doing and what that calls out in oneself as response. Freedom from the cognitive dissonance about God's ability to act in, with, and through Nature contributes significantly to remaining free and attentive to God's movements.

---

51. Carol Newsom's biblical work on Job offers some helpful language to articulate the phenomenon of nature impacting inner disposition. See Newsom, "Moral Sense of Nature," 9–27.

5. *Make a Tentative Decision.* In altering how humans see themselves, as part of Nature or as the middle-grounders in the universe, the science-religion dialogue influences the processes of weighing: rational, intuitive, imaginative, and one's sensory knowing.

6. *Bring Tentative Decision to God for Confirmation.* New touchstones from experiencing God in Nature contribute to the confirmation process. For example, belonging, humility, awe, wonder, praise, gratitude.

7. *Enact the Decision.* Attending to the idea that through discernment God calls a person to join in actualizing an existing potential, the enactment of a discerned decision puts the person into cooperative action with God and all of Nature.

8. *Evaluate the Discerned Decision.* Discern the discernment is a reprise of the first seven steps in order to continue growing in relationship with God.

In the end, the questions and choices that shape our daily lives involve both Christian ecological spirituality and discernment. Who we are in an interdependent, ecological system and what we claim about God's interaction with us shape our every decision. The ancient spiritual practice of discernment helps make those decisions more purposeful and, hopefully, more responsive to the One who creates, transforms, and inspires it all.

Bibliography

Au, Wilkie. "Holistic Discernment." *Presence* 11 (2005) 15–23.

Ayala, Francisco. "The Evolution of Life: An Overview." In *Evolutionary and Molecular Biology: Scientific Perspectives on Divine Action*, edited by Robert John Russell et al., 21–57. Berkeley, CA: Center for Theology and Natural Sciences, 1998.

Barbour, Ian. "Creation and Cosmology." In *Cosmos as Creation: Theology and Science in Consonance*, edited by Ted Peters, 115–51. Nashville: Abingdon, 1989.

Barbour, Ian. *Religion and Science: Historical and Contemporary Issues.* San Francisco: HarperSanFrancisco, 1997.

Bascom, Robert A. "Adaptable for Translation: Deuteronomy 6:5 in the Synoptic Gospels and Beyond." In *A Gift of God in Due Season*, edited by R. Weis and David M. Carr, 166–83. Sheffield, UK: Sheffield Academic, 1996.

Bohm, David. *Quantum Theory.* New York: Prentice-Hall, 1951.

Bondi, Roberta. *To Love as God Loves: Conversations with the Early Church.* Philadelphia: Fortress, 1987.

Burghardt, Walter. "Contemplation: A Long Loving Look at the Real." *Church* 5 (1989) 14–18.

Childs, Brian. "Experience." In *Dictionary of Pastoral Care and counseling*, edited by Rodney J. Hunter, 388–89. Nashville: Abingdon, 1990.

Clayton, Phillip. "Neuroscience, the Person, and God: An Emergentist Account." In *Neuroscience and the Person: Scientific Perspectives on Divine Action*, edited by Robert John Russell et al., 181–214. Berkeley, CA: Center for Theology and Natural Sciences, 1999.

Davies, W. D., and Dale C. Allison Jr. *A Critical and Exegetical Commentary on the Gospel According to Saint Matthew.* Edinburgh: T. & T. Clark, 1997.

Dreyer, Elizabeth, and Mark S. Burrows, editors. *Minding the Spirit: The Study of Christian Spirituality.* Baltimore: Johns Hopkins University Press, 2005.

Glimcher, Paul. *Decisions, Uncertainty, and the Brain: The Science of Neuroeconomics.* Cambridge, MA: MIT Press, 2004.

Graves, Mark. "Memory, Trauma, and Healing." Unpublished paper presented at the American Academy of Religion, November 20, 2006.

Hammond, P. "The Current Magnitude of Biodiversity." In *Global Biodiversity Assessment*, edited by V. H. Heywood and R. T. Watson, 113–38. Cambridge: Cambridge University Press, 1995.

Hick, John. *Evil and the God of Love.* San Francisco: Harper & Row, 1966.

Ignatius of Loyola. *Spiritual Exercises and Selected Works.* Edited by George Ganss SJ. New York: Paulist, 1991.

Janzen, J. Gerald. "The Claim of the Shema." *Encounter* 59 (1988) 243–57.

LeDoux, Joseph E. *Synaptic Self: How Our Brains Become Who We Are.* New York: Viking, 2002.

Liebert, Elizabeth. "The Role of Practice in the Study of Christian Spirituality." *Spiritus* 2 (2002) 32–49.

McFague, Sallie. *The Body of God: An Ecological Theology.* Minneapolis: Fortress, 1993.

Montague, Read. *Why Choose This Book: How We Make Decisions.* New York: Penguin, 2006.

Murphy, Nancey. "Supervenience and the Downward Efficacy of the Mental: A Nonreductive Physicalist Account of Human Action." In *Neuroscience and the Person: Scientific Perspectives on Divine Action*, edited by Robert John Russell et al., 147–64. Berkeley, CA: Center for Theology and Natural Sciences, 1999.

Newsom, Carol A. "The Moral Sense of Nature: Ethics in the Light of God's Speech to Job." *Princeton Seminary Bulletin* 15 (1994) 9–27.

Peacocke, Arthur. "The Sound of Sheer Silence: How Does God Communicate with Humanity?" In *Neuroscience and the Person: Scientific Perspectives on Divine Action*, edited by Robert John Russell et al., 215–48. Berkeley, CA: Center for Theology and Natural Sciences, 1999.

———. *Theology for a Scientific Age: Being and Becoming—Natural, Divine, and Human.* Minneapolis: Fortress, 1993.

Russell, Robert John. *Cosmology from Alpha to Omega: The Creative Mutual Interaction of Theology and Science.* Minneapolis: Fortress, 2008.

———. "Natural Sciences." In *The Blackwell Companion to Christian Spirituality*, edited by Arthur G. Holder, 325–44. Malden, MA: Blackwell, 2005.

———. *Theology and Science: Current Issues and Future Directions*. Berkeley, CA: Center for Theology and the Natural Sciences, 2000. Online: http://www.ctns. org/russell_article.html.

Saliers, Don E. *The Soul in Paraphrase: Prayer and the Religious Affections*. New York: Seabury, 1980.

Southgate, Christopher. "Critical Realism." In *Theology and Science: Current Issues and Future Directions*, edited by Robert John Russell, no pages. Berkeley, CA: Center for Theology and the Natural Sciences. Online: http://www.ctns.org/ russell_article.html.

———. *The Groaning of Creation: God, Evolution, and the Problem of Evil*. Louisville: Westminster John Knox, 2008.

Tracy, Thomas F. "Special Divine Action and the Laws of Nature." In *Scientific Perspectives on Divine Action: Twenty Years of Challenges and Progress*, edited by Robert John Russell et al., 249–83. Berkeley, CA: Center for Theology and the Natural Sciences, 2008.

Wiens, Nancy. *Discernment and Nature: Exploring Their Relationship through Christian Spirituality and the Natural Sciences*. PhD diss., Graduate Theological Union, 2007.

Wuthnow, Robert. *After Heaven: Spirituality in America Since the 1950s*. Berkeley: University of California Press, 1998.

8

Requiem for the Baiji

Liturgical Lamentation and Species Extinction

Timothy Hessel-Robinson

THERE IS AN INTEGRAL CONNECTION BETWEEN CHRISTIAN SPIRITUAL-
ity and liturgy. The corporate, ritual prayer of the church provides a
"context within which worshippers can experience the encounter with
God."[1] Further, liturgy forms its participants, linguistically, symbolical-
ly, and gesturally, in patterned expressions of the encounter with God.
That is, liturgy functions as a "school of prayer," modeling the form
prayer takes and "shaping the religious imagination out of which prayer
emerges" in a community.[2] As liturgical theologian Mary Margaret
Kelleher describes it, liturgy mediates a "horizon" of meaning, "a corporate vision of what it means to live as a Christian." This horizon offers a "public spirituality" that participants are invited to appropriate as
their own.[3] If it is the case that liturgy is a "school of prayer" mediating
a public spirituality, it is important to ask what vision of the Christian
life is being mediated, what kind of spirituality are worshippers invited
to appropriate when corporate worship largely excludes attention to
creation or nature? What sort of formation takes place when liturgy
promotes a dualistic spirituality that imagines communion with God
is to be achieved by escaping the material world? What forms should
Christian liturgical prayer take in light of the enormous threats now
facing Earth's ecosystems?

---

1. White, "Spirituality, Liturgy, and Worship," 44.
2. Ibid.
3. Kelleher, "Liturgy: An Ecclesial Act of Meaning," 494–95.

While interest in the relationship between ecology and liturgy seems to be growing, ecological issues have not been well integrated into either the practice of Christian worship or into liturgical scholarship.[4] As is the case with other areas of spirituality, liturgy must imagine how to mediate the experience of God within the material realities of Earth and cosmos. Liturgy must find ways to invite worshippers to live more sustainably when the biophysical life systems of the Earth are under severe strain. In this essay I suggest that one place to begin this work is by recovering the prayer of lament in relation to the Earth's wounds. By developing liturgies of lamentation for a despoiled Earth, Christian worshipping assemblies may offer a public spirituality that helps participants re-imagine the nature-human relationship.

Because spirituality is rooted in the concrete particularity of historical experience, I have chosen to focus my theological reflections a specific aspect of current ecological conditions. The extinction of the Yangtze River dolphin, or baiji, will be representative of violence perpetrated against the Earth and of the significant ecosystemic threats we now face. I attempt to answer the following questions: when faced with the eradication of an entire species of animal life, how might a Christian community pray? How can we begin to process the tragic finality of extinction when Christian scripture and testimony declares that all creatures have been lovingly created by God and blessed as good? First, I will introduce the case of the baiji. Next, I will survey the role of animals in Scripture and in the thought of selected figures from the history of Christian spirituality, focusing specifically on the way that animals have been imagined as mediators of divine revelation. This, in turn, leads to questions about the human condition and the absence of God within creation. Then, I will consider recent scholarship on lament in biblical studies and in practical theology. I will conclude by suggesting a provisional theology of eco-lamentation, suggesting five ways that lament can form Christian worshippers to respond to contemporary ecological tragedies like the extinction of a species: by affirming the blessedness of embodied life; by naming the forces that threaten the sustainability of

---

4. For an account of how nature has been generally excluded from Christian worship see Messenger, "These Stones Shall Be God's House." Recent attempts to integrate ecology and liturgy include Santmire, *Ritualizing Nature*; Mick, *Liturgy and Ecology in Dialogue*; McDougall, *Cosmos as Primary Sacrament*; Power, "Worship and Ecology;" Stuart, *Watered Garden*.

God's good creation; by offering a form by which to express a seemingly inexpressible grief; by helping worshippers to identify with other suffering creatures; by re-imagining the relationship between divine and human power and inviting worshippers to claim responsibility for action.

Susan White reminds us that the spiritual life has to do not only with individual relationships to God, but also with the individual's and God's involvement in the world. Liturgy offers "visions of genuine holiness" and "images of the future of the world and its contents." As liturgy mediates these visions and images, it "reorders all our dealings with others and casts a new light on the world."[5] As we face increasingly severe ecological challenges Christian liturgy must find ways to help worshippers name that which threatens creation, to genuinely express grief and fear about the future, and to empower worshippers to act on behalf of that which is vulnerable to destruction.

Witness to Extinction

Samuel Turvey's *Witness to Extinction* addresses the plight of the Yangtze River dolphin, or baiji, one of four known freshwater cetaceans in the world. The author chronicles his involvement in efforts to preserve the baiji from extinction. In the fall of 2006, Turvey traveled up and down the Yangtze River, the baiji's only known habitat, with a team of researchers looking for signs of the animal. Turvey was with a conservation team trying to determine how many baiji might be left in the river, and where they might be, so that a proposed captive recovery program could commence. After six weeks of searching the heavily trafficked and perilously polluted waterway, the survey team failed to locate a single baiji. Thus, the magnificent cetacean, after evolving as a distinct species in the Yangtze River basin for 20 million years, is now considered extinct.[6]

Baiji have inhabited not only the Yangtze River but also the Chinese cultural imagination for thousands of years, the oldest known literary reference dating at least from the Han dynasty (206 BCE to 8 CE). Chinese mythology renders the baiji's origins variously, but the legends commonly involve a young woman who is treated cruelly; she is

5. White, "Spirituality, Liturgy, and Worship," 44–45.

6. Turvey, *Witness to Extinction*." Turvey provides an brief overview of the evolutionary history of the baiji on pages 13–15.

either forbidden to marry the one she loves, threatened with being sold into slavery, threatened with being given in marriage to one she does not love, or threatened with sexual violence. Resisting these threats, the woman either throws herself into the river or is drowned in it. There she is changed miraculously into, or is reincarnated as, a white dolphin. "The Goddess of the Yangtze," as the baiji came to be known, became a symbol of peace, prosperity, and love.[7]

The animal's mythic status, however, could not prevent its rapid decline in the age of industrialization. A population of several thousand in the 1950s had dwindled to about 400 by the 1980s. A survey conducted in 1997 concluded that only a few dozen baiji remained. China placed the baiji in the "First Order of Protected Animals" category in the 1980s, outlawing many types of fishing that threatened the dolphins. This action did little to slow the decline. As one of the world's most heavily populated regions, the Yangtze River Valley is highly industrialized. The river is saturated with chemical and heavy metal pollutants from industrial discharge and from accidental spills. The Yangtze is also one of the world's busiest waterways, and many baiji have been killed in collisions with boats or fatally gashed by propellers.

Turvey's book chronicles his experience with international conservation efforts, and he offers substantial critique of these efforts. However, it also records his emotional responses to the ill-fated quest. His involvement in the efforts to preserve the baiji elicited in him a deep sense of affection for the animal, compassion for its plight, and zeal for its preservation. The ultimate failure to preserve the baiji produces a deep sense of loss, and the text is laced with the language of grief. Turvey writes that when he realized the survey had failed, that hopes for preserving the baiji were lost, he was overcome by a deep sadness. The trip turned into a "godawful, soul-destroying experience."[8] The whole enterprise had become "a travesty, and tragedy."[9] As the trip concluded, he found himself spontaneously weeping.[10] The disappearance of any species is tragic, he states with melancholy, but "if the baiji dies out, there would be nothing like it left on earth."[11]

7. Ibid., 3–5.
8. Ibid., 163.
9. Ibid., 197.
10. Ibid., 177.
11. Ibid., 104.

The disappearance of the baiji points to the troubles facing other cetaceans. Many fish and marine mammals are under stress because of pollution or overharvesting. From right whales to the vaquita, a small porpoise found only in the Gulf of California, nearly a quarter of all whale, dolphin, and porpoise species are considered endangered or threatened, according to the International Union for the Conservation of Nature (IUCN).[12] Turvey muses that "whales and dolphins have not really benefited from sharing a planet with humans for the past few millennia."[13] Further, the critical status of cetaceans is representative of the threats now facing tens of thousands of other species across the globe. Scientists estimate that roughly forty percent of all species on the planet should be considered endangered or threatened, including eleven percent of all bird species, twenty percent of all reptiles, twenty-five percent of both amphibians and mammals, and thirty-three percent of all fish species.[14] There have been five periods of mass extinction of biological species in the earth's history, the first coming some 550 million years ago in the Cambrian era and the last at the end of the Cretaceous period about 65 million years ago. Scientists tell us that we are now in the midst of the sixth period of mass extinction, the Holocene. Previous extinctions were caused by a variety of factors: meteor collisions, radical climate changes, and other occurrences scientists are still debating. The current destruction is distinguished from previous ones by one fact. Human beings are primarily responsible for the species extermination that has been rapidly accelerating over the past 200 years by destroying habitat, overharvesting on land and sea, and polluting soil, air, forests, oceans, rivers, and lakes. Humanity has become what one scientist calls "the current agent of mass destruction" upon the Earth.[15]

The reality and urgency of the situation is almost too much to comprehend. Even a scientist like Turvey who deals with these realities every day, wrestles with a deep sense of loss and gropes for words to process the emotional impact of the baiji's disappearance. The struggles of a scientist to convey his anguish about the loss of a species evokes questions for Christian spirituality. What shape can prayer take in

12. The IUCN "redlist," or data on the status of various species can be accessed at http://www.iucnredlist.org/.

13. Turvey, *Witness to Extinction*, 164.

14. Saier, "Species Extinction," 136. See Spray and McGlothlin, *Loss of Biodiversity*.

15. Saier, "Species Extinction," 136.

response to extinction? As our awareness of what we are losing grows, one of the challenges for Christian spirituality is to find ways of living with such awareness that open up possibilities for responding hopefully.

Animals as Revelatory in Christian Spirituality

Awareness of the scope of animal extinction now occurring necessitates some understanding of the role of animals within Christianity. Animals have been part of Jewish and Christian imagination and experience from the beginning. Frequently, in the Hebrew Bible and throughout the history of Christianity, animals have been regarded as bearers of divine revelation. While there are several dimensions to a full understanding of the role of animals in Christianity, here I focus on the way that animals have been understood as revealing God's presence and will.[16]

The Hebrew Bible contains many references to animals serving as messengers of God and witnesses to humans. Several biblical narratives are "saturated with the vocabulary of divine revelation" in which animals "see and know what the humans cannot." Animal speech and action "mediates between God and the humans, giving humanity access to God."[17] One of the most well-known examples appears in Numbers 22:22–35, the story of Baalam's "talking donkey." Balaam's is an unusual story in several ways. He is well known seer, a non-Israelite prophet, summoned by Balak, king of the Moabites, to curse the Israelites encamped on the plains of Moab, so that the Moabites might avoid conquest (Num 22:1–6). After consulting Yahweh, Balaam resists Balak's directive until God finally, seemingly, relents to allow Balaam's journey (Num 22:7–21). God, however, reverses course again and becomes angry as Balaam prepares to leave. When a weapon-wielding "angel of the Lord" is sent to block Balaam's path and prevent his errand, the donkey on which he is riding is the only being among Balaam's company who discerns the angel's presence. When the donkey veers off the road and lies down, sparing Balaam's life, Balaam responds with physical and

---

16. The literature on animals and religion is large and growing. Some recent works that focus on animals in Christianity include, Deane-Drummond and Clough, *Creaturely Theology*; Hobgood-Oster, *Holy Dogs and Asses*; Linzey, *Animal Gospel*; Wennberg, *God, Humans, and Animal*.

17. Howard, "Animal Speech as Revelation," 22.

verbal abuse of the animal. God opens the mouth of the donkey, who speaks in its own defense rebuking Balaam (Num 22:28–30). Only then is Balaam able to see God's messenger, finally realizing that the donkey has saved his life. Interestingly, the donkey not only acts as God's mouthpiece to Balaam, but, as Cameron Howard notes, when it protests Balaam's treatment the animal appeals to the companionship they share rather than pointing to the sword-bearing angel.[18] In the narrative, the donkey displays greater powers of discernment than the humans do: the animal is able "to see and know the ways of God when human beings cannot."[19] Through the donkey, God's will is revealed to Balaam.

One other example will suffice. In the book of Jonah, the starring animal role goes to the great fish appointed by God to swallow up the protagonist, thus saving his life when he is thrown into the sea. However, other animals—along with plants and the elements—play important roles in the story as "agents of God's instruction to the reluctant prophet."[20] A storm manifests God's displeasure at Jonah's disobedience and redirects his course. When the Ninevite king declares a penitent fast for the city his proclamation includes the animals, who are to join their human companions as they all "cry mightily to God" (Jonah 3:7–8). God "appoints" a bush to provide shade and relieve Jonah's discomfort (Jonah 4:6). God also "appoints" a worm to attack the bush and prepares a "sultry east wind," while the sun beats down on Jonah's head, all in order to get Jonah's attention and to teach him a lesson in compassion (Jonah 4:7–11). Finally, the book concludes with a phrase indicating that God is greatly concerned for the welfare of Nineveh's animals, as well as for its humans (Jonah 4:11). The book of Jonah notably displays, according to Kathryn Schifferdecker "the exquisite responsiveness of the natural world to God's call, a responsiveness noticeably lacking in the reluctant human prophet." Instead of Jonah, it is "the fish, the plant, the worm, and the repentant sheep, goats, and cattle . . . who teach us human beings how to respond when God calls."[21]

Animals do not play as dramatic a role in the New Testament, although occasionally they help to reveal the divine character and will.

18. Ibid., 27.

19. Ibid., 26.

20. Schifferdecker, "And Also Many Animals," 216. See also, Person, "Role of Nonhuman Characters in Jonah."

21. Ibid., 216–17.

Jesus, whose parables draw extensively on agrarian imagery, assured his listeners that God cares for them by proclaiming that God cares even for the humble sparrows (Matt 10:28) and ravens (Luke 12:24). A donkey assists Jesus in a dramatic action that initiates his passion (Matt 21:1–11). Elsewhere, something like a large sheet filled with all sorts of animals reveals to Peter God's will for the Gentiles (Acts 10:9–16), although the animals involved are to be killed and eaten. While there is not a great deal of attention given to animals in the New Testament, animals have figured prominently in the history of Christian reflection on divine presence.

For example, the great medieval Franciscan theologian Bonaventure (1221–74) regarded every creature as a unique representation of the creator. Bonaventure regarded nature and scripture as a "double book" of God's revelation. God made the universe as a reflection of the divine self, in order to reveal Godself to humanity. "The creation is a kind of book in which the Trinity shines forth," wrote Bonaventure.[22] Of animals he asserted, "Every creature is by its nature a kind of effigy and likeness of the eternal Wisdom."[23] The contemplative person may discern the way to God through meditation upon the creatures: "For these creatures are shadows, echoes and pictures of that first, most powerful, most wise and most perfect Principle, of that eternal Source, Light and Fullness . . . They are vestiges, representations, spectacles proposed to us and signs divinely given so that we can see God."[24] Despite the hierarchically-ordered medieval cosmology that shaped his thought, Bonaventure's work clearly affirms that Earth's creatures bear revelatory potential, serving to lead the attentive person toward union with God.

The contemporary Australian theologian Denis Edwards draws on Bonaventure's image of a stained-glass window to explain the Trinity in ecological terms: "as the one stream of light breaks up into different colors as it flows through a stained glass window, so the Creator is reflected in the different creatures we see around us. Each and every creature reflects a different aspect of the Creator. The exuberance of creation represents the infinite fecundity of God."[25] Drawing on both Bonaventure and Thomas Aquinas, Edwards goes on to assert that "no one creature,

22. Bonaventure, *Breviloquium*, 73–75.

23. Bonaventure, *Soul's Journey into God*, 77.

24. Ibid., 76.

25. Edwards, *Ecology at the Heart of Faith*, 77.

not even the human, can image God by itself."[26] Each creature uniquely reveals something about God.

Celtic Christian sources contain a great deal of attention to nature, frequently including animals in lists of blessings and hymnic verses. Celtic verses imagine animals as models to humans of true praise and virtue. The *Carmina Gadelica*, a nineteenth century collection of Gaelic religious verses that survived orally for several centuries in the Highlands and Western Isles of Scotland, is saturated with nature imagery. In the following verse, said to have been composed by a medieval woman suffering with leprosy, exiled from her community and living alone by the sea, plants and animals alike are regarded as being permeated with divine blessing. As bearers of divine goodness they reveal the presence of Christ and call humanity to worship, even as they offer their own praise.

> There is no plant in the ground
>   But is full of His virtue,
> There is no form in the strand
> But is full of His blessing,
>   Jesu! Jesu! Jesu!
>   Jesu! meet it were to praise Him.
>
> There is no life in the sea,
> There is no creature in the river,
> There is naught in the firmament,
> But proclaims His goodness.
>   Jesu! Jesu! Jesu!
>   Jesu! meet it were to praise Him.
>
> There is no bird on the wing,
> There is no star in the sky,
> There is nothing beneath the sun,
> But proclaims His goodness.
> Jesu! Jesu! Jesu!
>   Jesu! meet it were to praise Him.[27]

26. Ibid., 78. Aquinas stated that "God produced many and diverse creatures, so that what was wanting to one in the representation of divine goodness might be supplied by another. For goodness which in God is simple and uniform, in creatures is manifold and diverse. Hence the whole universe together participates in the divine goodness more perfectly, and represents it better than any single creature whatever." *Summa Theologiae* 1.47.1.

27. Davies and Bowie, *Celtic Christian Spirituality*, 95.

John Calvin (1509–1564), too, saw all of creation as reflecting God's character and presence. Calvin understood the universe as irradiated by the splendor of God's glory; God's presence is to be discerned in every element of the universe through the eyes of faith. Calvin described the world with metaphors like the "theatre of God's glory," the "living image of God," and the "beautiful garment" in which God wraps Godself in order to become visible.[28] The pages of Calvin's writings overflow with references to the cosmos and to creatures. Creation is the transparent vehicle disclosing God's splendor to Calvin: God has "in all parts of the world, in heaven and on earth, written as it were engraved the glory of his power, goodness, wisdom and eternity."[29] According to Peter Huff, "the world of nature is never separated from the realm of divine revelation" in Calvin's thought.[30]

Animals play a significant role in Calvin's theological reflections, supplying subjects for consideration as well as language and imagery with which to express his thought.[31] First, God cares for all creatures. Calvin's strong theology of providence is integrally linked to his theology of creation, the two being "inseparably joined."[32] God does not "idly observe from heaven what takes place on earth," but is intimately and immediately involved in the workings of nature and in human affairs.[33] Calvin asserts that God's loving providence is not exercised only with humans, but that God "sustains, nourishes, and cares for, everything he has made, even to the least sparrow."[34]

Beyond emphasizing God's care for animals, Calvin also strongly maintains the revelatory potential of the creatures for human beings. All creatures, "from those in the firmament to those which are in the center of the earth, are able to act as witnesses and messengers of his glory."[35] Like Bonaventure, Calvin claims that all of creation, and especially the animal world, entices human beings to seek God, "and

---

28. Zachman, *Image and Word in the Theology of John Calvin*, 25–49. Also, see Lane, "Spirituality as the Performance of Desire," 1–30.

29. Calvin, *Commentaries*, 59.

30. Huff, "Calvin and the Beasts," 68.

31. Ibid.

32. Calvin, *Institutes*, 1.16.1.

33. Ibid., 1.16:4.

34. Ibid., 1.16:1.

35. Calvin, *Commentaries*, 59.

after having found him, to meditate upon him and to render him the homage befitting his dignity."[36] In his instructions concerning how to achieve knowledge of God, Calvin warns "not to pass over in ungrateful thoughtlessness or forgetfulness those conspicuous powers which God shows forth in his creatures." Rather, one should attend to God's presence in creation and respond with grateful affection.[37] Alluding to Romans 1 Calvin writes, "For the little birds that sing, sing of God; the beasts clamor for him; the elements dread him, the mountains echo him, the fountains and flowing waters cast their glances at him, and the grass and flowers laugh before him."[38] Huff concludes "Calvin saw every living thing, no matter how humble or harmful, as a vehicle for the self-disclosure of its Maker."[39]

Numerous other examples could be cited, but these few give a sense of how animals have been regarded as revelatory in Christian scripture and history. Admittedly, this is not the whole story. Christian reflection on other than human creatures usually reveals an anthropocentric bias. For instance, when Calvin says that animals are witnesses to God's glory it is for the benefit of humans. Humans are "the most excellent" of God's works, according to Calvin: the entire universe was made especially for the sake of humankind.[40] Thus, one of the primary functions of animals is to provide food for humans.[41] Thomas Aquinas argued that human mastery over the animals is the natural order of creation, for God gave humans command over other creatures because of their usefulness to humans. Animals have value only in relation to humanity.[42] Regarding animal welfare, John Cobb has gone so far as to say that when compared to Judaism, Islam, Buddhism, and other religions, none have "a record quite as bad as Christianity."[43] Still, there is a significant strand running through various Christian traditions that regards animals, and other parts of nature, as agents of divine revelation.

36. Ibid., 59–60.

37. Calvin, *Institutes*, 1.14:21.

38. Calvin, *Commentaries*, 60.

39. Huff, "Calvin and the Beasts," 69.

40. Calvin, *Institutes* 1:14:4; 1:16:6.

41. Huff, "Calvin and the Beasts," 69.

42. Aquinas, "Man as Master Over Creation," 17–19.

43. Quoted in Wennberg, *God, Humans, and Animals*, 286.

In light of this witness, what are the implications for contemporary Christian spirituality in the face of mass extinction and potential ecosystemic collapse? If animals are bearers of divine revelation and presence, a question arises. As the rate of animal extinction accelerates, are the means of God's self-revealing obscured? Thomas Berry famously asserted that "when we destroy the living forms of this planet . . . we destroy modes of divine presence."[44] Denis Edwards puts it more sharply, stating that, "the human destruction of biodiversity is an act of contempt for the divine self-expression," and it reflects human arrogance and self-centeredness.[45] Samuel Turvey said that when the baiji had gone extinct, "there is nothing else like it in the world." This is true, also, for every other species of animal or plant life that passes into extinction. Each time this happens, according to much Christian reflection through the centuries, a unique manifestation of God's presence, a unique witness to God's loving providence and care, disappears. What implications does this have for Christian prayer? How should Christian liturgy respond to the tragic reality of the loss of animal life and diversity? The questions become even more pointed when we realize that humans are primarily responsible for this loss. Such a realization means that God has not simply removed Godself but that humanity, in causing the extinctions, is eclipsing the signs of divine presence. Cynthia Moe-Lobeda declares that humans have become the "uncreators."[46] Christian liturgy is deeply implicated by this.

Liturgical theologian David Power challenged a gathering of liturgy scholars around similar questions several years ago. Reflecting on issues of historical memory and theodicy, Power queried: "Can we in truth celebrate eucharist after the Nazi holocaust and in the face of imminent nuclear holocaust, and in a world half-populated by refugees, in the same way as we did before the occurrence of such horrors?"[47] Power asserted that worship and prayer "articulate before God our own experience of this world and of human history, our sense of the presence and absence of God in our time."[48] He warned that our spiritual and liturgical practices cannot retreat into an imagined golden past, a narrowly

44. Berry, *Dream of the Earth*, 11.

45. Edwards, *Jesus the Wisdom of God*, 161.

46. Moe-Lobeda, "Liturgy for Uncreators," 64.

47. Power, "Liturgy, Memory and the Absence of God," 328.

48. Ibid., 327–28.

focused, individualistic quest for personal salvation or fulfillment, or an "abstract universalism." If they do, we will find ourselves "doomed to silence by the inability to even face, let alone make any sense of, current reality."[49] For a people who remember Jesus and his witness to God's reign in worship, how does the Holocaust, the threat of nuclear annihilation, or the refugee crisis shape prayer? Such events challenge traditional notions of where and how God is to be encountered. Power later included the ecological crisis in his reflections: "What are we to say of the cosmic Christ and of the God of all creation in a world which may in time not be fit for human habitation because human greed has so exploited it? . . . Where is God in creation when the earth is raped?"[50]

For Power the violence done to the Earth, exemplified by the accelerating extinction rate, much like the Holocaust, raises significant questions about God's providence, God's goodness, and God's presence in the world. However, the recognition that these events result from predatory human actions against human and other-than-human creatures alike, also raises questions about the human condition and future. Mary Evelyn Tucker goes so far as to say that human-driven mass extinction calls into question the very viability of humanity as a species.[51] Power implies that these events mean we *cannot* celebrate eucharist, we *cannot* worship *in the same way* as before these events. How, then, *do* we pray in such a context?

Power suggests that such events and our knowledge of them threaten to overwhelm those who assemble for worship. The Holocaust, the prospect of nuclear annihilation, and the possibility of ecocide cause a "violent disorientation of beliefs, practices, and prayers which cuts to the very identity of a people in God."[52] Christian people often find it unbearable to question God's fidelity, even when confronted with such devastating circumstances, wanting somehow to reconcile their trust in God with the realities of climate change and massive species extinctions.[53] It is just as difficult to reconcile belief in the essential dignity and civility of humankind with the recognition that humans are principally responsible for ecological destruction. The reluctance to

49. Ibid., 328.

50. Power, "When to Worship is to Lament," 168–71.

51. Tucker, *Worldly Wonder*, 6.

52. Power, "When to Worship is to Lament," 162.

53. Ibid., 156.

name such realities in prayer or to admit their disorienting nature often leads to silence and paralysis.

Shierry Weber Nicholsen's book *The Love of Nature and the End of the World* is instructive on this point. Nicholsen explores the conditions of the public mind in which we recognize our dependence upon the natural world, we are aware of the grave threats to it, and yet we fail to speak and act to address such threats. As a psychotherapist, Nicholsen is interested in "the psychological forces that allow the destruction to continue."[54] Nicholsen contends that human selfhood is formed in relation to the natural world, especially through intimate experiences with particular places and beings in childhood. We form loving bonds with the natural world, identifying with other life forms in ways that expand our sense of self to include "greater wholes."[55] The recognition of these bonds, however, exposes our vulnerability, for to love something means that the self is exposed to the potential loss of that which is loved. What we love "can be lost, or harmed, and it can also betray us."[56] Nicholsen muses that identification with other creatures often comes through knowledge of their suffering, an experience that is likely to become more common as extinction rates increase.[57] In order to avoid such painful vulnerability we often deny the bonds and suppress any action or speech. Denial and silence about such things seems preferable to complete despair.

It is here that liturgy may contribute to a more sustainable spirituality by offering resources for articulating our sense of loss, grief, abandonment, and fear about the future of life. Among the many ways that liturgy needs to recover an emphasis on creation is by helping worshippers bring to expression the sense of despair about the Earth's conditions that Nicholsen analyzes. If Christian liturgy is to avoid the silence or glib irrelevance about which Power warned, it must directly confront current realities, like the threat of extinction, and find ways of "remembering God's apparent failure without loss of hope in the resurrection."[58] Also, with the recognition that humanity is the major contemporary threat to Earth's ecosystems, we must find ways of com-

54. Nicholsen, *Love of Nature and the End of the World*, 1.

55. Ibid., 42–51.

56. Ibid., 1–9.

57. Ibid., 51.

58. Power, "When to Worship is to Lament," 162.

ing to terms with human failure, encouraging changed behavior, and retaining hope without completely despairing over the human condition and vocation. The failure to address these realities is potentially ruinous. As Nicholsen puts it: "Loss not fully faced and mourned can lead one to fall under the spell of numbness and cruelty. It can lead to guilt and the wish to blot out the future."[59]

The Turn to Lament

Turning to the Hebrew Psalms of lament, Power suggests that they provide us with models and resources for coming to terms with the realities of our contemporary situation in corporate prayer. Biblical scholars have devoted a great deal of attention to lament in recent times.[60] Scholarship on the Psalms, especially, has demonstrated the importance of lament in the worship of ancient Israel. Laments make up over a third of the Psalter, appearing in other places throughout the Hebrew Bible as well. Biblical scholarship has prompted new reflection on lament, or "the prayer of pain and protest" as Kathleen Billman and Daniel Migliore term it, in liturgical theology, spirituality and pastoral theology.[61] Such scholarship notes the absence of lament and the lament Psalms from Christian liturgy in recent times. Claus Westermann, one of the pioneers in lament scholarship, asks how it is that lament has been "totally excluded from human relationship with God" in Western Christianity, especially from prayer and worship.[62] Lament Psalms are frequently excluded from the Psalm collections in denominational hymnals and worship books.[63] Carleen Mandolfo observes that, in general, western Christianity has "eschewed expressions of anger directed at God."[64] Even though raw emotionally-charged articulations of anger, desperation, and despair are found in the biblical Psalter, Christian prayer shies away

59. Nicholsen, *Love of Nature and the End of the World*, 179.

60. Westermann, *Praise and Lament in the Psalms*; Brueggemann, *Psalms and the Life of Faith* and *Spirituality of the Psalms*.

61 Billman and Migliore, *Rachel's Cry*, vii. Also, see Brown and Miller, *Lament*; Jinkins, *In the House of the Lord*.

62. Westermann, *Praise and Lament in the Psalms*, 265.

63. Meyer, "Lack of Laments in the Church's Use of the Psalter," 67–78.

64. Mandolfo, "Psalm 88 and the Holocaust: Lament in Search of a Divine Response," 155.

from appropriating such displays. According to Walter Brueggemann, another pioneer in lament studies, "texts that might protest against core claims have been quickly read over and swallowed up in a sustained act of expository denial."[65] However, when lamentation, biblical and liturgical, is excluded from corporate worship, the faith community loses a vital resource for coming to terms with disturbing, potentially shattering experiences. To dismiss the contents of Israel's and the church's traditions of lament from corporate worship is to reject "an essential resource in confronting the very emotions that terrify us, in a context where we might receive some help in admitting them, understanding them, and coping with them."[66] Without lament, according to Power, there is no space in liturgy for persons to contend with God about the realities of suffering in the world; the only recourse becomes to passively endure things as they are.[67] Power names the exploitation of the earth as one of the four "realities of contemporary existence" that call for Christian lament.[68] These realities, notes Power, already dwell in the conscious awareness of those who attend worship, but "they need to be invited into the assembly."[69] Power urges that "troublesome questions" and disturbing realities must be included at the heart of Christian liturgy, for only then can we try to make sense of them and begin to imagine ways to participate in a different future than would otherwise be possible.

A detailed exposition of recent scholarship on lament Psalms is beyond the scope of this study. However, Brueggemann identifies three main questions that emerge from the "disputatious questioning" central to Israel's lived faith and evident throughout the lament Psalms. Brueggemann's work is helpful for establishing the tenor of lament as it appears in the Psalter. The first question is "how long?" This arises when Israel recognizes the conditions of its experience are at odds with their professed faith in God's benevolent fidelity towards them. Israel has faith that God will act to deliver them from hopeless situations, but the hoped for deliverance does not come. In light of God's apparent failure to act, Israel insists on an accounting. According to

65. Brueggemann, "Fissure Always Uncontained," 67.

66. Billman and Migliore, *Rachel's Cry,* 14.

67. Power, "When to Worship is to Lament," 157.

68. Ibid., 166–70.

69. Ibid., 170.

Brueggemann, the question is "a restless insistence that amounts to a reprimand of Yahweh, who has not done for Israel what Israel has legitimately expected."[70] Examples include Psalm 6:3, in which the Psalmist is too overwhelmed to complete the utterance: "My soul also is struck with terror / while you, O Lord—how long?" Consider also Ps 13:1–2:

> How long, O Lord? Will you forget me forever?
> How long will you hide your face from me?
> How long must I bear pain in my soul,
> And have sorrow in my heart all day long?

Other examples are found in Ps 35:17 and Ps 62:3. Brueggemann argues that this bold and adamant question is intended to provoke God to act in ways consistent with Israel's understanding of God's character and commitment to Israel.[71]

The second question Brueggemann identifies is "why?" This question emerges from conditions of senseless suffering. Israel expects God to be "attentive and helpful," but God seems to be negligent, even absent. "Why, O Lord, do you stand far off? Why do you hide yourself in times of trouble?" queries the Psalmist (Ps 10:1). According to Brueggemann, the question is not meant to obtain reasons or justifications from God, but functions rather as an accusation against God who has failed to act according to God's promises to prevent suffering.[72] Other examples include:

> My God, my God, why have you forsaken me?
> Why are you so far from helping me,
> from the words of my groaning? (Ps 22:1)

> Rouse yourself! Why do you sleep, O Lord?
> Awake, do not cast us off forever!
> Why do you hide your face?
> Why do you forget our affliction and oppression? (Ps 43:2)

The third question is "where?" This question also interrogates God about the absence of attentive divine presence and care. "The point is that Yahweh's fidelity is *not here*, not in this circumstance of trouble,

---

70. Brueggemann, *Theology of the Old Testament,* 319.

71. Ibid.

72. Ibid., 320.

where it is needed and where it has been rightly anticipated," according to Brueggemann.[73]

> My tears have been my food day and night,
> while people say to me continually,
> "Where is your God?" (Ps 42:3)

For Brueggemann, these questions represent a "countertestimony" to Israel's core testimony that functions as a vigorous engagement with the God of the covenant. As such, it is a "form of serious faith."[74]

> The genre of complaint (lamentation) is an expression of candor about the reality of life experience that is incongruent with Yahweh; at the same time is it an expression of hopeful insistence that if and when the righteous Yahweh is mobilized, the situation will be promptly righted.[75]

Brueggemann and other scholars insist that lament is not an act of unfaith, nor does it indicate that the Psalmist or the community intends to abandon relationship with God. The acts of complaint, protest, and accusation found in the laments are viewed acts of radical trust. Most lament Psalms are structured so that complaint gives way to a confession of trust in God and is ultimately resolved in praise. This movement has been regarded as fundamental to the function and meaning of lament.[76] However, we should be cautious about moving too quickly from complaint to praise in response to situations like species extinction. Lament cannot become a way to assuage guilt, avoid facing the hard realities of our complicity in causing the crisis, and quickly restore equilibrium. Assertions like John Calvin's that God has "provided for the preservation of each species until the Last Day" have proven false, and the easy confidence to praise that such assertions inspire must be vigorously challenged.[77] Further, whereas lament Psalms often proceed on the assumption that God has withdrawn and is not acting according

73. Ibid.

74. Ibid., 321–22.

75. Ibid., 321.

76. Westermann, *Praise and Lament in the Psalms*, 265–66. Westermann argues that lamentation has no meaning in itself, but only as it gives way to the petition to remove suffering. Mandolfo argues differently, citing Psalm 88 as an example of a text in which "forsakenness has the last word." Mandolfo, "Psalm 88 and the Holocaust," 156.

77. Calvin, *Institutes* 1:14:20.

to the expectations of the covenant, in the case of species extinction we must come to terms with the fact that humans are the chief cause. We cannot demand that God stop exterminating God's creatures; we must accept responsibility for what is occurring. Still, Brueggemann has demonstrated that lament does not represent an abandonment of faith in the face of crisis, but is a way of faithful engagement with troubling, even shattering circumstances that challenge fundamental faith claims. In this way, the practice of lament may inform the way Christian prayer responds to the crisis of species extinction.

Toward a Theology of Eco-Lamentation

In light of the very real threats facing many of Earth's life-forms and of the serious questions that extinction raises for Christian spirituality, I want to develop a provisional theology of ecological lamentation to conclude. I will suggest five ways in which lament, integrated into Christian liturgy, can help to form a more ecologically responsible spirituality.[78] First, lament affirms the goodness of "embodied life."[79] Billman and Migliore cite numerous examples from the Psalms in which lamentation is "closely linked to the reality and vulnerability of embodied life." Laments call for deliverance from physical suffering as well as from emotional pain.[80] Billman and Migloire themselves connect lament to the ecological crisis here: "the prayer of lament for wounded bodies must include the "body of nature, ravaged by greed, exploitation, and reckless abuse."[81] In mourning the damage done to bodies—the bodies of humans and animals—lament confirms their value and protests their abuse. Billman and Migliore interpret the absence of lament as "a warning signal of a decline of commitment to the flourishing of all life created by God.[82]" The often violent ways in which animals like the baiji lose their lives, and the callousness with which human beings par-

---

78. Billman and Migloire develop a "pastoral theology of lament," consisting of nine ways the prayer of lament can "help to support the life of faith." *Rachel's Cry*, 103–27. My development here of how lament informs liturgy is significantly informed by their work.

79. Billman and Migliore, *Rachel's Cry*, 107.

80. Ibid., 107–8.

81. Ibid., 109.

82. Ibid.

ticipate in such violence indicates a failure to embrace and honor the dignity of other creatures. Further, it suggests a rejection of the value of human embodiment, while reminding us that our bodily existence is vulnerable to the same type of violence. Lamenting the baiji affirms that the creature and its millions-of-years embodied history matters; its loss is worthy to be mourned.

Second, lament names that which threatens creation's goodness and integrity.[83] Responding to current ecological realities requires naming them honestly and precisely. Nicholsen describes a "destructive narcissism" that results from our attempts to assert absolute supremacy over the rest of nature, assuming that humans have the *right* to dominate. Such narcissism lies at the heart of our crisis, threatening the very future of life. It must be named as the injurious force that it is and dismantled. However, dismantling it "entails experiencing despair, both despair over what we have deprived ourselves of, and despair over what we have wrought in our delusion."[84] The difficulty of naming it, of course, accompanies the reluctance to change, for we understand that something must pass away. "To accept something is really over, really finished, means to mourn, to grieve. We need to mourn for this dying way of life that we have lived," writes Nicholsen.[85] In lament, we resist the temptation to minimize the gravity of the situation. Brueggemann argues that one of the functions of lament is to "*evoke reality* for someone who engaged in self-deception and still imagines and pretends that life is well-ordered."[86] Lamenting means remembering the enormity and the gravity of losses like the baiji. But it also helps us to accept the need for change so that there may be a future for others.

Third, lament offers a form that helps us to express grief, fear, and sense of loss we feel in response to ecosystemic realities. I have noted how shattering experiences or realizations often result in traumatized silence. Billman and Migliore note that silence often becomes a "survival strategy" in dealing with the experience of suffering and feelings of hopelessness.[87] There are few resources for expressing that which seems beyond speech. Lament offers language and structure through

83. Ibid., 21.

84. Nicholsen, 179.

85. Ibid.

86. Brueggemann, *Spirituality of the Psalms*, 28.

87. Ibid., 106–7.

which to bring our wordless despair to expression. Lament becomes "the formfulness of grief," in Brueggemann's words.[88] Offered within a community of shared experience and support, lament allows us to emerge from paralyzing silence and to open ourselves to potential transformation. Billman and Migliore write: "In situations where all language has been shattered by suffering, the prayer of lament becomes a speech-enabling gift of God."[89]

Fourth, lament helps us to identify with other creatures who suffer. A common thread running through much contemporary ecotheology is that all things share a common evolutionary history, thus all things are a part of an interconnected, interdependent whole. Nicholsen goes further, grounding her work in the idea that human subjectivity itself is formed in relationship to other creatures. One of the foundational ideas in Thomas Berry's work is that the universe is a communion of subjects: "every reality of the universe is intimately present to every other reality of the universe and finds its fulfillment in this mutual presence."[90] Turvey's memoir demonstrates an evolving sense of connection with the baiji and its plight. His increasing sense of frustration, anger, and desperation emerges from his intimate involvement with the suffering of a particular animal species. Telling his story seems in some ways to be a therapeutic act, but not one that brings a sense of relief: rather, his despair in the end leads him to greater commitment to the cause of conservation. According to Billman and Migliore, lament "provides those who pray an opportunity to discover their solidarity with others who also suffer and long for salvation."[91] In discovering this solidarity, we may also be lending voice to those parts of creation whose testimonies are stifled or silenced altogether. Lament should not be seen as a kind of group therapy, but as a practice that involves us in the suffering of those who are most vulnerable. Our common lament invites us to more vigorous dedication to action on behalf of those who suffer.

Finally, lament provides opportunities for revising our understandings of the relationship between divine power and human action. As Brueggemann's work indicates, recent treatments of lament see it as a form of insistent demand that God act decisively to deliver the sufferer

88. Brueggemann, *Psalms and the Life of Faith*, 84–97.
89. Billman and Migliore, *Rachel's Cry*, 107.
90. Berry, *Dream of the Earth*, 106.
91. Billman and Migliore, *Rachel's Cry*, 122.

from a terrible situation. The worshipper implores God to act in ways consistent with what is believed to be the divine character and commitment to redeem. The worshipper's agency is seen in the proactive confrontation demanding divine action, since it is God who is seen as having all the power to make things right. Ultimately, the worshipper's complaint resolves in affirmations of faith and in doxology. However, we now have to face the reality that humanity, not God, is responsible for the current threats to creation. We may accuse God of abandoning the baiji to the destructive will of humanity, but the situation demands that we re-evaluate traditional notions of divine sovereignty, recognizing that humans have the power to destroy life and that we have willfully done so. There may not be immediate or effective replies to the questions echoing through the lament psalms ("How long? Why? Where?"). We may now have to face the possibility that God *is* absent or silent, and that destructive human dominance is obscuring modes of divine presence. Lament means that the nature of the faith we profess may have to undergo significant transformation as we search for answers. Further, biblical laments suggest a different understanding of God's power, demanding that we accept our role as responsible agents.[92] According to Billman and Migloire, lament calls for "redistributing the power relationship between God and petitioner."[93] We may confront God with God's seeming failure to protect creation, but we must also face the possibility that God is leaving us to accept responsibility for the destruction we have wrought, and expecting us to begin the hard work of re-ordering our lives in more sustainable, Earth-honoring ways. Billman and Migloire conclude:

> The act of lament, far from being the antithesis of hope and praise, is their necessary companion in a world full of suffering and injustice. Those who lament dare to name the brokenness of reality rather than denying it; they refuse to pretend it is other than it is; they want nothing to do with empty consolations. At the same time, they refuse to resign themselves to the given.[94]

92. Ibid., 116–17.
93. Ibid., 114.
94. Ibid., 126.

Conclusion

I do not want to overstate the potential of liturgical lament to form an ecologically responsible spirituality. However, liturgy has an important role to play in Christian spiritual formation. For centuries Christian liturgy has offered an Earth-transcending spirituality for consumption, and has been loathe to include the kind of disturbing, disorienting speech found in prayers of lament. However, as Douglas Burton-Christie has said, "if we hope to arrive at a deep and authentic response to this crisis, we will have to find a way to speak honestly about all we are losing and what this means to us."[95] By incorporating prayers of lament for the baiji, the Sumatran Tiger, the blue whale, the devastated mountaintops of Appalachia, and the oil-fouled Gulf of Mexico, Christian worship can begin to help its participants confront current ecological realities honestly, name a sense of loss and fear, admit the difficult questions about divine providence that extinction raises, and begin to imagine a different future. Lamenting our losses does not conclude our responsibility toward species lost and threatened. Rather, it invites Christian worshippers to embrace the human vocation to assist the rest of creation in achieving the fullness of divine intention for it. Lament invites those who lament to move from despair and silent fear to a renewed existence in which we vigorously take up the work of restoring a damaged world.

Bibliography

Aquinas, Thomas. "Man as Master Over Creation." In *Animals and Christianity: A Book of Readings*, edited by Andrew Linzey and Tom Regan, 17–20. New York: Crossroad, 1988.

Berry, Thomas. *The Dream of the Earth*. San Francisco: Sierra Club, 1988.

Billman, Kathleen, and Daniel Migliore. *Rachel's Cry: Prayer of Lament and Hope of Rebirth*. Cleveland: United Church Press, 1999.

Bonaventure. *Breviloquium*. Translated by Erwin Esser Nemmers. London: Herder, 1947.

———. *The Soul's Journey into God*. Translated by Ewert Cousins. New York: Paulist, 1978.

Brown, Sally, and Patrick D. Miller, editors. *Lament: Reclaiming Practices in Pulpit, Pew, and Public Square*. Louisville: Westminster John Knox, 2005.

Brueggemann, Walter. "A Fissure Always Uncontained." In *Strange Fire: Reading the Bible After the Holocaust*, edited by Tod Linafelt, 62–75. New York: New York University Press, 2000.

95. Douglas Burton-Christie, "Gift of Tears."

————. *The Psalms and the Life of Faith,* edited by Patrick D. Miller. Minneapolis: Fortress, 1995.

————. *The Spirituality of the Psalms.* Minneapolis: Augsburg/Fortress, 2002.

————. *Theology of the Old Testament: Testimony, Dispute, Advocacy.* Minneapolis: Fortress, 1997.

Burton-Christie, Douglas. "The Gift of Tears: Loss, Mourning and the Work of Ecological Restoration." unpublished paper presented at the American Academy of Religion, November 2007.

Calvin, John. *Calvin: Commentaries.* Library of Christian Classics. Translated and edited by Joseph Haroutunian. Philadelphia: Westminster, 1958.

————. *Institutes of the Christian Religion* (1559). Translated by Ford Lewis Battles. Philadelphia: Westminster, 1960.

Davies, Oliver, and Fiona Bowie, editors. *Celtic Christian Spirituality: An Anthology of Medieval and Modern Sources.* New York: Continuum, 1995.

Deane-Drummond, Celia, and David Clough, editors. *Creaturely Theology: On God, Humans, and Other Animals.* London: SCM, 2009.

Edwards, Denis. *Ecology at the Heart of Faith.* Maryknoll, NY: Orbis, 2008.

Hobgood-Oster, Laura. *Holy Dogs and Asses: Animals in the Christian Tradition.* Urbana and Chicago: University of Illinois Press, 2008.

Howard, Cameron. "Animal Speech as Revelation in Genesis 3 and Numbers 22." In *Exploring Ecological Hermeneutics,* edited by Norman Habel and Peter Trudinger, 21–30. Atlanta: Society of Biblical Literature, 2008.

Huff, Peter. "Calvin and the Beasts: Animals in John Calvin's Theological Discourse." *Journal of the Evangelical Theological Society* 42 (March 1999) 67–75.

Jinkins, Michael. *In the House of the Lord: Inhabiting the Psalms of Lament.* Collegeville, MN: Liturgical, 1998.

Kelleher, Mary Margaret. "Liturgy: An Ecclesial Act of Meaning." *Worship* 59:6 (1985) 482–97.

Lane, Belden. "Spirituality as the Performance of Desire: Calvin on the World as the Theatre of God's Glory." *Spiritus* 1 (Spring 2001) 1–30.

Linzey, Andrew. *Animal Gospel.* Louisville: Westminster-John Knox, 2000.

Mandolfo, Carleen. "Psalm 88 and the Holocaust: Lament in Search of a Divine Response." *Biblical Interpretation* 15 (2007) 151–70.

McDougall, Dorothy. *The Cosmos as Primary Sacrament: the Horizon for an Ecological Sacramental Theology.* New York: Peter Lang, 2003.

Messenger, Troy. "These Stones Shall Be God's House: Tools for Earth Liturgy." In *Earth Habitat: Eco-Injustice and the Church's Response,* edited by Dieter Hessel and Larry Rasumussen, 173–83. Minneapolis: Fortress, 2001.

Meyer, Lester. "A Lack of Laments in the Church's Use of the Psalter," *Lutheran Quarterly* 7 (Spring 1993) 67–78.

Mick, Lawerence. *Liturgy and Ecology in Dialogue.* Collegeville, MN: Liturgical, 1997.

Moe-Lobeda, Cynthia. "Liturgy for the Uncreators." *Studia Liturgica* 38 (2008) 64–80.

Nicholsen, Shierry Weber. *The Love of Nature and the End of the World: The Unspoken Dimensions of Environmental Concern.* Cambridge, MA: MIT Press, 2002.

Person, Raymond F. "The Role of Nonhuman Characters in Jonah." In *Exploring Ecological Hermeneutics,* edited by Norman Habel and Peter Trudinger, 85–90. Atlanta: Society of Biblical Literature, 2008.

Power, David. "Liturgy, Memory, and the Absence of God." *Worship* 57 (July 1983) 326–28.

———. "When to Worship is to Lament." In *Culture and Theology*, 155–74. Washington, DC: Pastoral, 1990.

———. "Worship and Ecology." *Worship* 84:4 (July 2010) 290–308.

Saier, Milton. "Species Extinction." *Environmentalist* 26 (2006) 135–37.

Santmire, H. Paul. *Ritualizing Nature: Renewing Christian Liturgy in a Time of Crisis.* Minneapolis: Fortress, 2008.

Schifferdecker, Kathryn. "And Also Many Animals: Biblical Resources for Preaching About Creation." *Word and World* 27:2 (Spring 2007) 210–23.

Spray, Sharon and Karen McGlothlin, editors. *Loss of Biodiversity.* Lanham, MD: Rowan & Littlefield, 2003.

Stewart, Benjamin. *A Watered Garden: Christian Worship and Earth's Ecology.* Minneapolis: Fortress, 2011.

Tucker, Mary Evelyn. *Worldly Wonder: Religions Enter Their Ecological Phase.* Chicago: Opencourt, 2003.

Turvey, Samuel. *Witness to Extinction: How We Failed to Save the Yangtze River Dolphin.* Oxford, UK: Oxford University Press, 2008.

Wennberg, Robert. *God, Humans, and Animals: An Invitation to Enlarge our Moral Universe.* Grand Rapids: Eerdmans, 2003.

Westermann, Claus. *Praise and Lament in the Psalms.* Atlanta: John Knox, 1981.

White, Susan J. "Spirituality, Liturgy, and Worship." In *The New Westminster Dictionary of Christian Spirituality*, edited by Philip Sheldrake, 44–48. Louisville: Westminster John Knox, 2005.

Zachman, Randall. *Image and Word in the Theology of John Calvin.* Notre Dame, IN: University of Notre Dame Press, 2007.

9

Water as Earth's Bloodstream

Latina Ecofeminist Spirituality and Water Justice

Laura A. Stivers

> "The rivers are the Earth's bloodstream, and if they are contaminated, death will circulate throughout the body."
>
> —Doris Muñoz, Chilean ecofeminist theologian [1]

CARRYING A FLASK OF WATER WITH DROPS FROM THE SEA OF GALILEE, Japan's Mt. Fuji, and other sites, twenty-five runners from the Hopi tribe in Northern Arizona ran relay-style to Mexico City in time for the March 16th–22nd Fourth World Water Forum in 2006. It is their tradition to carry important messages through running, and in the words of Vernon Masayesva, executive director of the Black Mesa Trust, they are "carrying a prayer for water to this important meeting." [2] The contentious debate today is how water should be viewed: as a commodity, a right, or as the sacred source of all life. Many of the participants who could afford the $600 entrance fee for the World Water Forum argue for water as a commodity that should be privatized and sold at "full-cost pricing."

However, many social justice organizations, in line with the United Nations Declaration of Human Rights, make the important claim that water is a human right, not a want, and thus should not be privatized, commodified, traded, or exported for commercial gain. Latin American ecofeminists and many indigenous organizations go steps

1. Ress, *Ecofeminism in Latin America*, 167.
2. Hawley, "Hopis' trek to tell world about water."

further, offering a cosmology of relationship and claiming that water is not simply a right, but is the source of all life and the connection for living beings. In this cosmology humans see themselves in connection to water, as embodied sensuous beings who are all born in water, not as rational consumers of a commodity. Bolivian indigenous women, fighting to make water a public good that all have access to, have said it best: "¿Acaso no han crecido en las barrigas de sus madres dentro de una bolsa de aqua? El agua es nuestra, el aqua es sagrada, el agua es la vida" (Weren't you raised in the wombs of your mothers in a sac of water? Water is ours, water is sacred, water is life).[3] While Latina ecofeminist theologians draw on theological resources to frame a relational cosmology, their spiritual practices and communal life experiences provide equally important foundations.

Latina ecofeminist activism for water justice arises from their embodied creation-centered spirituality. Latina ecofeminist cosmology views humans as ecologically connected to all of creation, and water as the earth's bloodstream. In this essay I will map out a Latina ecofeminist spirituality and relate this perspective to both environmental and social justice in relation to water use and distribution. That is, I will claim that Latina ecofeminist spirituality entails that we have a sustainable relationship with this sacred source of life, and that water should be a public good that supports the flourishing of all life, not simply the lives of those who have the resources to pay for it.

Privatization of Water

Proponents of the privatization of water include the World Bank and the International Monetary Fund (IMF), as well as the major transnational corporations, who stand to gain the most, Suez and Vivendi (recently named Veolia Environnement) of France, and RWE-AG of Germany. All three are in the top 100 corporations in the world and control more than 40 percent of the private water market.[4] The privatization of nationally owned enterprises has been a key component of structural adjustment programs since the 1980s, but since the late 1990s the privatization of public services has increasingly been a component of

3. "Las Mujeres en La Defensa del Agua Como Derecho Humano Fundamental," 17.

4. Barlow and Clarke, "Water Privatization"; and "Public Citizen Report Reveals World Bank Loans Continue to Promote Water Privatization."

debt rescheduling and a requirement for further IMF loans. A random review of forty countries in the year 2000 showed that the IMF loan agreements with twelve countries included conditions of water privatization or requirements of cost recovery (that is, user fees by consumers must cover water system costs).[5] The countries with such stipulations were the smallest and most debt-ridden: eight are within sub-Saharan Africa and three are in Central America.

The main argument the World Bank makes in support of privatization is that it raises private finance for investment in infrastructure in low-income economies. The core argument in support of cost-recovery is that with higher payments from consumers, private companies will have revenues and incentive to invest in pipes for communities relying on water trucks or unclean sources. Generally, full-cost pricing has been a prerequisite to privatization (so companies will have incentive to invest). The assumption undergirding privatization is that by treating water as a commodity and an economic good, water will be more efficiently distributed to a greater number of people. The World Bank website sums up this assumption well: "Effective water resource management requires that water be treated as an economic good," and that "private participation in water and wastewater utilities has generally resulted in sharp efficiency gains, improved service, and faster investment in expanding service."[6]

Experiences have shown that in countries with privatized water, increased infrastructure in poor communities has been the exception not the rule, and full-cost recovery has meant that the poor use less or go without. For example, when water delivery was privatized in Cochabamba Bolivia in 1999 and full-cost recovery was instituted, rates increased by 100 percent. Water bills were over $20 a month at a time when the minimum wage was less than $65 a month.[7] In Aquascalientes Mexico, French transnational Vivendi increased rates but left the city's aquifer in a state of collapse.[8] The push for profit leads transnational corporations to "cherry pick" the best customers and to forget the rest. It does not lend to democratic participation in deciding how water is distributed.

5. Grusky, "Privatization Tidal Wave."
6. Siregar, "World Bank and ADB's Role in Privatizing Water in Asia."
7. Ibid.
8. Marrero, "Water Privatization in Latin America."

The corporate emphasis on profit over people and the earth has had negative effects on poor communities in Latin America. Lack of access to clean water causes millions of people to suffer needlessly from disease and, according to the United Nations Development Programme, kills more than two million children a year.[9] The link between dirty water and infectious disease is clear. In the 1990s, cholera, a disease caused by lack of clean water and sanitation, resurfaced in Latin America.[10] Limited access to clean water also leads to increased poverty and depressed education levels, especially for girls who are kept from school to collect water (often requiring several hours). Furthermore, political instability increases when 1.1 billion people in the world lack access to clean water and competition over water resources intensifies.[11]

While public as well as private management of water systems can be based on water as a commodity tradable to the highest bidder, the large transnational corporations who are managing water systems clearly do not view water as a right for all. The 2006 United Nations Development Report notes,

> From Argentina to Bolivia, and from the Philippines to the United States, the conviction that the private sector offers a "magic bullet" for unleashing equity and efficiency needed to accelerate progress towards water for all has proven to be misplaced. While these past failures of water concessions do not provide evidence that the private sector has no role to play, they do point for the need of greater caution, regulation and a commitment to equity in public-private partnerships.[12]

When water is not treated as a public good that is accessible to all, communities lose out. While poor communities suffer disproportionately, everyone is negatively affected by increased disease, pollution, and political instability.

In 2000 *Fortune* magazine predicted that "water is the oil of the 21st century."[13] Transnational corporations view water as a prime commodity to market for profit, especially as clean water resources become scarce. These corporations are not particularly concerned

9. Ruxandra, "Lack of Clean Water."

10. Arbona and Crum, "Medical Geography and Cholera in Peru."

11 Watkins et al., *Beyond Scarcity*, 5.

12. Ibid., 10.

13. Public Citizen, "Water Privatization Overview."

about sustainable use of water, putting profits before people and the flourishing of creation. Water becomes simply another economic resource that transnational corporations seek to conquer and control, rather than a crucial source of life. Ecofeminist Vandana Shiva refers to this conquest and control as "cowboy economics." The first settlers in the American west who forcefully gained control of water got exclusive rights to the detriment of other people (especially Native Americans) and the environment (rivers were drained and polluted by mining).[14] The corporate view is one of self-interested individuals competing over scarce resources, with no sense of the many communities who have cooperatively managed water in sustainable and equitable ways.

Social justice organizations argue that if water is a human need, not a want, it should be a right and not serviced by the private sector. They claim that corporations should not be able to sell a right, especially for a profit. To be fair, social justice organizers have also critiqued the public sector for not ensuring water as a right for all. For example, when the Mexican government decentralized water management to the municipal level in the 1990s to open the way for management by private companies, the state did not acknowledge that many communities, due to the lack of state funded infrastructure, had already been fending for themselves and communally provided and managed water on their own for years.[15] In effect, the state defined the existing communal (e.g., private) management of water as public so that it could transfer the management to large private investors.[16] A social justice perspective, in contrast to the Darwinian corporate view, argues that people have a right to life, and therefore resources that are necessary for life, such as water, must also be rights.

14. Shiva, *Water Wars*, 22–23.

15. "Although 27 percent of Mexico's population report having inadequate access to drinking water, this is most serious for rural areas where 45 percent of the population report having inadequate access to drinking water, versus the 10 percent of the population in urban areas that report a similar problem." Ennis-McMillan, "A Paradoxical Privatization," 31.

16. Ibid., 45.

Latina Ecofeminist Spirituality

Although Latina ecofeminist theologians and activists support the idea of water as a right for all, their perspective is more communally oriented and not couched in individualistic rights language. A Latina ecofeminist spirituality offers an alternative foundation for resisting oppressive realities. It is concerned with the material lives and realities of people and the ways in which humans participate in sin and evil while also emphasizing the embodied, relational, and ritual yearnings of humans. My description of Latina ecofeminist spirituality is drawn from a small, but powerful, group of ecofeminist theologians who have been in dialogue with others throughout Latin America. Their work is most notably publicized through the collective "Con-spirando" (breathing-together-with-others).[17] The ecofeminist spirituality that has emerged from this collective stems from the life experiences of injustice and oppression that these women have faced both individually and within particular communities. Several of these women were participants in the liberation movements against oppression in the 1960s and 70s in Latin America and most were influenced by the tenets of liberation theology.

Although these ecofeminist theologians continue to resist injustice and oppression, they have moved away from liberation theology's emphasis on resistance and revolution and towards a more constructive "ethics of life." Through exploration of Jungian archetypes they found they had overdeveloped their warrior archetypes in leading the fight for rights and were ready to recharge their erotic and wise women energy fields.[18] Thus, while Latina ecofeminist theologians continue to connect social analysis and theology, they also emphasize ritual, worship, and beauty as components of salvation. Brazilian ecofeminist Ivone Gebara writes, "My ecofeminism is shot through with the staunch conviction that beauty is important in healing people. It might be the beauty of sounds, of colors, of words, of faces, of food

17. Con-spirando is a collective of women who share an interest in feminist spirituality and theology. They first gathered in Santiago, Chile in 1991, after which they formed a collective. In 1993 they began publishing a journal entitled *Con-spirando: Revista Latinoamerciana de Ecofeminismo, Espiritualidad y Teología*. See their website http://conspirando.cl/.

18. The Con-spirando Collective explored the feminine archetypes proposed by Toni Wolff, a protégé of Jung, namely Mother, Heteria (Lover), Amazon (Warrior), and Medium. Ress, *Ecofeminism in Latin America*, 145.

and drink, or of embraces. Like my friend Rubem Alves, I too can vouch for 'salvation through beauty.'"[19]

Holistic Spirituality

A Latina ecofeminist ethics of life embraces a holistic view of spirituality, that is, a "conscious and deliberate way of living" oriented towards ultimate good, often termed God/dess, but also including what is life giving in this world for all of creation.[20] Latina ecofeminist theology assumes relatedness as our ethical and cosmic reality. Spiritual wholeness for Latina ecofeminist theologians entails working towards a world that supports relationships of respect and reciprocity between humans, and for the earth's ecosystems. Thus, spirituality is connected to the ethical task of challenging life-denying factors in our world and promoting sustainable and life-affirming practices. Spirituality for them is not simply a private affair of personal prayer and virtuous living, but is intricately connected to ethical and political realities such as water distribution. Access to clean water is necessary for life and thus a component of spiritual wholeness. For Latina ecofeminist theologians, theology, ethics, and spirituality are intricately related to one another. As ecofeminist Mary Judith Ress writes of Latina ecofeminist theologians, ". . . they also are looking for a spirituality that will water present and future struggles."[21]

Latina ecofeminist theology and spirituality emerges from the life experiences of communities, especially from their activist challenges to life denying realities. While Latina ecofeminist theologians celebrate life and beauty, theological reflection has been born from the suffering that communities have undergone. Gebara says, "I sense that ecofeminism is born of daily life, of day-to-day sharing among people, of enduring together garbage in the streets, bad smells, the absence of sewers and safe drinking water, poor nutrition, and inadequate health care."[22] In particular, the suffering of women's bodies has been the starting point for theological and ethical reflection and action and for the formation of spiritual practices for healing.

19 Ivone Gebara, quoted in Ress, *Ecofeminism in Latin America*, 134.

20. Schneiders, "Approaches to the Study of Christian Spirituality," 16.

21 Ress, *Without a Vision, the People Perish*, 58.

22 Gebara, *Longing for Running Water*, 2.

When poor Latina women protest against the destruction of the environment, they do so out of the lived experience of having to deal with such things as polluted water, smoggy air, landfills, and other environmental ills. Numerous environmental protests have been led by women, especially when the issue affects the home, as access to water clearly does. [23] The most famous victory against water privatization occurred in Cochabamba, Bolivia in 2000 when Bechtel was forced to turn over water management to the state.[24] Indigenous women were at the forefront of the movement to force Bechtel out. In the Junin region of Peru, women from the "Glass of Milk" committees[25] filled fourteen streets demanding that the mayor stop water privatization.[26] Currently El Salvadoran women are working with organizations like the Centre for Defense of the Consumers to make water a human right and ban water from being sold into private hands in their country.[27] Latina women do not have to identify themselves as ecofeminists to know that the privatization of water does not support an ethics of life.

Mestizaje Spirituality

Challenging life-denying realities has led Latina ecofeminist theologians to reflect theologically on evil. They define evil as the human species' excessive desire to take possession of life and make it our own, noting that due to patriarchy, it is white men who run and profit from the multinationals who are appropriating water. Women and people of color are regarded as secondary by the "self-appointed proprietors of the earth."[28] Latina ecofeminists are careful, however, to identify patriarchy, colonization, and unequal power relations on all levels. They

23. See the following for an historical example of women protesting and organizing for better services. Bennett, *Politics of Water*.

24. This did not stop Bechtel from filing a lawsuit for compensation for lost profits. Due to bad publicity, Bechtel settled the $50 million lawsuit for a symbolic amount of about 30 cents on January 19, 2006.

25. Peru's Glass of Milk Program is designed to provide breakfast to children under the age of six and to pregnant and nursing mothers.

26 Avendaño, "Fight for a New Ideal," 22.

27. Uruguay, Ecuador, and Bolivia have successfully done this. Costa Rica has a bill pending votes. Mexico and El Salvador have lobbying campaigns underway. Gómez, "New Definition of Hope," 15.

28. Gebara, *Longing for Running Water*, 168.

are not interested in idealizing indigenous worldviews that also include unequal class, property, and gender relations. For example, they would probably commend communities in rural Mexico who use non-market principles to regulate access to and distribution of drinking water, yet they would critique those same communities if they used water sanctions to pressure individuals to conform to community customs not directly related to water management, especially since such practice often leads to oppression and exclusion.[29]

Gebara starts her book, *Longing for Running Water: Ecofeminism and Liberation*, with a chapter on epistemology, for she argues that we have to change our way of knowing away from a hierarchical, androcentric, and universalist perspective to a more holistic, ecocentric, contextual, and affectively oriented perspective.[30] In other words, a way of knowing that supports and celebrates life, instead of one that possesses and destroys life. However, Latina ecofeminist theologians are wary of positing dualisms (e.g. liberation theology's clear identification of the oppressor and oppressed). Their experience is a *mestizaje*: a mixture of indigenous, African, and European. They seek to find power in the mixture, not simply to appropriate whiteness for power or to claim whiteness as evil.

While Latina ecofeminist theologians critique any form of oppression or destruction and support any celebration of life, they understand the diverse social locations people inhabit and the complexity of structural oppression. For example, it is clear that Latina ecofeminists would support social and economic policies that promote sustainable non-polluting practices that ensure the accessibility to the sustenance of all life, water. Yet they would be careful to critically evaluate private, public, or mixed options of water management according to an ethics of life based on criteria such as sustainability, equity, and participation, and not by a simplistic view of privatization as evil.

Latina ecofeminist theologians are not interested in idealizing or romanticizing either earth or women. They are fully aware that humans (male and female) as well as nature can be a source of both destruction and creation. Gebara claims that there was no pre-existent essence before the fall, but we were all born with the ability to build or destroy. Thus, rather than concentrating on where evil comes from, we should

29. Ennis-McMillan, "A Paradoxical Privatization," 40.

30. Gebara, *Longing for Running Water*. 19–65.

envision how to "escape the destructive process in which we are all in-volved with different degrees of guilt."[31]Latina ecofeminist theologians direct most of their energy to a spirituality and ethics of life.

Embodied Spirituality

While not interested in idealizing women's experience, Latina ecofemi-nist activism and spirituality is thoroughly embodied, that is, the body and bodily experiences of women are central to their theology, spiritual-ity, and ethics. Latina ecofeminist theologians do not argue that women are necessarily closer to "nature," but they are aware that the negative effects of environmental destruction, and in this case water privatiza-tion, are disproportionately borne by women. Women are overwhelm-ingly responsible for the reproductive labor in the household, which in poor households includes gathering water and ensuring the health of children against numerous environmental threats. As an El Salvadoran peasant woman put it, "We are the root from which the whole people sustains itself and grows."[32] Since theology stems from lived experience, and spiritual wholeness is connected to healthy relatedness between bodies, it makes sense for Latina ecofeminists to uplift the bodily expe-riences of the "root sustainers" of community life.

While the body is the locus of theology, spirituality, and ethics, Latina ecofeminist theologians avoid exclusive focus on individual bodies by redefining who we are as humans. While each human per-son is unique, all are connected to a larger cosmos. Urugayan Fanny Geymonat-Pantelís says, "We form part of a process of ongoing creation by a wise and ever-present transcendent energy . . . We form part of a planetary ecosystem that is dynamically interrelated."[33] Bolivian Alcira Agreda draws on her indigenous roots to give a fuller human anthro-pology, "The indigenous speak of the physical body, the emotional body, the mental body, and vital Energy—and all are interrelated . . . I have also discovered that I live within an ecosystem and that I am not in any way superior to other beings."[34] This depiction of individual selves as embodied in the larger web of life and exhibiting Divine energy

31. Ibid., 95.
32. Canas, "In Us Life Grows," 24.
33. Ress, *Without a Vision, the People Perish,* 160–61.
34. Ibid., 161–62.

critiques the corporate view of people as simply individual consumers and the environment as simply a resource that is dispensable. An interrelated cosmic self can also offer a deeper normative foundation for an ethics of life than an emphasis on human rights can.

Gebara asserts that the exaggerated Western emphasis on the autonomy of the human person has not only suppressed communal understandings of human nature but has also led to unrestrained power and domination. While autonomy was originally connected in Christianity to respect for every person, increasingly countries, social institutions, and even transnational corporations use the notion of autonomy to justify actions that do not respect people or local communities.[35] Gebara instead lifts up a relational Jesus who was extremely sensitive to human suffering and proclaimed abundant life for all. An emphasis on interdependence and a relational, incarnate Jesus challenges water distribution systems that in the name of corporate autonomy promote unsustainable use of water and limit accessibility.

The view of in interrelated cosmic self is also extended to our ancestors and future generations, often through nature. Life and death are not separate for Latina ecofeminist theologians. Geymonat-Pantelís claims,

> Even after someone dies, he or she lives on in the memories of the family, the community, in the hills and in the Pachamama herself . . . My ancestors rise in me, as I will in my descendants. Life and death are interactive, continuous parts of the great matrix of oikoumene, where individual life is only a cell in the universe.[36]

Brazilian Silvia Regina de Lima Silva says, "These ancestors continue in nature, perhaps as rocks or rivers."[37] Chilean Doris Muñoz notes, "I like the idea of becoming part of the earth, a seed that flowers in another form, that can give life to others."[38] Making a connection to future generations of life is central for thinking normatively about sustainability. Corporate conquest of water for profit is counter to sustainable use. Latina ecofeminist theologians know that the flourishing of life into the

---

35. Gebara, *Longing for Running Water*, 71–73.

36. Ress, *Without a Vision, the People Perish*, 203.

37. Ress, *Ecofeminism in Latin America*, 178.

38. Ress, *Without a Vision, the People Perish*, 205.

infinite future depends on humans being responsible for future generations by living in sustainable harmony with the larger cosmos.

Many Latina ecofeminist theologians connect the healing of the
earth to the healing of women's bodies. Regina de Lima Silva sees her
recent cancer as part of the disequilibrium in the cosmos, most notably
rampant pollution. Her recovery included care for her own body as well
as the earth's body. Connecting the destruction of mining in Bolivia
with violence against women, Agreda writes, "For me, to speak of the
Earth as Body is to speak of my own women's body. As a woman, I
need to make that connection if we are going to heal our ecosystem and
ourselves. The Earth and we humans are one; I am part of her and she
is part of me."[39] For these women, all material bodies are part of Divine
energy and are thereby sacred. Thus we are called to heal bodies that
have suffered at the hands of human sin.

Sacred Life

The Latina ecofeminist claim that all life is sacred serves as a normative
critique of the conquest and commodification of water for profit. The
sacredness of life stems from a view of God/dess as energy, presence, and
ground of being, rather than an autonomous being with "His" own will
external to humans and creation. Rather God/dess is the Sacred Body
that connects all of creation. Agreda says, "The divine or sacred Energy
is circular. It is like a current that flows and infuses life. It makes all life
blossom forth and grow, not just human life but the entire ecosystem."[40]
For these theologians, "no reality is outside sacred space."[41] Yet, while
God/dess is in all, God/dess is also much more and remains the "Great
Mystery." Thus all of our representations of God/dess are partial and
limited by our own history and experience.

Latina ecofeminist theologians regularly refer to the sacred, not
only in reference to God/dess but also in reference to all of life, especially in relationships with one another and with nature. Brazilian Sandra
Rawuew says of her community's beliefs,

39. Ibid., 233.

40. Ress, *Ecofeminism in Latin America,* 169.

41. Ress, *Without a Vision, the People Perish,* 199.

> We have a very strong sense of the presence of the Sacred, a profound respect for the forces of Nature—and this for me defines my sense of ancestral belonging . . . this sacred space that strengthens you, finds you, is revealed to you, affirms you. It is having a dimension of life where our relationship to Nature is valued as are relationships with others . . . I see myself as a human-divine person with all the complexity of Mystery that is revealed in time.

For Latina ecofeminist theologians the sacred is more about relationality than about something outside ourselves. They believe Jesus himself challenged the idea that God dwelt only in the Temple, as illustrated by his care for the sick, prayer in nature, and critique of oppressive practices connected to the Temple. Ress argues that the sacred takes us beyond ourselves and is born in us. It is about a quality of life and an attitude of connection to the whole. Latina ecofeminist theologians do not view spirituality as solely an individual reality but instead connect the spiritual health and pain of individuals to a larger whole or what Gebara calls the "Sacred Body of the cosmos."[42] Healthy stewardship and unhealthy contamination of creation both affect the sacred "Energy, Force, and Spirit" of individuals and communities.[43]

Ritual and Activist Spirituality

Both social activism and feminist rituals have nourished the ability of Latina ecofeminist theologians to be spiritually alive in their efforts to heal the disconnections in the world. Acreda says, "I am watered by the rituals we do as women that are connected in some way to the Earth, and to healing rites for women, the Earth, and our ecosystem."[44] The Con-spirando collective of women have made ritual a central part of their gatherings and their annual summer schools. Often their rituals are held outside under the trees with song and dance. Their rituals reflect the *mestizaje* of the women by including elements from the various cultures and traditions of Latin America, such as the indigenous Mapuche or Aymara traditions, or the African traditions brought over with slavery. Reenactments of ancient myths that support feminist con-

42. Gebara, *Longing for Running Water*, 53.

43. Ress, *Ecofeminism in Latin America*,167.

44. Ibid., 190.

sciousness are also a feature of their rituals. While these women are Christian, many of them do not find spiritual nourishment from the patriarchal images and language in the worship services of their churches. They are looking for a post-patriarchal form of Christian spirituality.

Both women's bodies and the earth body are always central to these rituals. One participant recounts, "In our gatherings (of women), we celebrate our bodies and everything that surrounds us—we celebrate the elements, the lives of other women; we celebrate life with our women's bodies."[45] In their rituals the women celebrate their own lives and their relations with one another and their ancestors, as well as their connections to nature and all of creation. While many of the rituals involve movement and dance, others emphasize mind-body practices of mediation and contemplation. Rituals include time to commune with nature as well as space to share with one another.[46] These women gather spiritual strength in communal rituals to continue the struggle against the many life-denying realities in their local regions, the privatization of water being one of many challenges they face.

While Latina ecofeminists continue to organize and resist forces that are destructive to people and the earth, they are at the same time joining together to celebrate and worship the beauty of the natural world and the intricate and complex web of relationships within it. Their rituals and worship are not meant to romanticize or idealize the connectedness women feel to the earth, but instead render their ethics of life and the beliefs connected with such an ethic theologically, naming all of life as sacred. All life has the ability of creation and destruction, and all life is intricately interconnected with God/dess as the energy and presence within all of creation.

The cases of water privatization in Latin America have clearly been destructive, a way to hoard resources and profit for a few at the expense of the poor, especially people of color and women. When water is a market commodity, profit comes before environmental sustainability and social justice. When water is viewed simply as a human right, human interconnection with the rest of creation can be forgotten. Latina ecofeminists hold that water should be viewed as earth's sacred bloodstream, to be treated with reverence and respect, and to be used sustainably by all of creation.

45. Ress, *Without a Vision, the People Perish*, 217.
46. Ress, *Ecofeminism in Latin America*, 211.

Ethical Implications for Water Use and Distribution

While Latina ecofeminist theologians are on the forefront in resisting corporate control of water, their theological and spiritual grounding calls for a fundamental transformation of consciousness that moves us towards a positive vision of flourishing life, and not simply a mode of resistance (although they are astute enough about human sin to know that resistance will always be necessary). They promote moving away from a worldview in which people and nature are viewed as resources or commodities to exploit for short-term profit, to a worldview in which people and nature are viewed as part of a living cosmos imbued with divine spirit, and thus subject to care towards long-term sustainability. While Latina ecofeminist theologians in their spiritual rituals emphasize the personal transformation that is required, they never lose sight of what an ethics of life means on a broader level. Personal and political arenas as well as spiritual and ethical realities are intricately connected. Thus, they are aware that a vision of flourishing life requires major structural change, especially of a global economic system based on a worldview of conquest, control, and commodification.

Free trade policies and structural adjustment programs that seek to open up economies for corporate investment and profit in the name of economic growth and development will often consider certain groups of people (e.g., the poor, disproportionately people of color) and the environment as expendable in a utilitarian cost-benefit analysis. Justificatory rhetoric claims that growth and development will benefit all, but the corporate privatization of water illustrates otherwise. Over the years, the World Bank and the IMF have addressed protection of the environment and vulnerable groups, but they never radically change the logic of domination that is implicit in their structures and policies. Distributing a few resources to poor communities does not change the structures that cause inequality and inequitable use of resources, does not open the doors for communities to participate in decisions affecting them, and does not acknowledge and respect the culture and local ways of economic management that communities have developed over years.

A new vision based on Latina ecofeminist spirituality would rule out unregulated control of water by large transnational corporations. Corporate privatization of a basic life source such as water is simply a new form of colonization that threatens the earth as well as indigenous cultures and communities. Beyond ruling this option out, however, there are many ways that water might be equitably managed and distributed, including both public and private options. Crucial to an adequate vision is the ability of communities to have some local control in water use and distribution. Local control, of course, does not ensure justice, thus criteria for just management are still necessary. Local control also does not ensure capital to build needed infrastructure, thus local control cannot be separated from larger global structural changes that would redistribute wealth worldwide.

Several ethical criteria for assessing management of water use and distribution emerge from Latina ecofeminist spirituality. First, water should be viewed not as a commodity or as a right, but as a life source that needs to be accessible to all of creation. This means that we must protect water as a public good and resist efforts of a handful to hoard water at the expense of others. Protection of water as a public good should be done so that all living species that require water for sustenance are served, not just humans. If all life is interconnected and sacred, then our management of water should be a reflection of these theological and spiritual claims.

Second, water needs to be equitably distributed and consumed. Sustainable use needs to start with those communities and businesses that consume the most. Poor communities conserve out of necessity. Viewing water as a public good does not mean that water needs to be offered as a free resource to all. Clearly, conservation in a capitalist system requires putting a price on water. The pricing of water, however, should be done in a way that ensures accessibility to those with little means and should provide incentive to conserve for those who use substantial amounts of water. As it stands now, the poor pay more for water because they do not have direct links to water networks and must rely on expensive intermediaries to receive water (e.g., truckers, vendors, or other carriers). One study showed that the poorest 20 percent of households in Argentina, El Salvador, Jamaica, and Nicaragua spent more than 10 percent of their income on water. Half of these households live below the $1 a day extreme poverty threshold.[47]

Agriculture and industry need to shift to low impact technology that does not inefficiently use large amounts of water, and high-income communities need to drastically cut their water consumption. Irrigated

47. Watkins et al., *Beyond Scarcity*, 51.

agriculture accounts for 80 percent of water use in developing coun-tries, and in many cases there are subsidies that encourage overuse of water by agriculture and industry.[48] No community, human or other-wise, should be denied water due to human hoarding and exclusion. On one hand, water pricing should reflect the scarcity of water. On the other hand, water should not be given only to those who can pay for it. Sustainable use also requires that we care for the health of our watersheds, which means minimal pollution both from corporate and individual sources. The Latina ecofeminist emphasis on the continuous nature of life calls us to accountability for all forms of life, both in the present and indefinitely into the future.

Third, there should be processes for meaningful participation by marginalized groups in decision-making around water use and distribu-tion. There is no one water management plan that fits all communities, but clearly transnational corporations that are focused on profit and are based miles away from most communities will not voluntarily be open to the influence of marginalized groups on their decision-making about water systems. Urban-focused state governments have not generally been open to such participation either. The Latina ecofeminist empha-sis on gender, race, and class justice demands that those communities that rarely have their needs addressed should be the first to be consulted on such a vital need as water.

Conclusion

The suffering of women's bodies and the earth body as the starting point of Latina ecofeminist theological reflection has meant that theol-ogy, spirituality, and ethics are intricately related in the writings, rituals, and everyday lives of Latina ecofeminist theologians. For these women, embracing a holistic spirituality entails addressing material realities that negatively affect certain communities, like lack of access to clean water and sanitation. While ethical reflection and action are imperative for healing destructive practices, Latina ecofeminist theologians have found that a spiritual cosmology centered on beauty, relatedness, and the sacred offers a deep foundation for an ethics of life. Their view that relatedness is our ethical and cosmic reality and that all of life is sacred with God/dess as the unifying energy and presence leads them to see

48. Ibid., 14.

water as the sacred bloodstream within creation. Thus, they hold that we must protect water sources from contamination and use water sustainably so that all life that relies on this bloodstream for nourishment, both in the present and into the indefinite future, can have access to it.

While many Latina women have resisted corporate conquest and control of water in the name of profit, Latina ecofeminist theologians offer spiritual nourishment for such activism. One way they remain spiritually alive in their everyday practices of life-giving resistance and healing is through the communal practice of post-patriarchal rituals where women's bodies and the earth body are central. Latina ecofeminists are not naïve in their embrace of beauty and worship but know that escaping destructive practices requires both staying focused on Divine energy that connects the cosmic web of life we are part of and being involved in communities of life-giving support.

While Latina ecofeminist theologians clearly resist viewing water as a commodity to be sold for profit, they realize that ethical issues such as water distribution are complex and that all humans are complicit in practices of creation and destruction. Thus, they evaluate *all* water distribution policies and practices by the norms of sustainability, equity, and participation. A Latina ecofeminist spirituality and ethics of life will uplift policies and practices that support the sustainable and equitable use of water and that ensure participation in decision-making of those who are most negatively affected by water distribution policies. In closing, Latina ecofeminist theologians would support the Hopi prayer for water and hold that more prayers be sent to future World Water Forums to encourage policymakers to do all they can to protect our rivers of life and to treat water as a public good that sustains all life.

Bibliography

Arbona, Sonia, and Shannon Crum. "Medical Geography and Cholera in Peru." Boulder: University of Colorado, 1996. Online: http://www.colorado.edu/geography/gcraft/warmup/cholera/cholera.html.

Avendaño, Nelly. "The Fight for a New Ideal." In *Changing the Flow: Water Movements in Latin America,* edited by Beverly Ball et al., 20–22. Food and Water Watch, 2009. Online: http://documents.foodandwaterwatch.org/ChangingTheFlow.pdf.

Barlow, Maude, and Tony Clarke. "Water Privitization: The World Bank's Latest Market Fantasy." *Global Policy Forum* (January, 2004). Online: http://www.globalpolicy.org/socecon/bwi-wto/wbank/2004/01waterpriv.htm.

Canas, Mercedes. "In Us Life Grows: An Ecofeminist Point of View." In *Women Healing Earth: Third World Women on Ecology, Feminism, and Religion*, edited by Rosemary Radford Ruether, 24–28. Maryknoll, NY: Orbis, 1996.

Ennis-McMillan, Michael. "A Paradoxical Privatization: Challenges to Community-Managed Drinking Water Systems in the Valley of Mexico." In *Protecting a Sacred Gift: Water and Social Change in Mexico*, edited by Scott Whiteford and Roberto Melville, 27–48. La Jolla: Center for U.S.-Mexican Studies, University of California, 2002.

Gebara, Ivone. *Longing for Running Water: Ecofeminism and Liberation*. Minneapolis: Fortress, 1999.

Grusky, Sara. "Privatization Tidal Wave: IMF/World Bank Water Policies and the Price Paid by the Poor." *The Multinational Monitor* 22:9 (September 2001). Online: http://www.multinationalmonitor.org/mm2001/01september/sep01corp2.html.

Hawley, Chris. "Hopis' Trek to Tell World about Water." *Arizona Republic* (March 2, 2006). Online: http://www.azcentral.com/arizonarepublic/local/articles/0302hopiruno302.html.

"Las Mujeres en La Defensa del Agua Como Derecho Humano Fundamental." Comite de Mujeres de la Alianza Social Continental (July 2004).

Marrero, Carmelo Ruiz. "Water Privatization in Latin America" (October 28, 2005). Online: http://www.globalpolicy.org/component/content/article/215-global-public-goods/46063-water-privatization-in-latin-america.html?tmpl=compon ent&print=1&page.

Public Citizen. "Water Privatization Overview." Online: http://www.citizen.org/cmep/Water/general/.

"Public Citizen Report Reveals World Bank Loans Continue to Promote Water Privatization." *Common Dreams* (April 22, 2004), Global Policy Forum website: http://www.globalpolicy.org/socecon/bwi-wto/wbank/2004/0422water.htm.

Ress, Mary Judith. *Ecofeminism in Latin America*. Maryknoll, NY: Orbis, 2006.

———. *Without a Vision, the People Perish: Reflections on Latin American Ecofeminist Theology*. Santiago, Chile: The Con-spirando Collective, 2003.

Ruxandra, Adam. "Lack of Clean Water Kills 2 Million Children Per Year" (November 10, 2006). Online: http://news.softpedia.com/news/Lack-of-Clean-Water-Kills-2-Million-Children-a-Year-39814.shtml.

Siregar, P. Raja. "World Bank and ADB's Role in Privatizing Water in Asia." *Jubileesouth* (December 12, 2003). Online: http://www.jubileesouth.org/news/EpZyVyEyylgqGYKXRu.shtml.

Schneiders, Sandra M. "Approaches to the Study of Christian Spirituality." In *The Blackwell Companion to Christian Spirituality*, edited by Arthur Holder, 15–34. Malden, MA: Blackwell, 2005.

Shiva, Vandana. *Water Wars: Privatization, Pollution, and Profit*. Cambridge, MA: South End, 2002.

Watkins, Kevin, et al. *Beyond Scarcity: Power, Poverty and the Global Water Crisis*. New York: United Nations Development Programme, 2006.

10

Alice Walker and the Emergence of Ecowomanist Spirituality

Melanie L. Harris

ALICE WALKER IS A PULITZER PRIZE-WINNING AUTHOR AND GLOBAL activist committed to a liberating vision of justice for humanity and the earth. Active in many movements such as the Civil Rights movement, the Feminist movement, the Anti-Nuclear War movement, and the Peace movement Walker is a leading writer whose work consistently lends a prophetic voice to the work of social justice. As the author of more than thirty books that span the genres of fiction, non-fiction, personal essay, and poetry, Walker's breadth of literary artistry makes her one of the most prolific writers of our time. Her style of uncovering women's stories, especially African American women's stories, shows the rich cultural wisdom alive in these communities that contributes to the humanity of all peoples. Beyond a focus on human community, however, Walker's work also opens possibilities for readers to more deeply consider the interconnections between humanity and nature. Promoting a sense of oneness that views plants, animals, and human beings as coming from one sacred source, Walker honors the "Earth as God—representing everything—and Nature as its spirit."[1] Reflecting on her own connection with the earth as the daughter of hardworking sharecroppers in Georgia, Walker's work enlivens a commitment to see nature as divine, to create life sustaining ways for the whole earth community, and to fight for environmental justice.

This essay will focus on Alice Walker's ecowomanist spirituality, showing how her fluid spirituality serves as a foundation for an

---

1. Walker, "Only Reason You Want to go to Heaven," 3–27.

emerging integration of eco-justice and womanism. Examination of Walker's non-fiction essays about ecowomanist spirituality reveals an important ethical imperative for womanist ethical analysis: earth justice. In addition to analyses of racism, classism, sexism, and heterosexism, traditional in womanist thought, I argue that studying Walker's non-fiction work summons us to add earth-justice to womanist religious ethical analysis. Ecowomanist spirituality, and its focus on the interconnections between the oppressions faced by women of African descent and the unjust treatment of the earth, becomes a new aspect of theo-ethical discourse whereby we are moved to heal our own bodies and communities in connection with healing the body of the Earth. Alice Walker's spirituality helps us chart our course.

Womanism and Ecowomanism

The heart work of womanist religious thought is to uncover the voices, wisdom and critical theological reflection that emerge from the lives, moral values, and experiences of women of African descent. Womanist perspectives entered religious discourse in the early 1980s as African and African American theologians, ethicists, sociologists, and historians began to problematize traditional European theological worldviews that did not include intersectional race, class, and gender analysis. Scholars including Katie G. Cannon, Jacquelyn Grant, Delores S. Williams, and Renita J. Weems argued that the theological lenses used by women of African descent prompted them to interpret theological categories such as evil, redemption, sacrifice and suffering differently.[2] Heavily influenced by the social protest tradition of such figures as Harriet Tubman, Sojourner Truth, Ida B. Wells, and Ella Baker, womanist religious thinkers found that white feminists who also claimed the significance of these historical women for the women's liberation movement were not always self critical about the absence of race analysis in their work. That is to say, even though some white feminists claimed these historical women as figures paramount in the struggle for gender justice, white feminists often sidestepped talk about the racial injustice these historical women faced, avoiding discussion about how racism

2. For more on first-generation womanist perspectives on Christian categories including sacrifice, servanthood, and unmerited suffering see Williams, *Sisters in the Wilderness*; Grant, *White Women's Christ and Black Women's Jesus*.

impacted women of color much more than white women. They refused to recognize race as a central and connected issue in the women's movement. It was as if race didn't matter in the minds of some white feminists. For many African American women and womanist scholars, not only did race matter, but gender, class, sexual orientation, religion and earth-relationship also mattered as points of analysis in any true fight for social justice. As Womanist scholars began to point out how some white feminist theological perspectives were infused with racially biased perceptions that assumed a white, middle-to-upper class woman's experience as normative and universal, their own perspectives became more focused. Rather than bury some of the most significant differences among women based on race, class, sexual orientation, religion and more, Womanist scholars chose to unearth the false image of the "universal woman" used in the quest to liberate all women and encouraged a focus on particularity and the diversity of woman as a source of strength from which the women's movement could gain power. This approach countered the seemingly inherent perpetuation of racial oppression alive in some of the writings of white feminists, and supported an embrace of gender as a unifying element in the feminist movement even as particularity and difference were also celebrated.[3]

Having engaged the work and perspectives of white feminists with their focus on gender justice, Womanist religious scholars also began to mine their own racial and cultural history for sources of empowerment. Noting the importance of intersectional analysis, and attempting to highlight the category of race in justice work, Womanist religious scholars turned to Liberation Theology to glean methods that used racial analysis in theological discourse. The race analysis missing in many white feminist theological perspectives was primary in many forms of liberation theology, including black male liberation theology. Emerging from the rich cultural tradition alive in black intellectualism and the traditions of black Christianities (largely in the U.S.), black male liberationists celebrated race analysis as central to theological inquiry. They posed such questions as, "Is God A White Racist?"[4] and "Isn't Jesus

---

3. For more on the origins of feminism, see Hooks, *Feminism is for Everybody*. Also, see Eugene et al., "Appropriation and Reciprocity in Womanist/Mujerista/Feminist Work," 88–120.

4. Jones, *Is God a White Racist?* 185–202.

Black?"[5] Black male liberation theology celebrated the Civil Rights Movement as a primary locus of the development of black theology. However, these scholars, at least initially, gave little attention to gender analysis. Some black theologies were framed around sexist ideologies, culturally accepted patriarchal behaviors, and biblical interpretations that set women's humanity underneath their male counterparts. Naming these roots as unhelpful and unhealthy for black women, womanist scholars sought full liberation for themselves, their communities, and the earth. As I have described their efforts elsewhere,

> They found it necessary to push black male theologians to incorporate the voices, experiences and theological perspectives of black women in their ideas of black liberation theology . . . Calling sexism a necessary category of contemplation for black church leaders and arguing that interrelated black feminist race-class-gender analysis be used in the methods, practice and pedagogy of black liberation thought, the "confessional" generation of womanist theology and ethics moved to establish a new theological perspective, *womanism,* that would center the theological voices and theo-ethical reflections of black women.[6]

Boldly claiming a connection with the vision and term "womanist," coined by Alice Walker,[7] these African American women scholars in religion and theology aligned the project of Womanist theology and ethics with the lineage of African American women's literature, naming it a valid and authoritative source from which to glean values, virtues, and theological perspectives from women of African descent. In this move, the works of literary artists including Zora Neale Hurston, Alice Walker, Jamaica Kincade, and Ntozake Shange are treated as important sources for theological reflection and inquiry, and resources from which values, ethics, interpretations of justice, and examples of moral action can be derived. The moral imperative to honor African and African American women's connection with the earth is also found in literature. This can be noted most especially in essays by Alice Walker in which she investigates the similarities between structural systems of oppression that dehumanize people and logics of domination that attempt to subdue and control the earth. These actions most often have a devastat-

---

5. Cone, *Black Theology and Black Power.*

6. Harris, "Womanist Humanism: A Deeper Look," 392.

7. Walker, *In Search of Our Mothers' Gardens.*

ing effect on women around the globe, decreasing their chances of hope and survival. The focus on women's shared status with and connection to the earth opens dialogue between womanist ethics and environmental ethics in that it honors the spiritual and historical connections between the two and proposes methods of eradicating structural evil that impacts the lives of women, while also healing the planet.

Ecowomanism then, is an approach to environmental ethics that centers the perspectives, theo-ethical analysis, and life experiences of women of color, specifically women of African descent, giving voice to their views and their solutions for environmental problems. It asserts that the voices of women of African descent contribute new attitudes, theories and ideas about how to face ecological crises. The approach applies womanist intersectional analysis to issues of environmental concern in order to engage the complex ways racism, classism, sexism, and heterosexism operate in situations of environmental injustice, including numerous cases of environmental racism.

Environmental racism "refers to the disproportionate impact of environmental contamination on communities of color." According to Charles Lee,

> It refers to racial discrimination in formulating and carrying out environmental policy. It refers to the decisions to put hazardous waste facilities and other unwanted land uses in predominantly poor and people-of-color communities. It refers to the adverse health effects that result from the unkind treatment of the environment in these communities.[8]

This description of environmental racism is helpful in illuminating part of the task of ecowomanism. In addition to investigating cases wherein landfills and other potentially hazardous facilities are deliberately placed in racially identified and lower-income neighborhoods, ecowomanism examines how these placements uniquely impact women's lives. The interdisciplinary conversation also embodies a religious perspective that highlights the sacred ties women of color often have with the earth and how this relationship informs moral action. More specifically it uncovers the roots of African cosmology, indigenous religious traditions, interconnectedness, and connection to ancestors expressed in many religious traditions practiced by peoples of color

---

8. Lee, quoted in Barnes-Davis, *Environmental Racism*, 3.

and women of African descent around the globe. Analysis of how these beliefs prompt and motivate care for the environment also serves as entry points into ecowomanist dialogue.

An examination of the titles of ecowomanist writings such as "Green Lap, Brown Embrace, Blue Body: The Ecospirituality of Alice Walker," by Pamela Smith and "Ecology Is A Sistah's Issue Too: The Politics of Emergent Afrocentric EcoWomanism," by Shamara Shantu Riley reveals the significance of Alice Walker's life of activism and writings for eco-womanism.[9] Many of the theorists cited here glean values, strategies for earth-justice activism, and inspiration from Walker. Just as the emergence of womanism owed much to the inspiration of Alice Walker's life and work, so her frequent attention to issues of earth-justice and earth-healing is also foundational for the emergence of ecowomanism.[10]

It is Alice Walker's care for women and the earth, and her deep cherishing of all humans living in creation that prompts her activist writings in the area of eco-justice. Noting how these passions emerged into a religious orientation for her, Walker shares in an interview with Scott Winn, entitled "Moved to Speak," that her love for humans and the earth has led her to explore many spiritual paths.[11]

Alice Walker's Spirituality

> I'm probably tri-spiritual. I was raised as a Christian. Now I love Buddhism and I love earth religion.
>
> —Alice Walker, *Moved to Speak*[12]

9. Smith, "Green Lap, Brown Embrace, Blue Body, 471–87; Riley, "Ecology Is A Sistah's Issue Too," 191–206. Other ecowomanist writers include Baker Fletcher, "A Womanist Journey," *Sisters of Dust, Sisters of Spirit,* and *Dancing With God;* Holmes *Race and the Cosmos.*

10. Ecowomanism also embodies several perspectives on earth-justice and honors the multi-racial identities that many women of African descent carry especially in the North American context. Many African descended women in the North America also have Native American. Thus, it is important to acknowledge the presence of "Native Womanism," as a part of the religious and spiritual perspective that influences Ecowomanism. See Guerreo, "Native Womanism," 37–54.

11. Walker, "*Moved to Speak.*"

12. Ibid.

The fluid spirituality that Alice Walker embodies features aspects of a variety of religious traditions that shape her religious, ethical, and moral perspectives, expand her sense of community, and ground her connection to and with the earth. In the interview with Winn she identifies herself as a "pagan Buddhist who was brought up as a Christian."[13] Noting how all of these traditions show up in her writings and interviews regarding her spirituality Karla Simcikova writes about Alice Walker's fluid spirituality in her book, *To Live Fully, Here and Now: The Healing Vision in the Works of Alice Walker*. Simcikova attempts to "fully understand Walker's complex and multilayered concept of spirituality that developed in the mid-1980s and that has continued to evolve," as a way of understanding how her earth-orientation develops on a continuum often influenced by religious traditions she has practiced in the past.[14]

Walker's fluid and evolving spirituality can be best understood by first presenting Walker's concept of spiritual plateaus. Rather than one's spiritual development moving along a linear progression, the metaphor of the plateau suggests that a "multilayered spiral, a process that incorporates the wisdom or lessons learned from the past or prior plateaus, in which the 'truths' embedded . . . become a part of the irreducible core of . . . [an] existing belief system, a foundation in which a new spiritual impetus may take root."[15] Instead of one's spiritual development being measured linearly, spiritual plateaus suggest that one's spiritual practice is seen as a process or journey of becoming aware, knowing the self, the community, the divine realm, nature and the earth in deeper tones.

In analyzing the fluid spirituality evident in Walker's writings, Simcikova names at least three major shifts in Walker's thought. These shifts of thought coincide with the shifts in Walker's spiritual becoming. Beginning with her own racial and cultural identity as an African American woman raised in the South during the Jim Crow era, and as an African American southern writer who critiqued the Christianity of her parents because it embraced patriarchy and preached the subordination of women, Simcikova claims that the inquisitive nature found in the term *womanist* rightly fit the initial phase of Walker's writing and spiritual identity. However, as Walker embraced her own Native American (Cherokee) identity as part of her "tri-racial" self, welcoming

13. Cited in Simcikova's *To Live Fully, Here and Now,* 20.

14. Ibid., 4.

15. Ibid., 10.

Native American spiritual practices into her fluid spirituality, her writings began to reflect this consciousness and revealed a deeper level and more global reach. Simcikova claims that this shift places Walker "beyond womanism."

> To fully understand Walker's complex and multilayered concept of spirituality . . . we have to move beyond the womanist model to include, incorporate, and/or accommodate all influences that have had a significant impact on Walker's way of seeing and participating in the world, particularly her interest in Native American spirituality . . . Walker's preoccupation is no longer only with the survival of her people, but also, and perhaps more importantly, with the survival of the whole planet.[16]

While acknowledging that womanist consciousness grounds much of Walker's work and initial identity, as clearly seen in works like *In Search of our Mothers' Gardens* and *The Color Purple*, Simcikova claims that womanism was only the first phase of Walker's literary identity. Simcikova sees a change in Walker's second collection of non-fiction essays, *Living By The Word,* suggesting that Walker's embrace of her identity as Native American produces a great shift not only in her writing focus but also in her spirituality and self awareness. This shift to another spiritual plateau breaks Walker from her womanist identity and gives her a new global and earth consciousness that eventually leads to a third shift in her spiritual identity: earth-based spirituality.[17]

While the explanation of the spiritual plateau metaphor is extremely helpful in understanding Walker's fluid spirituality, Simcikova incorrectly assumes that womanist spirituality is concrete and unbending. Simcikova seems to believe that womanist spirituality is focused narrowly on African American culture and life and embedded within a specific tradition of Christianity, instead of being the fluid creation that it is. She mentions significant work in womanist theology and ethics by Delores S. Williams, Katie G. Cannon and Jacquelyn Grant. However, her reading of their works ignores the diversity of perspectives, varied tones, shifts of thought, and movement of spirit alive in womanist spirituality today. Many womanists—Christian, Muslim, Yoruba, and Buddhist—describe womanist spirituality as encompassing a number of religious traditions, rites, and rituals that are life-affirming to women

16. Ibid., 4.

17. Ibid., 9–26.

of African heritage. This indicates that spiritual fluidity and religious plurality is at the heart of womanist spirituality.[18] Central to all womanist spirituality is an emphasis on justice for the wholeness of humanity and creation. Emilie M. Townes describes womanist spirituality as "a social witness . . . grounded [in] . . . the deep kneading of humanity and divinity into one breath, one hope, one vision." This witness, she explains, is "not only a way of living, it is a style of witness that seeks to cross the yawning chasm of hatreds and prejudices and oppressions into a deeper and richer love. Womanist spirituality is the working out of what it means for each of us to seek compassion, justice, worship, and devotion in our witness."[19]

Since womanist spirituality embraces a number of varied religious practices, and religions, and at the same time acknowledges the fluid nature of African descended peoples' spirituality that has flowed for centuries, Walker's fluid spirituality is at home in this concept of womanist spirituality. Rather than having moved "beyond womanism," Walker's spirituality, as indicated in her writings, has moved deeper into it as womanism itself grows deeper and broader.

Walker speaks directly about the fluid nature of her spirituality in the essay, "The Only Reason You Want to Go To Heaven Is You've Been Driven Out of Your Mind, (Off Your Land and Out of Your Lover's Arms) Clear Seeing Inherited Religion and Reclaiming the Pagan Self,"

18. Coleman, "Must I Be A Womanist?" 85–96. Also, see Hucks and Stewart, "Authenticity and Authority in the Shaping of the Trinidad Orisha Identity," 176–85.

19. Townes, *In a Blaze of Glory,* 11–13. Townes's work shows that fluidity is a key dimension of womanist spirituality. In *In a Blaze of Glory* she refers to God and Jesus as important aspects of her womanist spirituality, but just over a decade later Townes uncovers a shift in her own thought based on the fact that she does not often see Christianity truly being lived out in a way that promotes social witness. Elsewhere she writes: "for many years, I have been a somewhat reluctant Christian. From childhood, I listened to and took seriously what the older folks told me about what being a Christian meant and I watched with equal care as almost no one ever came close to being one. It was for me, as a child, a strange disconnect and in many ways I thought (and continue to think) that Christianity is a wonderful religion but hardly anyone is actually doing it. What I found far too often, however, is a Christianity that sanctions oppression as holy or a religiosity that separates spirituality and social witness." In "Womanist Dancing Mind," 239. Townes' more extensive analysis on the importance of expanding womanist discourse appears in her groundbreaking work, *Womanist Ethics and the Cultural Production of Evil* where she argues that womanist scholarship must expand its focus to the multiplicity of religious understandings and belief systems held by peoples of various faiths across the African Diaspora.

a detailed account of her spiritual journey.[20] The essay is also a good summary of the earth-reverencing dimension of her spirituality. It reveals a spiritual path grounded in respect, honor, even worship, of the Earth as divine. It shows that Walker's Earth orientation is informed by aspects of Native American spirituality and emphasizes the interconnectedness of all beings, women's experiences, and the Earth as "Mother." Originally presented at Auburn Seminary in New York in 1995, Walker engages a theological audience, accounts for the shifts in her thought, and claims her own spiritual path as earth-honoring. The essay begins with her earliest memories of feeling shelter and experiencing the deep love of community offered by her biological family, as well as by the religious, Christian family among whom she and her family worshipped in the black, segregated Christian Methodist church of her youth in rural Georgia.

Naming the important values of community and love for humanity and creation as central aspects to her fluid spirituality, Walker comments in the essay that these values emerged from her parents and, at least initially, from the religious community that welcomed her into life. However, she also expresses her deep convictions that Christianity and its roots in patriarchal doctrines were not for her. Recalling moments at three and seven years of age when she questioned the sexism embedded in her parents' Christianity, Walker writes that she disagreed with several doctrines of the church, including the doctrine of original sin.

> I had a problem with this doctrine at a very early age: I could not see how my parents had sinned . . . I did not see that they were evil, that they should be cursed because they were black, because my mother was a woman. They were as innocent as trees, I felt.[21]

Instead of accepting the God her parents worshiped, "a picture of a blond, blue-eyed Jesus Christ . . . son of God . . . his father: an older version of him," Walker shares how she began to conceptualize an image of God as Nature at a young age.[22] In a poem entitled "Baptism" she recalls the moment of her baptism in the murky waters of a rural Georgia creek. She remembers neither the doctrine of salvation nor the

20. Walker, "Only Reason You Want to Go to Heaven," 3–28.

21. Ibid., 19.

22. Ibid., 9.

teachings on repentance, but rather the feel of the soggy earth around her feet welcoming her into the family of creation. She recalls being lifted from the "brooklet" covered in "bullfrog spoores gluing up my face," feeling as if she had truly encountered the love of God through the touch and feel of Mother Nature. Walker goes on to not only articulate her nuanced understanding of God as Nature in the essay, but also to problematize doctrines dealing with sin and heaven. Noting her early dismissal of heaven as some far-away place, she claims that paradise is in the here and now.

Walker brings one of her strongest critiques of Christianity to bear when examining the inherent sexism and violence embedded in the biblical texts. Patriarchal interpretations of the Bible that viewed women as vessels of evil (Eve), pieces of property to be exploited (Tamar), and human persons mostly valued for their ability to give birth to sons, strongly shaped the sexist ideology that undergirded the theology practiced in the black church of Walker's childhood. Male church leaders also used the Bible to devalue the contributions of women. According to Walker, women's voices in their church community were considered less important than men's. She speculates about the reasons that women were not allowed to speak in church:

> They might have demanded that the men of the church notice Earth. Which always leads to revolution . . . For the other, more immediate and basic, reason my mother and the other women were not permitted to speak in church was that the Bible forbade it. And it is forbidden in the Bible because, in the Bible men alone are sanctioned to own property, in this case, Earth itself. And woman herself *is* property, along with the asses, the oxen, and the sheep.[23]

Throughout the essay Walker questions the nature of God as she wrestles with the notion of a *loving* God who would "curse women" and sanction the murder of women and children. By critiquing sexist interpretations of the Bible, which were used to legitimate the sexist practices of the black church in which she was raised, Walker not only critiques the sexist and patriarchal structure of the church, but the sexism innate to Christianity itself.

Walker's belief in Christian doctrine waned during her high school and college years: "As a college student I came to reject the Christianity

23. Ibid., 14–15.

of my parents, and it took me years to realize that though they had been force-fed a white man's palliative, in the form of religion, they had made it into something at once simple and noble."[24] At the same time her belief in activism, humanity, and her connection to the earth was strengthened. During her involvement in social movements like the Civil Rights Movement, the Feminist Movement, the Black Women's Literary Movement, the Anti-Nuclear War Movement and the Peace movement, Walker began to embrace a spirituality that honored the multiplicity of religious paths, remaining open to wisdom born of experience that celebrated women's stories and offered reverence to earth.

In essays such as, "Nuclear Madness,"[25] "Only Justice Can Stop A Curse,"[26] and "The Universe Responds: or, How I Learned We Can Have Peace On Earth,"[27] Walker's deep concern for the earth shines clearly as she gives examples of ecological disasters, explains how they impact the life of the earth, as well as human life, and urgently appeals to readers to get involved in the environmental movement. One example of how she does this is found in "Nuclear Madness: What You Can Do." In this review of a book by Helen Caldicott, Walker praises the author for providing helpful analysis and attempting to answer the question of why people have stopped becoming active in the environmental justice movement. Walker writes in urgent tones to encourage readers to become active in the anti-nuclear 'Save the Earth' movement. Personifying the Earth as a mother with universal status and drawing connections between racism as an oppression suffered by people of color, and potential nuclear action as an oppression suffered by the earth, Walker writes, "The good news may be that Nature is phasing out the white man, but the bad news is that's who She [Mother Earth] thinks we all are."[28] The connection between racism and earth injustice that Walker implies here illuminates the link between injustices, in this case racial injustice and earth injustice. For ecowomanism, this reemphasizes the point that oppressions are connected and that womanist intersectional analysis is necessary in order to see the damning effects earth-injustice can have on people of color, the earth, and *all* earthlings.

24. Walker, *In Search of Our Mother's Gardens*, 17–18.
25. Ibid., 343–46.
26. Ibid., 338–42.
27. Walker, *Living by the Word*, 187–93.
28. Walker, *In Search of Our Mother's Gardens*, 146.

"Nuclear Madness" is also an example of how Walker attempts to make people of color more aware of their important role in the environmental justice movement. Early in the essay Walker points out that while the environmental justice movement is traditionally viewed as a "white persons" movement there is a deep connection between the abuse of the earth and the abuse of people of color. "Individuals must join others. No time to quibble about survival being 'a white issue.' No time to claim you don't live here, too," she writes.[29] Walker peels away the glaze of assumed apathy that can hinder people of color from getting involved with the environmental movement.[30] Whether people of color are not involved because they are busy fighting for racial justice, basic human rights, or equality, Walker presses people of color to get involved. She writes, "We must save Earth, and relieve those who would destroy it of the power to do so."[31]

Walker also addresses the significant link between oppressions faced by peoples of color and oppressions faced by the earth in "The Universe Responds: or, How I Learned We Can Have Peace On Earth."[32] The essay also reflects upon the possibilities for world peace. Noting that Nature is trying to alert humanity that the planet is in trouble, Walker proposes that if humanity would earnestly love the Earth, and turn from the practice of exploiting nature, then violence towards and on the Earth would cease.

> I think I am telling you that the animals of the planet are in desperate peril, and that they are fully aware of this. No less than human beings are doing in all parts of the world, they are seeking sanctuary. But I am also telling you that we are connected to them at least as intimately as we are connected to trees. Without plant life human beings could not breathe.[33]

Here she notes the interconnections humans have with trees, as plants are a major source of the oxygen humans need to breathe. Walker also draws a bodily connection between humans and trees in *The Color*

29. Ibid., 345.

30 On the intersections of race and the environment, see Taylor, "Race, Class, Gender, and American Environmentalism"; and Cone, "Whose Earth Is It Anyway?" 23–32.

31. Walker, *In Search of Our Mother's Gardens*, 146.

32. Walker, *Living By the Word*, 187–93.

33. Ibid., 190–93.

Purple, where the arm of a black woman, Shug Avery, is explained as an extension of Mother Nature—the Earth.

> Here's the thing, say Shug. The thing I believe. God is inside you and inside everybody else . . . one day when I was sitting quiet and feeling like a motherless child, which I was, it come to me: that feeling of being part of everything, not separate at all. I knew that if I cut a tree, my arm would bleed.[34]

Walker makes a direct connection between black women's identity and Nature suggesting that the two are so intimately connected that they are in fact one in the same.

She continues to emphasize the relationship between humanity and the Earth in her essay "Everything Is A Human Being." Here she argues that humanization ought to be extended to parts of nature so that trees, birds, lakes, rivers, mountains and streams existing in "safe" sanctuaries such as public parks cannot be torn down and polluted. [35] In the essay she contends that the wisdom offered by Native American spiritualities is important because it sees the connection between people (humans) and the earth. In comparing the detrimental effects of logging in California to the cutting down of "old sisters and brothers" Walker notes the relational nature between herself as a human and the trees. In grieving tones she writes, "I saw the loggers' trucks, like enormous hearses, carrying the battered bodies of the old sisters and brothers, as I thought of them, down to the lumberyards in the valley . . . It was of this endless funeral procession that I thought as I lay across the feet of the sick old relatives whose "safe" existence in a public park (away from logging trucks) had not kept them safe at all."[36] By drawing a familial connection between the trees and humans Walker insists that everything, all creatures, all nature, and all humans be treated more humanely. She writes that humans must "restore the Earth," pointing to "its dignity as a living being." Only by doing this will humans realize their own intimate connection with the earth and with their own humanity. According to Walker, being accountable for and to the Earth is a moral imperative for one operating within an understanding that the Earth, nature, divinity, and humanity are interrelated.

---

34. Walker, "The Only Reason You Want to Go to Heaven," 7–14.
35. Walker, *Living by the Word*, 139–52.
36. Ibid., 141.

But finally, after much discourse, I understood what the trees were telling me: Being an individual doesn't matter. Just as human beings perceive all trees as one . . . all human beings, to the trees, are one. We are judged by our worst collective behavior . . . The Earth holds us responsible for our crimes against it, not as individuals, but as a species—this was the message of the trees. I found it to be a terrifying thought. For I had assumed that the Earth, the spirit of the Earth, noticed exceptions—those who wantonly damage it and those who do not. But the Earth is wise. It has given itself into the keeping of all, and all are therefore accountable.[37]

Conclusion

The impact of Walker's ecowomanist spiritual lens reaches far beyond those who identify as womanists. For example, Larry L. Rasmussen, a Christian social and environmental ethicist, draws on Walker's connection between the human arm of Shug Avery and the branches of trees, signaling that there is significant meaning in human—nature interrelatedness for Christian environmental ethics. Rasmussen's reference to the work and poetry of Alice Walker helps to shape his construction of an ethical methodology for Earth Ethics in his book, *Earth Community, Earth Ethics.*[38] Rasmussen interprets the connection that Walker makes between human beings and Nature in theological terms. Explaining the web of existence that unites humanity to the Earth, Rasmussen notes how the passage from *The Color Purple* illustrates the "intimacy of blood and sap, life and resistance."[39] Referring to the spiritual awakening of Shug Avery, and the scene in which she teaches Celie how to walk away from the oppressive image of a white, male God and to accept herself as a divine being intimately connected to Nature, Rasmussen points to Walker's theological understanding that everything is a part of everything as a way of describing the interconnectedness of divine creation.[40] Citing Shug's statement, "if I cut a tree, my arm would bleed,"[41] Rasmussen writes, "Arms bleed when trees are cut. Everything is that

37. Ibid., 142.
38. Rasmussen, *Earth Community Earth Ethics.*
39. Ibid., 203.
40. This is also an understanding of Walker's Goddess Spirituality.
41. Walker, "Only Reason You Want To Go To Heaven," 8.

much a part of everything else, something like using the same word for sap and blood."[42]

The blood of the earth is flowing in us all. Acting in grace to honor this heritage requires a recognition that just as the cosmic dust of eons ago that floated in the universe is divine, so too are we billions of years later. We are as old as the earth, and as young as the new baby being born this very minute. To discount or dishonor this fact of life is to cut ourselves off from the flow of the universe, the nurturing care of creation and the joy of life. Alice Walker's prophetic testimony and her fluid spirituality are models for us to walk humbly on the earth and to honor the generations that are coming. She encourages us to continually seek justice. Noting the similarities between injustices fought against by women, peoples of color and the Earth, Walker calls to us is to move towards honoring the earth in every way possible, and to live into a determination that we all can be saved as we help to save the Earth.

Bibliography

Baker Fletcher, Karen. "A Womanist Journey." In *Deeper Shades of Purple: Womanism in Religion and Society*, edited by Stacey Floyd-Thomas, 158–75. New York: New York University Press, 2006.

———. *Dancing With God: The Trinity from a Womanist Perspective*. St. Louis: Chalice, 2006.

———. *Sisters of Dust, Sisters of Spirit: Womanist Wordings on God and Creation*. Minneapolis: Fortress, 1998.

Barnes-Davis, Rebecca. *Environmental Racism: An Ecumenical Study Guide*. Washington, DC: National Council of Churches USA, undated.

Coleman, Monica A. "Must I Be A Womanist?" *Journal of Feminist Studies in Religion* 22 (2006) 85–96.

Cone, James H. *Black Theology and Black Power*. New York: Harper & Row, 1969.

———. "Whose Earth Is It Anyway?" In *Earth Habitat: Eco-justice and the Church's Response*, edited by Dieter Hessel and Larry Rasmussen, 23–32. Minneapolis: Fortress, 2001.

Eugene, Toinette, et al. "Appropriation and Reciprocity in Womanist/Mujerista/Feminist Work." In *Feminist Theological Ethics*, edited by Lois Daly, 88–120. Louisville: Westminster John Knox, 1994.

Grant, Jacquelyn. *White Women's Christ and Black Women's Jesus: Feminist Christology and Womanist Response*. Atlanta: Scholars, 1989.

Guerreo, J. A. Jaimes. "Native Womanism: Exemplars of Indigenism in Sacred Traditions of Kinship." In *Indigenous Religions: A Companion*, edited by Graham Harvey, 37–54. New York: Cassell, 2000.

42. Rasmussen, *Earth Community, Earth Ethics*, 203.

Harris, Melanie L. "Womanist Humanism: A Deeper Look." *CrossCurrents* 57:3 (2007) 391–403.

Holmes, Barbara A. *Race and the Cosmos: An Invitation to View the World Differently.* Harrisburg, PA: Trinity, 2002.

hooks, bell. *Feminism Is for Everybody.* Cambridge, MA: South End, 2000.

Hucks, Tracy, and Dianne M. Stewart. "Authenticity and Authority in the Shaping of the Trinidad Orisha Identity: Toward an African-Derived Religious Theory." *The Western Journal of Black Studies* 27 (2003) 176–85.

Jones, William R. *Is God A White Racist? A Preamble to Black Theology.* Boston: Beacon, 1973.

Rasmussen, Larry L. *Earth Community Earth Ethics.* Maryknoll, NY: Orbis, 1996.

Riley, Shamara Shantu. "Ecology Is A Sistah's Issue Too: The Politics of Emergent Afrocentric EcoWomanism." In *Ecofeminism and the Sacred,* edited by Carol J. Adams, 191–206. New York: Continuum, 1993.

Simcikova, Karla. *To Live Fully, Here and Now: The Healing Vision in The Works of Alice Walker.* New York: Lexington, 2007.

Smith, Pamela A. "Green Lap, Brown Embrace, Blue Body: The Ecospirituality of Alice Walker." *CrossCurrents* 48:4 (1998/99) 471–87.

Taylor, Dorceta E. *Race, Class, Gender, and American Environmentalism.* Portland, OR: United States Department of Agriculture, Forest Service, Pacific Northwest Research Station General, 2002.

Taylor-Smith, Chandra. "Earth Blood and Earthling Existence: A Methodological Study of Black Women's Writings and Their Implications for a Womanist Ecological Theology." PhD diss., Vanderbilt University, 2001.

Townes, Emilie M. *In A Blaze of Glory: Womanist Spirituality as Social Witness.* Nashville: Abingdon, 1995.

———. "The Womanist Dancing Mind: Speaking to the Expansiveness of Womanist Discourse." In *Deeper Shades of Purple: Womanism in Religion and Society,* edited by Stacey Floyd-Thomas, 236–47. New York: New York University Press, 2006.

———. *Womanist Ethics and the Cultural Production of Evil.* New York: Palgrave MacMillan, 2006.

Walker, Alice. *In Search of Our Mothers' Gardens: Womanist Prose.* New York: Harcourt Brace Jovanovich, 1983.

———. *Living By The Word: Selected Writings 1973–1987.* New York: Harcourt Brace Jovanovich, 1988.

———. *Moved to Speak* interview by Scott Winn on November 15, 2000. http://www.realchangenews.org/2000/2000_11_15/features/walker_moved_to.html.

———. "The Only Reason You Want to Go to Heaven Is That You Have Been Driven Out of Your Mind (Off Your Land and Out of Your Lover's Arms) Clear Seeing Inherited Religion and Proclaiming the Pagan Self." In *Anything We Love Can Be Saved: A Writer's Activism,* 3–28. New York: Random House, 1997.

Williams, Delores S. *Sisters In The Wilderness: The Challenge of Womanist God-Talk.* Maryknoll, NY: Orbis, 1993.

11

"Surely the Woods Are God's Tabernacle"

Considering Emily Carr's Ecospirituality Today

Colleen Mary Carpenter

CANADIAN ARTIST EMILY CARR (1871–1945) IS BELOVED IN HER OWN country if almost unknown in the U.S.A. A native of Victoria, British Columbia, Carr is best known for her stunning modernist depictions of the coastal British Columbian rainforest and her work depicting the totems and villages of Pacific Northwest First Nations peoples. In her posthumously published journal, *Hundreds and Thousands*, Carr gives voice to the spiritual vision underlying both her painting and her passion for the forest—or jungle, as she calls it:

> Working on jungle. How I want to get that thing! Have not succeeded but so far it fascinates . . . Should you sit down, the great, dry, green sea would sweep over and engulf you . . . If you face it calmly, claiming relationship, standing honestly before the trees, recognizing one Creator of you and them, one life pulsing through all, one mystery engulfing all, then you can say with the Psalmist who looked for a place to build a tabernacle to the Lord, I "found it in the hills and in the fields of the wood" . . . Surely the woods are God's tabernacle. We can see Him there. He will be in His place. It is God in His woods' tabernacle I long to express.[1]

Emily Carr's work has profound theological and spiritual implications for a time of global ecological crisis. Carr's insistence, in both paint and prose, on the deep connection between God, the forest, and art can illuminate for us a new way to imagine—and thus a new way to

---

1. Carr, *Hundreds and Thousands*, 283.

see and know—God's suffering creation. Carr wrote in her journal that "seeing things the Christ way, [the world is] dipped in love."[2] This is the vision I want to pursue. Carr's steady gaze at a world traumatized by human greed and violence yet redeemed by the love of Christ enabled her to see and to paint the stunning yet profoundly damaged forests around her in a new and deeply moving way. Carr saw and did not shy away from destruction, yet she also saw hope. Like Carr, we too are faced with a profoundly damaged world, and many people have fallen into despair because of the dire predictions of climatologists and other environmental scientists. My seven year-old son recently asked me, "Mom, will the world still be here when I'm sixteen?" Carr's way of looking at the world can help us gather the courage to make the changes needed in order to ensure that the world is in fact here for future generations.

In what follows, I offer a brief introduction to Carr, the forests she loved, and the way she portrayed them. I then argue that in Carr's work, we encounter a spirituality of brokenness woven seamlessly into a spirituality of resurrection. This is a truly Christian spirituality, one that walks lightly and surely past the two most common pitfalls of superficial Christian practice: Carr neither embraces a bloody atonement that never acknowledges the joy of the resurrection, nor ignores the pain and loss of sin and death in favor of a too-easy jump to Easter Sunday. With respect to how this spirituality can manifest itself today in our relationship with the traumatized world around us, I believe that Carr suggests not that we seek salvation in her beloved forests, but that we must abandon any overly romantic notions of a salvific, transcendent Nature—a Nature somehow separate from and "better than" human existence. Instead, through Carr's paintings, we find that our own brokenness and the brokenness of the world around us are inextricably bound up together, and that this brokenness is the very place where the presence of God shines forth around us, and as the place where we can and must see the resurrection happening even now.

Emily Carr

Emily Carr was born in 1871, and grew up as the youngest girl in a family of four daughters and a son. The Carrs were a comfortable middle-class family living in Victoria, a small city on the southeastern coast of

2. Ibid., 209.

Vancouver Island, British Columbia. Both of Carr's parents died when she was in her teens, leaving her oldest sister in charge of the family. In 1890, Carr traveled to San Francisco to study art at the California Institute of Design. She spent three years there but did not complete a degree, returning home at the end of 1893 due primarily to financial pressures. Once back in Victoria, Carr began teaching art classes and saving for a trip to England, where she planned to further her art studies. She left for England in 1899 and spent four years there, although not all that time was spent painting. Instead, she spent eighteen months in an English sanatorium after a breakdown; the headaches, vomiting, and exhaustion that plagued her were diagnosed as hysteria, "a common enough illness at the turn of the century."[3]

Carr returned home to Victoria in 1904, and then moved to Vancouver, where she established herself as an art teacher. She was popular as a teacher and earned a good living, but had almost no time to pursue her own work. During summer breaks from teaching, she had begun to struggle with how to paint the forests of British Columbia, and discovered that the techniques and traditions she had learned in England were no help to her. Carr wrote in her journal that she wished desperately to capture on canvas the "appalling solemnity, majesty, and silence . . . the Holiest thing I ever felt," but was not able to manage it. Her frustration was directed both at her own artistic abilities and at the trees—she wrote of being "resentful at how tightly they sealed their secrets from me, resentful at my foolish art, humble and pleading before the great trees."[4] Her work was judged at the time to be "charming," "quaint," and "pretty," words that in no way can be applied to the trees she was trying to portray, and are equally unlikely to be used to describe her mature paintings.[5]

In 1907, Carr took a cruise to Alaska with her sister Alice. This was "a transformative experience, giving purpose and direction to her

3. Tippett, *Emily Carr: A Biography*, 57. "For turn-of-the-century doctors, hysteria was the rubric for what would today be termed, among other things, neurasthenia, hypochondriaisis, depression, conversion reaction, or ambulatory schizophrenia. On the Continent an increasing level of sophistication in diagnosis and treatment was being achieved . . . but in Britain, very little was known about the condition," 57. Carr endured six weeks of experimental shock therapy in 1903. Tippett opines that "the severity of her treatment likely prolonged her confinement," 60.

4. Ibid., 73, quoting from Carr's unpublished journals.

5. Ibid.

life and her art."[6] It was during this trip that Carr first truly encountered First Nations artwork: the totems and villages she saw overwhelmed her with their strange beauty—a beauty utterly unlike that of a traditional English landscape. When she returned to Vancouver, she began an ambitious project to produce a documentation in paint of First Nations culture, which she and her contemporaries assumed was dying out. Over the next several years, she made several sketching excursions up along the coast of Vancouver Island. She also spent a year in France studying the new modernist techniques of painting, and it was when she returned from France that she finally had the tools she needed to engage the British Columbian landscape and its First Nations art. She produced many paintings of totems, holding an exhibition in 1913, which she supplemented with a public lecture on her understanding of the artistic value of the totems. She argued that they "are fast becoming extinct; every year sees some of their number fall, rotted with age; and bought and carried off to museums in various parts of the world."[7]

In her early forties at this point, Carr's hope was that the provincial government would purchase all of her totem paintings in order to preserve this significant aspect of the history of British Columbia. She was disappointed, however. The government was not interested, and indeed, many of the people who viewed her exhibition saw her work as shockingly modern and lacking in any artistic or historic value. At this point, Carr gave up. She returned to Victoria, bought an apartment house and worked as a landlady for the next 15 years. Painting rarely during this time, she had clearly abandoned any idea of life as a professional artist.

However, a quiet life as a landlady and sheepdog breeder was not to be her fate. In 1927 Carr was invited to participate in an exhibition held at the National Gallery in Ottawa entitled "Canadian West Coast Art: Native and Modern." This exhibition brought together both First Nations and Anglo-Candian art. Carr was hailed as a visionary and embraced by the prominent eastern Canadian school of artists known as The Group of Seven.[8] Lawren Harris, a central figure in the Group

6. Stewart and McNair, "Reconstructing Emily Carr in Alaska," 20.

7. Tippett, *Emily Carr: A Biography*, 114.

8. The Group of Seven came together in the 1920s, determined to paint Canada in a uniquely Canadian way and to celebrate the spirit of the "North." Insisting that they were no longer reliant on European techniques or training, the members of the Group of Seven celebrated the Canadian landscape, which, they claimed, gave rise to its own styles and forms of art. See Silcox, *Group of Seven and Tom Thomson*, and Harris, *Story*

of Seven, became a treasured friend and mentor: his enthusiasm for her work and his support for her unique vision brought her to life again. She returned to Victoria newly determined to paint, and in 1928 made another major expedition to First Nations villages on the coast of Vancouver Island. By 1929, she was regularly included in national exhibitions and had begun her greatest work. The 1930's saw her greatest artistic achievements. She moved away from totems, but returned to them later. She experimented with oil on paper, which enabled her to achieve the fluidity and movement she had long sought. She finally found a way to express the holiness she felt in the forest.

However, this great spurt of artistic growth and creativity came in her late fifties and early sixties, and her health was declining precipitously by this time. She suffered a series of heart attacks and was unable to keep up her journeys into the forest. By the end of the 1930's, she regularly turned to writing when she was too ill to paint. A collection of short stories about her experiences travelling to First Nations villages, *Klee Wyck*, was published in 1941 and won the Governor General's Award the following year. Her stories were read on CBC radio on Sunday evenings through the war years, and Canadians fell in love with her depictions of the western "pioneer" life she experienced as a child and young adult. No longer scorned as too modern or too odd, her painting was embraced by both the art establishment and the general public in Canada, who came to believe that she had captured on canvas the unique sensibility of their country. Carr died in 1945, after she had been told of but shortly before being awarded what she saw as a definitive acknowledgment of her artistic achievements: an honorary doctorate from the University of British Columbia.

The Forests of British Columbia

Carr's central achievement was discovering a way to paint the strange, overwhelming forests of the west coast of Canada. The forests that Emily Carr knew differ dramatically from the broadleaf deciduous forests found across much of the rest of the continent.[9] British Columbian

---

of the Group of Seven.

9. The exception, of course, would be the coastal forests of the Northwest, especially the great redwood forests of California.

forests are temperate rainforests caught between the ocean and the mountains, and the forests begin immediately at the water's edge:

> The forest simply takes over where the tide wrack ends, erupting full-blown from the shallow, bouldered earth. The boundary between [the ocean and the trees] is unstable, and the sea will heave stones, logs, and even itself into the woods at every opportunity . . . The air is at once rank and loamy with the competing smells of rotting seaweed and decaying wood.[10]

While this may sound like an environment rather inhospitable to tree growth, the trees here are among "the biggest freestanding creatures on earth," with the redwood, spruce, pine, cedar and fir trees all reaching the status of giants of their kind.[11] Trees tower 150, 200, even 300 feet in the air. Innumerable life forms thrive both on the forest floor and far overhead in the canopy. The sea-sodden atmosphere deadens sound even as it encourages wild growth. Canadian journalist John Vaillant describes the forests Carr knew as "awesome . . . huge, holy, and eternal-feeling, like a branched and needled Notre Dame." He quickly adds, however, that these forests are neither comfortable nor safe:

> You can be twenty paces from a road or a beach and become totally disoriented; once inside, there is no future and no past, only the sodden, twilit now. Underfoot is a leg-breaking tangle of roots and branches and, every fifty feet or so, your way is blocked by moss-covered walls of fallen trees that may be taller than you and hundreds of feet long. These so-called nurse logs will, in turn, have colonnades of younger trees growing out of them, fifty years-old and as orderly as pickets. In here, boundaries between life and death, between one species and the next, blur and blend: everything is being used as a launching pad by something else; everyone wants a piece of the sky.[12]

The rainforest is simply too much for some people. It is obviously inhospitable to human life and flatly dangerous to the unwary or unprepared. It is no surprise, then, that Carr's awe and wonder at the forest was not shared by her contemporaries. For most people, she confided to her journal, the forest is a terrible place:

10. Vaillant, *Golden Spruce*, 7.

11. Ibid., 9.

12. Ibid., 8.

The loneliness repels them, the density, the unsafe hidden foot-
ing, the dank smells, the great quiet, the mystery, the general
mix-up (tangle, growth, what may be hidden there), the insect
life. They are repelled by the awful solemnity of the age-old
trees, with the wisdom of all their years of growth looking down
upon you, making you feel perfectly infinitesimal—their over-
powering weight, their groanings and creakings, mutterings
and sighings—the rot and decay of the old ones—the toadstools
and slugs among the upturned, rotting roots of those that have
fallen, reminding one of the perishableness of even those slow-
maturing, much-enduring growths.[13]

It is too much. It is too "Other." It is both alive and dead in terrifying
ways. Yet Carr finds God in these forests. She recognizes her beloved
Christ not only in the forest but in her struggle to capture the forest on
canvas as well.

To eyes other than Carr's, however, what was (and still is today)
most apparent in viewing the forest was potential profit, enormous
potential profit, as enormous as the outsized trees, some of which
were hundreds of years old and upwards of 300 feet tall. Large-scale
industrial logging began in the 1860's in British Columbia, and by the
1930's, when Carr's greatest forest paintings were done, intensive clear-
cutting had become the norm, resulting in "a radical transformation of
the landscape."[14] The old giants were gone. The B.C. Forest Service was
trying to push the logging industry towards something approaching
"sustainability." Government surveyors roamed the province, "taking
careful inventory of the remains of the natural forest and the areas of
recent replanting."[15] The surveyors recorded their data in both maps
and photographs. Indeed, the recent exhibition of Carr's work, "Emily
Carr: New Perspectives on a Canadian Icon,"[16] featured Carr's forest
paintings juxtaposed with B.C. Forest Service archival photographs
from the 1930's. The contrast between the two is staggering: the photographs show a blasted, destroyed landscape, unutterably ugly, while
Carr's paintings are renowned for their spiritual beauty. This contrast

13. Carr, *Hundreds and Thousands,* 282.

14. Hunter, "Emily Carr: Clear Cut," 204.

15. Ibid., 205.

16. Travelling exhibition that began at the National Gallery of Canada (Ottawa) in
the summer of 2006 and finished in Calgary, at the Glenbow Museum, in January of
2008.

is the key to what makes Carr significant for us today. What was she looking at? How did she take in the devastation of the landscape she loved and find a way to see it with hope instead of grief? In order to answer these questions, we will first need to carefully examine the forests not as the photographers saw them, but as Carr painted them. Setting aside her paintings of First Nations villages and totems, Carr's paintings of the British Columbian rainforest can be divided into two groups: those that seem to be paintings of untouched wilderness, and those that deliberately incorporate evidence of industrial logging and human destruction.

Carr's Paintings: The Forest as Wilderness

Many of Carr's forest paintings are devoid of any human presence: they are paintings simply of trees, or of trees intersecting with the sky. They are haunting in their close-up vision of a world where human beings simply have no place. The colors are rich: deep greens and browns, startling blues, a sudden bright slash of golden sunlight. The shapes are somewhat stylized, often leaning towards the abstract. Most are not landscapes in a traditional sense. Instead of capturing a sweeping expanse spread out before the viewer, these paintings depict small snippets of a landscape clearly too large for human comprehension. We cannot take in the sheer size of the forest, nor even of a single tree, and so we see a glimpse: a few branches, a section of trunk. Moreover, these "small" glimpses are often overwhelmingly large, reinforcing the viewer's sense of being utterly dwarfed by Carr's "jungle." I will briefly discuss three of these paintings. There are dozens more, each equally enticing, but this should suffice as an introduction.

"The Red Cedar" (c. 1931–1933) is one of Carr's most famous works. Here she focuses tightly on a single mature tree whose trunk rises majestically out of the foreground, dominating the smaller trees and soft, swirling, pale yellow-green undergrowth to either side. The canvas is nearly four feet tall and over two feet wide. Its height is enough that the viewer must either stand well back to take in the full image, or else focus on small sections at a time. Standing close to the image gives the viewer a claustrophobic, overwhelmed feeling: the tree is far too large to be contained in the canvas, let alone grasped in a single view. The trunk's crevices and lines draw the eye upward towards the great swirl of dark, richly green branches that fill the upper third of the canvas. At the center of the trunk, exactly at the center of the canvas, the reddish-browns of the trunk dissolve into a flash of purest red. The heart of the tree, the throbbing life of the tree, provides the energy of the piece. The dramatic movement of the branches flows forth from this heart.

Another painting of a single tree, titled simply, "Cedar" (1942), is even more tightly focused, more close-up to the viewer, and shakes with greater movement. This painting was done during the final year that Carr was able to paint in oil; it is a work of her maturity. The branches of this great cedar almost reach out to envelop the viewer in their sweeping embrace; the trunk is obscured behind a multi-layered screen of swaying green. There is nothing human, nothing controllable here: instead, size, darkness, and raw power overwhelm human frailty. The branches could be of a single tree or a tangle of many; there is no ground, no sky, no place to get one's bearings. The sweeping sea of green is everywhere. Critic Doris Shadbolt describes the mood of this and other 1942 canvases as one of "lyrical tranquillity,"[17] but I find nothing tranquil here. Standing before this painting, I find the sheer size and awe-fullness of the forest to be both disturbing and beautiful. Carr's forests have striking elements of *mysterium tremendum et fascinans*.

Still, Carr's forests are not always dark, not always intimidating. Carr captures the startling brightness of the sky glimpsed between young trees in a trackless wood in "Blue Sky" (c. 1932–1934). Here too there is no sign of human life, but there is at least room to breathe. No forest path wends its way between the trees, however; no cabin is glimpsed in the distance. Like her other wilderness paintings, "Blue Sky" depicts a world entirely without humans. The most striking thing about this particular painting is the blue of the sky; it is not at all a soft blue, or a gentle blue, but rather a deep, rich, royal blue that struck me at first as being an obvious example of Carr's modernist love for dramatic color. Surely no sky in a wild, dimly-lit forest could look like that! I discovered, however, while wandering in a provincial park near Victoria—a place Carr is known to have visited, camped, and sketched—that the blue of the Canadian sky on a summer's day is as dramatic as she portrayed it. The blue is shocking next to the deep greens and browns of the forest; it shines with a fierceness that makes the sky itself, rather than the sun, seem to be the source of light.

17. Shadbolt, *Art of Emily Carr*, 182.

Carr's Painting: Human Devastation in the Forest

Carr's paintings of the forest as untamed and untamable wilderness are stunning. They are beautiful, dramatic, and disturbing. But her most powerful paintings all include some sort of human intrusion into the forests, an intrusion that can only be described as devastation. In paintings such as "Odds and Ends," "Scorned as Timber, Beloved of the Sky," Above the Gravel Pit," and "Loggers' Culls," Carr depicts the world that human rapaciousness and greed have left in their wake.

"Odds and Ends" (1939) depicts a recently-logged landscape as a sea of stumps, with only a few small, scraggly trees left in a field that was clearly once a great forest. This is indeed a landscape. Unlike her wilderness paintings, "Odds and Ends" portrays an expanse of torn-up sand and earth in the foreground, stumps filling the middle ground, and still-green hills in the distance. The blue sky above is as richly, deeply blue as in "Blue Sky," but is no longer swirling and dancing. Instead, it is painted in short, sharp vertical strokes, hinting at rain, perhaps, or tears.

The lone tree at the center of "Scorned as Timber, Beloved of the Sky" (1935), perhaps her most dramatic painting, reaches its impossibly long, spindly, useless trunk into the blazing heavens above. It is hauntingly bereft, yet the skies surrounding its peak explode in beauty. About 90 percent of this painting is the sky. It is a sky of transcendent, breathtaking glory. Most viewers take a long time to re-focus their gaze downward and see, with no small shock, the devastated land at the base of the canvas. Stumps and a few small, shrub-like trees surround the bare, stripped base of the central tree in oddly tiny, shrunken form. The glowing clouds above seem to belong to another world entirely. This seemingly odd image of a single tree remaining after a clear-cut is in fact a realistic depiction of a common logging practice of the time:

> a single large tree (a home or spar tree) anchors the site of harvest and supports the extensive cable system used to lift and move sawn logs onto waiting rail cars . . . the land has been cleared to the soil, and the fringes of the site are choked with brush and slash, the dangerously dry material that was so often set alight by the adjacent machinery. Stripped bare, the spar tree

stands alone, like some prisoner of war forced to collude in his comrades' demise.[18]

The title of the painting, "Scorned as Timber, Beloved of the Sky," emphasizes the contrast between what the loggers see in the forest and what Carr sees. It also hints at the complex mixture of rejection and triumph/glory that informs a crucifixion scene. The spar tree stretches out across the sky much as a cross would. It is abandoned and alone, yet somehow not destroyed.

A different approach to the mixture of life and death in the loggers' forest appears in "Pines in May" (c.1929–1930). Here the stumps cluster in the center, and the smaller, new growth around them is eye-catching in its brightness. Pale greens, yellows and blues flow in free, swooping arcs, leaving the viewer not with a firm view of any particular tree but rather with the impression of many small trees in motion. Carr described the setting in her journal:

> It has been liberally logged and few giants are left, but there are lots of little frivolous pines, very bright and green as to tips. The wind passes over them gaily, ruffling their merry, fluffy tops and sticking-out petticoats. The little pines are very feminine, and they are always on the swirl and dance in May and June.[19]

The life and gaiety of the "little frivolous pines" is not at all the transcendent hope of the skies in "Scorned as Timber." Rather, the hope in this painting is smaller, sweeter, and more child-like. The sky is distant and tends towards purple, not gold. The life and light here is decidedly in the trees, not above or beyond them.

Carr returns to the glory of the skies in "Above the Gravel Pit" (1937). This breathtaking canvas is primarily a painting of a sky—a swirling, moving, sun-streaked, royal blue sky—that is so beautiful that it almost distracts the viewer from the death and devastation below. Carr's skies have been likened to Van Gogh's, and this is one painting in which the similarity is striking.[20] Two lonely stumps mar

18. Hunter, "Emily Carr: Clear Cut," 204.

19. Carr, *Hundreds and Thousands*, 185.

20. Tippet, *Emily Carr: A Biography*, 238: in noting that the comparison of Carr's work to Van Gogh's was both frequently made and appropriate, Tippet notes, "The short brush strokes and shimmering light that created a unity of movement in such mid-1930's oil-on-paper sketches as "Stumps and Sky" called to mind Van Gogh's Provençal landscapes."

the foreground; stumps also litter the mid-ground on the far side of the pit, just before the sky takes over. Carr described this painting as a "skyscape":

> I started a new canvas today, a skyscape with roots and gravel pits. I am striving for a wide, open sky with lots of movement, which is taken down into dried greens in the foreground and connected by roots and stumps to sky. My desire is to have it free and jubilant, not crucified into one spot, static. The colour of the brilliantly lighted sky will contrast with the black, white, and tawny earth.[21]

Her use of the word "crucified" here is of great interest. The emphasis she wants in this painting is life rather than death, movement rather than stasis. Like the spar tree at the center of "Scorned as Timber," the stumps here remind us that death is obvious and inescapable. Yet the swirling open sky speaks of hope, transcendence, and new life.

Finally, "Logger's Culls" (1935) combines elements of all of these: the lone tree at the center, the field of stumps in the foreground, new young growth at the edges, and the swirling sky above. The juxtaposition, even integration, of beauty and devastation is particularly disturbing in this stunning, lovely canvas. What can it mean to look at a clearcut forest and see something so beautiful? The large stump in the left foreground is especially striking: several times as large as anything nearby, it is clearly the remains of an old-growth giant. The stump is not cut cleanly across; instead, there is a clean, straight cut across a bit more than half of the stump, and the rest is jagged, split, ripped apart. This rough tearing of the tree was particularly important to Carr and her understanding of what it was she was looking at in these logged landscapes:

> There's a torn and splintered ridge across the stumps I call the "screamers." These are the unsawn last bits, the cry of the tree's heart, wrenching and tearing apart just before she gives that sway and the dreadful groan of falling, that dreadful pause while her executioners step back with their saws and axes resting and watch. It's a horrible sight to see a tree felled, even now, though the stumps are grey and rotting. As you pass among them you see their screamers sticking up out of their own tomb-

---

21. Carr, *Hundreds and Thousands*, 391.

stones, as it were. They are their own tombstones and their own mourners.[22]

The large stump and screamer dominating the foreground of "Logger's Culls" marks the entire landscape as a graveyard—yet the joyous blue of the sky overwhelms any sense of mourning.

Carr's work insists over and over again on a mixture of life and death, joy and sorrow, hope and loss; I believe it is by exploring this central tension in her painting that we see most clearly how her vision can inform our own. There are two key issues here, and we will examine each in turn: first, Carr's focus on brokenness; second, her ability to move through brokenness to resurrection hope.

Brokenness and the Presence of God

Christians today have much to gain from contemplating Emily Carr's vision of the meeting of humanity and the wilderness. First and most importantly, Carr gives us a glimpse of the way death and new life are tangled up together. Of course, this is a central teaching of Christianity: neither the cross nor the resurrection stands alone. Yet, throughout Christian history believers have struggled to hold these two in tension without over-emphasizing one or the other. Certain cultures and time periods lose their balance more dramatically than others: medieval Europe, for example, embraced a bloody spirituality of atonement, all

22. Ibid., 187–88.

but ignoring the resurrection. In contrast, the triumphalist piety of the conquistadors celebrated the glorified Christ, crowned and regnant over the universe. Today, various groups of Christians lean toward one side or the other. It can also happen within an individual person's faith journey that the crucifixion is at the center of one's piety at a given time in life, and all but ignored at another. Further, differences remain between cultures: when North Americans first encounter the Catholic spirituality of the poorest areas of Central and South America, comfortable North Americans are often shocked and disturbed by the bloodied, disfigured images of Christ common in the South.[23]

By contrast, in Carr's forests neither death nor resurrection obscures the other. Both the horror of death and the surprising renewal of life are inescapable. The "frivolous pines" dance next to the stumps and screamers of the trees that lived and died before them. This insistence on the forest as a site not only of life but of death that leads to new life grew out of Carr's patient attention to what she saw and experienced in the woods. She did not see the woods as fundamentally separate from the rest of her life. Carr loved the forests, but she loved her garden and the "cow yard" near the barn as well.[24] She recognized each of these places as home. She did not have either a naively romantic attachment to the forest as a uniquely spiritual realm, nor a pious disdain for the forest as someplace that cried out for taming and civilizing. Science is demonstrating today what Carr took for granted a century ago: the world around us is not separate from us, and the Earth cannot be divided into pristine wilderness and smog-smeared civilization.[25] Rather, it is all one, and it is all broken. Novelist Marilynne Robinson says it quite bluntly:

> Wilderness has for a long time figured as an escape from civilization, and a judgment upon it. I think we must surrender the idea of wilderness, accept the fact that the consequences of human presence in the world are universal and ineluctable, and invest our care and hope in civilization, since to do otherwise

23 Peruvian sculptor Edilberto Merida's portrayal of the crucified Christ, which appears on the cover of Gustavo Gutierrez' A Theology of Liberation is a terrific example of this. My students tend to see the grotesquely exaggerated hands and feet, and Christ's mouth twisted in obvious agony, as not just disturbing but as somehow embarrassing, even shameful.

24 Carr, Book of Small, 27–37.

25 Johnson, Woman, Earth, Creator Spirit, especially chapters 3 & 4.

risks repeating the terrible pattern of enmity against ourselves, which is truly the epitome and paradigm of all the living world's most grievous sorrows.[26]

By investing our care and hope in civilization, Robinson is certainly not advocating that we simply pave over the last remaining wild places and be done with it. Rather, she is arguing that human civilization is not separable from the rest of the world, and that if we recognize that and care for the world around us as an act of gentle and generous self-care, then and only then will we have a chance of living sustainably on our small planet.

Our wilderness is, in a real sense, gone. Wild places remain, to be sure, but all of them have been deeply affected by human activity, human presence, and human violence. Even though she lived in a time of industrial logging and the deliberate destruction of First Nations cultures, Carr would not, I suspect, have been able to imagine where we have ended up only a few generations after her death. "Ecocide" was not a word that existed in her time. Still, her struggles with the death and destruction of her own time, and her persistent vision of new life in the midst of that death can help us as we make the turn away from fantasizing about a separate wilderness and towards investing our care and hope in the civilization that is all there is.

Caring for the world around us will in the end require that Christians choose to embrace, rather than deny, the woundedness and imperfection of humanity and of the Earth.[27] Locating perfection, transcendence, beauty, and purity in the heavens and in the wilderness, away from ourselves, as Robinson points out, only results in "enmity against ourselves," destruction, and sorrow. Carr's forest spirituality is a spirituality that squarely faces that woundedness and brokenness. It is precisely here, I think, that she has found a way to live in the face of destruction, to live, as it were, in the face of death.

This is the task of human living: to find life and hope in the midst of the death all around us. In Belden Lane's marvelous book on desert and mountain spirituality, *The Solace of Fierce Landscapes*, he describes three elements of a spirituality of brokenness that show us "how to live in the face of death."[28] First, Lane reminds us, "grace rarely comes as a

26. Robinson, "Wilderness," 254.

27. Woods, *Christian Spirituality*, 275.

28. Lane, 32.

gentle invitation to change. More often than not it appears in the form of an assault, something we first are tempted to flee."[29] Carr's logged landscapes are shocking next to her paintings of a single cedar tree, or of the sky peeking through dense forest. It is easier to rest in front of the beauty of the swirling blues and greens and browns of her forest work. Still, it is not enough; it is not, in the end, *true* enough. When confronted by *Loggers' Culls*, or by *Odds and Ends*, we are disturbed and saddened, but also fascinated. There is no escape here. This is, after all, exactly where we live: in the midst of our own violence and in the midst of beauty; in the midst of loss and in the midst of hope.

Lane's second element of a spirituality of brokenness is "a rethinking of what it means to be human."[30] To be human is not to be rational or whole or beautiful or productive or successful: any of the things that our culture assumes and insists on. Rather, we all share our humanity with the most broken among us: the physically and mentally disabled, the dying, the elderly suffering from profound dementia, the "marginal and despised."[31] Further, just as it is all too human to be "broken" in some way, so too does being human include the ability to break things (and people): anger, aggression, hatred, and war shape us all, and there is no escaping the destruction and violence that are part of who we are as human beings. Carr's logged landscapes are landscapes of destruction, of the dramatic and heartbreaking way human violence ravages the Earth. To ignore it is a lie.

Finally, Lane describes the "third and last requirement of a spirituality of brokenness . . . [a] call to reconsider the ways we've learned to picture God."[32] For some, to find God in the wilderness is to find God in the raw power and beauty of nature untouched by human hands. Yet Carr and Lane offer us an alternative vision of what it means to find God in the wilderness. Although "we may be ready like Peter on the mount of transfiguration to concede God's presence in stupefying splendor . . . [that] image of God doesn't prepare us for

29. Ibid.

30. Ibid.

31. Lane, 33. Lane is of course not the only one to make this argument. Jean Vanier, founder of L'Arche, also insists that to be human is to encounter the broken among us. See especially Vanier, *Becoming Human*.

32. Lane, 34.

a truth realized in brokenness."[33] Brokenness is the strange and disturbing location of truth in Christianity, the crucified Christ who rose with his wounds, the God who persistently manifests Godself in the small and outcast and unlikely. Perhaps, then, God is to be found in the logged-over, destroyed landscape Carr knew so well. Can we see God there, in the screamers and the stumps, in the trees that are now "their own tombstones and their own mourners"?[34] Lane reminds us that "repeatedly in biblical faith we discover a broken and despised people calling upon a God made accessible in pathos and tears." What we see in the screamers can be viewed either a reflection /projection of our own experience, or as an extension of it into the experience of nonhuman Creation. As Lane goes on to say:

> The God of scripture is equally revealed in vulnerability and in triumph . . . Divine love is incessantly restless until it turns all woundedness into health, all deformity into beauty, all embarrassment into laughter. In biblical faith, brokenness is never celebrated as an end in itself. God's brokenness is but an expression of a love on its way to completion.[35]

Carr's work, too, is an expression of unfinished love, love that both embraces what is and moves forward to what is not yet. Carr looked at the clearcuts and did not see only the devastation I see, or the positive if regrettable signs of positive human progress that the logging companies saw. Instead she saw a landscape in trauma that was, nevertheless, held in God's embrace. That embrace is a promise of resurrection. And so she painted what she saw, the dynamic whole of what she saw, rooted in her experience of the world and in her trust in God. For her, the world was still dipped in love, still held in the embrace of Christ. And looking with her, imagining with her, constructing our experience with her and interpreting the world with her, we may well find ourselves able to stare down death until we too can see the love and hope even here, even in the midst of death and destruction. When we see the broken world as Carr did, then we can conclude with Carr that our fragility is in fact our route to new life in God:

---

33. Ibid.

34. Carr, *Hundreds and Thousands*, 188.

35. Lane, *Solace of Fierce Landscapes*, 35.

We are still among material things [Carr tells us]. The material is holding the spiritual, wrapping it up till such time as we can bear its unfolding. Then we shall find what was closed up in material is the same as is closed up in our flesh, imperishable—life, God. Meantime bless the material . . . we cannot elude matter. It has got to be faced, not run away from. We have got to contact it with our five senses, to *grow* our way through it. We are not boring down into darkness but through into light.[36]

Bibliography

Carr, Emily. *The Book of Small*. Vancouver: Douglas & McIntyre, 2004.

———. *Hundreds and Thousands: The Journals of Emily Carr*. Vancouver: Douglas & McIntyre, 2006.

Harris, Lawren. *The Story of the Group of Seven*. Toronto: Rous & Mann, 1964.

Hunter, Andrew. "Emily Carr: Clear Cut." In *Emily Carr: New Perspectives on a Canadian Icon*, edited by Ian M. Thom and Charles Hill. Vancouver: Douglas & McIntyre, 2006.

Johnson, Elizabeth. *Women, Earth, Creator Spirit*. Mahwah, NJ: Paulist, 1993.

Lane, Belden. *The Solace of Fierce Landscapes: Exploring Desert and Mountain Spirituality*. New York: Oxford University Press, 1998.

Robinson, Marilynne. "Wilderness." In *The Death of Adam: Essays on Modern Thought*, 245–54. New York: Picador, 1998.

Schneiders, Sandra. *Women and the Word: The Gender of God in the New Testament and the Spirituality of Women*. Mahwah, NJ: Paulist, 1986.

Shadbolt, Doris. *The Art of Emily Carr*. Vancouver: Douglas & McIntyre, 1979.

Silcox, David. *The Group of Seven and Tom Thomson*. Buffalo: Firefly, 2003.

Stewart, Jay, and Peter MacNair. "Reconstructing Emily Carr in Alaska." In *Emily Carr: New Perspectives on a Canadian Icon*, edited by Ian M. Thom and Charles Hill. Vancouver: Douglas & MacIntyre, 2006.

Tippett, Maria. *Emily Carr: A Biography*. Toronto: House of Ansani, 2006.

Vaillant, John. *The Golden Spruce: A True Story of Myth, Madness, and Greed*. New York: Norton, 2005.

Vanier, Jean. *Becoming Human*. Mahwah, NJ: Paulist, 1998.

Woods, Richard. *Christian Spirituality: God's Presence Through the Ages*. Maryknoll, NY: Orbis, 2006.

36. Carr, *Hundreds and Thousands*, 269.

12

Love of Nature and Love of God

A Christian Ecological Spirituality

Ray Maria McNamara, RSM

Since the middle of the twentieth century there has been an increasing awareness of our natural world. This developing ecological consciousness has heightened human concern for the plight of the plants and animals as well as the sustainability of inanimate systems such as water, air and soil. This increased awareness has also produced a developing sense of the interdependent relationships which exist in and among earth's ecosystems, relationships that weave together the lives of multiple and diverse life forms with each other and the various systems which support that life. Coupled with this emerging concern for the planet's well being has been a growing understanding of the place and role of humanity within these interdependent relationships. Writers like conservationist Aldo Leopold and paleontologist Loren Eiseley have filled several volumes with essays describing and interpreting their own informed observations of nature. Repeatedly they attempted to articulate their own sense of humanity's embeddedness in and dependence on the natural processes that constitute the natural world and, in the process, they helped shed light on a new understanding of the human relationship with nature.

Eco-spirituality, developing parallel to this emerging ecological consciousness, locates the human quest for meaning within the context of the human-nature relationship. There is an abundance of literature illustrating that humans who turn towards nature in a spirit of awe and genuine concern are moved and often transformed by the experience.[1]

1. For example, see: Burton-Christie, "Feeling for the Natural World"; Cummings,

However, an eco-spirituality placed within a religious context, specifically Christian, shifts the locus of meaning from the human-nature relationship to the God-human relationship. This shift is best illustrated in the definition of Christian spirituality. Theologian Sandra Schneiders defines Christian spirituality as "the experience of conscious involvement in the project of life-integration through self-transcendence toward the ultimate value one perceives: where the "horizon of ultimate value is the triune God revealed in Jesus Christ," within the context of the Church community through the gift of the Holy Spirit.[2] God is the source and the focal point of this spirituality. The Christian relates to the whole of life in a specifically Christian way.[3] Christians articulate their spirituality in terms of the God-human relationship. This has led some critics to claim that Christianity is exclusive of the natural world and is, therefore, anti-ecological.[4] As a result, efforts within the Christian community to be more inclusive of creation have often created a pendulum effect: a constant swinging from the God-human to the human-nature relationships. The effect of this back-and-forth shift of focus is a dualistic perception of what it means to be in the world while focused on union with God. This essay will illustrate that a direct, hands-on experience of the natural world, can break down this either/or stance towards life. A contemplative attitude towards creation and towards God unites the human quest for meaning in such a way that the human person can be attentive to the needs and concerns of the natural world while remaining focused on a quest for God.

This chapter is divided into three sections. Part one describes an integrated world view in which the human community is recognized as a part of the whole of creation. Aldo Leopold's "Land Ethic" will serve as an example of how to understand the human community's embedded-ness within nature. Carolyn Merchant's Partnership Ethic will suggest that an attitude of attentive listening is a way for human persons to be attentive to nature's needs. Part two examines an essay by

---

Ecospirituality; Eiseley, *Immense Journey*; Hettinger, "Ecospirituality: First Thoughts"; Jung, *We Are Home*; Leopold, *Sand County Almanac*; Milton, "Nature is Already Sacred"; Rolston, "Ecological Spirituality"; and Taylor, "Earth and Nature-Based Spirituality."

2. Schneiders, "Study of Christian Spirituality," 1, 3.

3. Ibid., 3.

4. For example, see White, "Historical Roots of Our Ecologic Crisis."

paleontologist Loren Eiseley entitled "The Flow of the River." This shift from the work of environmental philosophers Leopold and Merchant to a contemporary nature writer, Eiseley, will illustrate that a direct experience of nature can give shape to an understanding of the human-nature relationship that is ecologically conscious and allow for the possibility of a human relationship with a Divine Other. Finally, I will conclude this essay by focusing on the God-human relationship inclusive of the human-nature connections by drawing a correlation between Eiseley's direct experience of nature and Athanasius' notion of the spiritual journey found in his *Life of Antony*. This correlation will illustrate that a God-human relationship, a life focused on a journey towards God, can take place within the context of an ecologically responsible life. To begin this exploration it is important to identify a holistic view of the natural world.

A Holistic World View

"The Land Ethic"

Aldo Leopold (1887–1948), often referred to as a wilderness ecologist and father of modern day conservationism, was a very strong influence in the development of an ecological consciousness in American culture. Throughout his life, both as an academic and a nature writer, he worked to balance his thirst for knowledge with his fascination with the beauty of the nature around him. While it is notable that Leopold had a very successful academic career, he is most remembered for his collection of ecological essays entitled *A Sand County Almanac: And Sketches Here and There*. In these essays, Leopold demonstrates a genius for setting up an interaction between a deep reflection on his hands-on fieldwork and a scientifically trained intellect. He is able to recreate a specific scene, reflect on it using his scientific knowledge, while proposing a way of seeing the beauty of nature, thus instilling a sense of awe and respect in his reader. "The Land Ethic" is a unique example.

Published in 1949, "The Land Ethic" is a composite of three essays written over a fourteen-year period, masterfully woven together with newer material composed in 1948. In writing this Leopold was able to "broaden the scope of his ideas," thus creating "an argument stronger than the sum of its parts."[5] The integration of old with new makes this essay neither a wholly new creation nor a mere stringing together of old material. It is a "new expression of old thoughts."[6] While the length of this paper does not allow an examination of the entire essay, I believe the section entitled "The Community Concept" is representative of his environmental ethic and provides a sufficient picture of an ecocentric human-nature relationship to adequately represent this relationship in a Christian ecological spirituality.

Basic to Leopold's land ethic is the idea of community, a system of parts that function interdependently, both competing with and cooperating with each other. To illustrate this, he begins "The Community Concept" section of "The Land Ethic" with the observation that all ethics are grounded in the understanding "that the individual is a member of a community of interdependent parts."[7] In his land ethic, Leopold expands this notion of the human community to include soils, plants and animals; he names this expanded community "the land."[8] By including the whole of creation, animate and inanimate, within the concept of "community," Leopold understood that this attitude towards each and all of the component parts of nature would "affirm their right to continue existence and at least in spots, their continued existence in a natural state."[9] At first glance it appears that Leopold's land ethic is an extensionist ethic, simply enlarging the boundaries of the community concept to include "soils, waters, plants, and animals, the Land" as moral subjects."[10] However, Leopold did much more than expand the list to moral subjects. He re-imagined the very structure of the biotic community and, even more importantly, the place and role of the human within this community.

Leopold's idea of the biotic community challenges the idea that humans are positioned at the top of the biotic structure, superior to and slightly removed from the rest of creation. Leopold locates *Homo sapiens* within the very fabric or framework of the biotic community rather than in a hierarchical place in relationship to non-human nature.

5. Meine, "Building 'The Land Ethic,'" 174–75.

6. Ibid., 174.

7. Leopold, "Land Ethic," 203.

8. Ibid., 204.

9. Ibid.

10. Fern, *Nature, God, and Humanity*, 50.

He states: "In short, a land ethic changes the role of *Homo sapiens* from conqueror of the land-community to plain member and citizen of it."[11] This shift of awareness calls for the human community to change its basic attitudes towards the rest of creation, from that of conqueror who knows what natural needs to that of participant in the dynamic and intricate combinations of relationships that constitute the natural world. The needs and desires of humans no long take center stage. Rather, Leopold's concept of the biotic community is holistic, shifting the focus from one species in the community to the community and its needs as a whole. "A thing is right when it tends to preserve the integrity, stability, and beauty of the biotic community. It is wrong when it tends otherwise."[12] In other words, Leopold's "Land Ethic" is quite radical, redefining the place of humans in relation to the rest of nature and calling for a totally transformed sense of self and its "role in the formation of a genuinely holistic ethic of nature."[13]

In addition to his inclusive image of the biotic community and the human species' place and role as an ordinary citizen of this community, Leopold also emphasizes the importance of relationships. For him, it is not enough to simply name the biotic community as the point of focus; he takes it one step further by emphasizing the give-and-take among species as well as between human beings and non-humans that actually creates and sustains this community. One way he does this is by suggesting that, through an ecological interpretation of history, one is able to see that many "historical events, hitherto explained solely in terms of human enterprise, were actually biotic interactions between people and land. The characteristics of the land determined the facts quite as potently as the characteristics of the men who lived on it."[14] Leopold, seeing humanity as a "member of a biotic team," identifies the impact the land has had in helping to shape human history. For example, soil types determine grass types that, in turn, attract human settlement and result in human activities like planting and/or the grazing of cattle. Furthermore, these human relationships with the soil impact what grass will grow in an area, which, in turn, determines the continued success of that grass or its regression to a less useful plant, which then affects the

11. Leopold, "Land Ethic," 204.

12. Ibid., 224–25.

13. Fern, *Nature, God, and Humanity*, 50.

14. Leopold, "Land Ethic," 205.

long-term human settlement. Clearly, from this one can see that there are recognizable relationships that exist between and among the various citizens of the biotic community, including the human population.

Leopold stresses the need for humans as sentient elements of the biotic community to continually evaluate their actions from a reflexive point of view, seeing themselves in relationship to the land and, therefore, responsible for preserving the rhythm of natural systems.[15] In order to preserve this rhythm, humans need to see themselves not only in relationship with the land in general, but, more importantly, as a dynamic part of the intricate web of relationships, interacting with ecosystems as well as the individual components, animate and inanimate, of these ecosystems. For the sake of the integrity, stability and beauty of the biotic community, humans have an obligation to attend to the quality of the relationships that bind them to this community. Leopold makes this argument clear in his use of the metaphor of friendship. "Harmony with the land is like harmony with a friend; you cannot cherish his right hand and chop off his left."[16] Given the embedded nature of the human connection to the biotic community, it would seem, then, that our own flourishing is interdependent with the flourishing of the land and its multiple sets of relationships.

Leopold's land ethic was a revolutionary concept. He took a mechanistic world view where nature was seen as a machine, a passive object for study and control by science for the sole use and benefit of the human community and, through his idea of nature as a community, converted this worldview into an organic view of nature. In his model the land is seen as an organism with interdependent and highly diverse parts comprising a dynamic whole. In this community model of the world, humans are placed in the midst of this diversity, needing to receive as well as contribute to the flow of energy necessary for the health and preservation of the land. Carolyn Merchant's partnership ethic provides a view of how this mutually beneficial complex of relationships can work.

---

15. Oelschlaeger, *Idea of Wilderness,* 206.
16. Leopold, "Round River," 189.

Partnership Ethic

Recognizing the social, economic and political aspects of human cultures and the intrinsic value of non-human nature, environmental philosopher Carolyn Merchant suggests an ethic that brings the human and non-human together as partners in a relationship. She locates this partnership ethic in the notion that people have the capacity to live in relationships as helpers, partners, and colleagues" and that basically nature and humans are "equally important to each other."[17] Given the unique cultural reality of the human community, the human ability to function in partnerships, and the intrinsic value of the myriad non-human species and communities, Merchant states that "a partnership ethic is a synthesis between an ecological approach based on moral consideration for all living and non-living things and a human-centered approach based on the social good and the fulfillment of basic human needs."[18] Key to this partnership ethic is a consciousness of nature on the part of human persons that sees nature as having its own worth or value, allowing nature to be recognized as an equal partner.[19] In this ethic the realities of both the human and non-human communities are included in creating a sense of the both/and dynamic that identifies a viable partnership. Instead of the generally accepted cultural view of humans as higher than, outside of, and superior to non-human creation, Merchant's partnership ethic is inclusive, considering what is good for both the human and more-than-human communities in one overarching moral stance towards the natural world. In being in and with a particular set of circumstances, within the context of a partnership ethic, an individual or group of persons is expected to consider the needs and limitations of the environment alongside considerations for the needs and limitations of the human community. The image of partner as one's companion in a dance can illustrate this point.

When ballroom dancing is done well, differences, whether they are partner-roles, hand placement or directionality, are brought together by the rhythm and pace of the music to create an exquisite display of flow and harmony, pleasing to both participants and observers. However, in order for a waltz, for example, to be a successful venture between two

17. Merchant, *Reinventing Eden*, 223.

18. Merchant, "Partnership with Nature."

19. Merchant, *Earthcare*, 200.

persons, communication is crucial. Each partner must listen for and to the many non-verbal signals shared between them in order to sense the music and to move, as one, across the dance floor. The essential nature of non-verbal communication for a dance can be applied to the type of communication required for the human/nature connection to be a true partnership. It is crucial that humans learn to listen to what nature is saying about itself, its needs and limitations, whether nature is fish, bird, mammal, insect, mountain, river, or desert. Most important, though, is not only the listening to but the hearing of nature's voice. Merchant tells us that both nature and humans have voices and in order for a true partnership to exist, humanity must listen to the voice of nature and interact with it.[20] Merchant further points out that nature's voice is "tactile, sensual, auditory, odoriferous, and visual," providing a "visceral understanding of nature that is communicated through our hearts into our minds."[21] In this she underscores the significance of direct encounters with nature. Just like the dance partners above, placing oneself in the presence of the natural world makes one available to receive the multitude of non-verbal clues that can give the person a felt sense of nature, making a strong, viable partnership possible: where the connections between people and the environment are made visible, motivating the human community to find "new cultural and economic forms that fulfill vital needs, provide security, and enhance the quality of life without degrading the local or global environment."[22]

Merchant's partnership ethic, with its stress on the importance of listening to nature's voice, is a blending of an ecocentric ethic where nature is recognized as an independent value center and a homocentric ethic where the needs of human cultures and its members are also recognized and addressed. Partnership ethics indicates the need for humans to listen to nature's voice in order to more truthfully and adequately address nature's needs and limits while handling the needs of human persons. Merchant suggests that humans need to be in better contact with nature, giving careful and deliberate attention to the various elements of a local ecosystem in such a way that nature is able to teach humans what it needs in order to continue its own existence, including sustaining the multiple connections and interactions with other

20. Merchant, *Reinventing Eden*, 227.
21. Ibid.
22. Ibid., 228.

factors of the ecosystem. Engaging in this type of listening requires that the human partner be present to the non-human partner, attending in whatever way possible, in order to hear the unspoken voice as it reveals the reality of the one being seen. As needs and limits are revealed, humans will be drawn to respond from a sense of moral responsibility that comes from looking into the "eyes" of the other. In this listening, humans will not only meet the natural word "face-to-face," but will also come to experience themselves as connected and interactive with the animate and inanimate elements of creation. Human persons, with a habit of attentiveness to nature's story of shared resources and vibrant interconnections, will learn about their own embeddedness in nature with its responsibilities and inherent sense of wonder and awe. A partnership ethic offers a way for the human community to live in and with the natural world so that both benefit. Contemporary nature writers such as Loren Eiseley provide concrete examples of the transformative effects of an attentive listening relationship with the natural world.

"The Flow of the River"

Loren Eiseley (1907–1977), a paleontologist, spent his entire life searching both the outer and inner landscapes, looking for a sense of at-homeness in the world and within himself. Eiseley's essays provide a classic example of the contemporary nature writing genre where, according to Douglas Burton-Christie, the author combines the knowledge and thick descriptions of nature that come from the natural sciences like biology and geology, with the deep reflective, aesthetic and interpretive sensibilities of the arts.[23] This combination allows the nature writer and his/her reader to take nature as it is while at the same time exploring new ways to imagine the relationships that exist between humankind and the rest of creation. In other words, the art of contemporary nature writing takes nature as itself while probing for new understandings of the place of the human community within the complex web of ecological relationships. It is precisely this direct and intense encounter with the natural world that opens up the possibility for mystery. I have selected the essay "The Flow of the River" because Eiseley trained professionally as a scientist, giving him a very specific and technical view of nature. Because of his training, he tends initially to view the natural

23. Burton-Christie, "Feeling for the Natural World," 175.

world in a literal and analytical way, reflecting an ability to discern the individual voices amid the symphony of sounds made by the many creatures inhabiting a specific geographic region.

> Every spring in the wet meadows and ditches I hear a little shrilling chorus which sounds for all the world like and endlessly reiterated "We're here, we're here, we're here." And so they are, as frogs, of course . . . After a while the skilled listener can distinguish man's noise from the katydids' rhythmic assertion, allow for the offbeat of a rabbit's thumping, [and] pick up the autumnal monotone of crickets.[24]

While Eiseley published scholarly works in the field of science, he is most remembered for his poetry-like reflections on his own experiences of nature, combining his knowledge of science with remarkable artistic sensibilities. Finally, because Eiseley was not religious, he did not set out to look for the sacred in nature. So, while he did not go looking for mystery, his essays consistently reflect a "breaking in" of mystery and awe.

> I would say that if "dead" matter has reared up this curious landscape of fiddling crickets, song sparrows, and wondering men, it must be plain even to the most devoted materialist that the matter of which he speaks contains amazing, if not dreadful powers, and may not impossibly be, as Hardy has suggested, "but one mask of many worn by the Great Face behind."[25]

"The Flow of the River," published in 1946 in a collection of essays entitled *The Immense Journey*, is a classic example of contemporary nature writing, combining evocative descriptions of nature enhanced by Eiseley's training as a scientist with his probing search for deeper meaning making. In this essay, Eiseley is exploring his life-long fascination with water as he recounts two different experiences, the first along the Platte River in Nebraska and the second, along a tributary of the same river. In the first story, Eiseley describes a time when he floated down the Platte on a hot summer day. An eye-to-eye encounter with a fish during the winter, frozen in a small tributary to the Platte, constitutes the second tale. For the purpose of this chapter, I will focus only on the first story.

24. Eiseley, "Flow of the River," 25.
25. Eiseley, "Secret of Life," 210.

Eiseley begins "The Flow of the River" with a recounting of a day when, hot from scientific field work, he decides to strip off his clothes and float, naked, down the river to cool off. He first describes the river by naming its geographic location: "It leaves the Rockies and moves downward over the high plains towards the Missouri."[26] He follows this with a description of the river itself.

> In the spring floods, on occasion, it can be a mile-wide roaring torrent of destruction, gulping farms and bridges. Normally, however, it is a rambling, dispersed series of streamlets flowing erratically over great sand and gravel fans that are, in part, the remnants of a mightier Ice Age stream bed. Quicksand and shifting islands haunt its waters. Over it the prairie suns beat mercilessly throughout the summer.[27]

Tucked into this description of the river is a reference to his own particular interpretive lens, "remnants of a mightier Ice Age stream bed." Here he makes reference to a time long removed from the mid-twentieth century, a time when geologic events left markers to be discovered by modern day archaeologists. For Eiseley, it is in this looking back into geologic time, collecting evidence of evolutionary processes, that he is able to discover the deep and unbreakable bonds shared by humans with the rest of creation.

> I was streaming over ancient sea beds thrust aloft where giant reptiles had once sported; I was wearing down the face of time and trundling could-wreathed ranges into oblivion. I touched my margins with the delicacy of a crayfish's antennae, and felt great fishes glide about their work.[28]

As he continues to recount his experience along the Platte River, in just a few words Eiseley shifts from simply describing the experience of floating in the water to an awareness of being connected to much more than the water surrounding him.

> Then I lay back in the floating position that left my face to the sky, and shoved off. The sky wheeled over me . . . For an instant, as I bobbed into the main channel, I had the sensation of sliding down the vast tilted face of the continent. It was then that I felt

26. Eiseley, "Flow of the River," 17.

27. Ibid.

28. Ibid., 19.

the cold needles of the alpine springs at my fingertips, and the
warmth of the Gulf pulling me southward. Moving with me . . .
was the immense body of the continent itself, flowing like the
river was flowing, grain by grain, mountain by mountain, down
to the sea.[29]

In paying attention to the sensual experience of the water, his imagination, shaped by his studies, became tuned to the fact that as he floated in the water he was linked with the river's source, its destination and all the creatures who came in contact with the water.

Turtle and fish and the pinpoint chirpings of individual frogs
are all watery projections, concentrations—as man himself is a
concentration—of that indescribable and liquid brew which is
compounded in varying proportions of salt and sun and time.[30]

In a few short sentences Eiseley transcends the present moment, becoming conscious of the very flow of time as it moves from the dark and distant past, through the current moment and out into the unknown future.

With a renewed sense of wonder at the pervasive presence of water in all of life, Eiseley concludes this story by describing his emergence from the Platte River, tottering against the pull of gravity as human's ancient ancestors did long ago, with a reluctance to "break contact with that mother element."[31] He returns to solid ground with a new "vision" of the relationship that exists between humans and nature.

As for men, those myriad little detached ponds with their own
swarming corpuscular life, what were they but a way that water has of going about beyond the reach of rivers? I, too, was a
microcosm of pouring rivulets and floating driftwood gnawed
by the mysterious animalcules of my own creation. I was three
fourths water, rising and subsiding according to the hollow
knocking of my veins.[32]

Connecting humans to nature using water, Eiseley highlights an almost seamless link with the environment. For him, a direct experience of nature, a listening to the evolutionary story contained in the voices of

29. Ibid.
30. Ibid., 20.
31. Ibid.
32. Ibid.

water, sand, and animals, gave him an understanding of human bond-ed-ness to the rest of creation. Each person is dependent on the natural world because we share not only the same evolutionary history but also participate in the same evolutionary processes that helped shape the natural world of the twenty-first century.

In "The Flow of the River" Eiseley demonstrates that an open and receptive experience of nature can enable a person to hear in nature's voice the common links shared by humans and the rest of creation, links which reveal the interdependent rather than the dominating character of the human/nature relationship. However, Eiseley also shows in this essay that intense attention to nature can move one beyond an aware-ness of our deep embeddedness in the natural world. At the end of this essay, following his two reflections on water, he concludes with the ob-servation of the intricate pattern of a snowflake that has just fallen on his sleeve. Noting that there is no utilitarian purpose for a snowflake, no logical reason for its existence, he describes it as merely water that has "leapt out of vapor and thin nothingness in the night sky to ar-ray itself in form."[33] He finishes by saying that water, like evolution, is "an apparition from that mysterious shadow world beyond nature, that final world which contains—if anything contains—the explanation of men and catfish and green leaves."[34] Thus, in an essay that begins with a rich description of floating along the Platte River, an experience requir-ing the use of all of his senses, Eiseley concludes by suggesting that a focused and intentional attention to nature not only reveals characteris-tics of the human/nature relationship, but also alludes to a mystery that is beyond the natural world. The voice of nature, therefore, is capable of speaking of its own needs and limits, revealing truths to the human community about itself, while hinting at something more than itself.

Through a rich description of the Platte River, Eiseley communi-cates the River's past as well as its present, its source and its destination. As he probes for deeper meanings, Eiseley come to experience the hu-man connection to the rest of the natural world as a shared history and shared role in the evolutionary process. In other words, "The Flow of the River" shows that a direct experience of nature can draw attention to the interdependent, mutually beneficial roles nature and humans share with each other. Finally, Eiseley's essay highlights the possibility that a

33. Ibid., 27.
34. Ibid.

direct encounter with nature offers the possibility of a transformation that can lead one beyond a recognition of "relationship" to an awareness of the mystery that lies beyond nature. Nature writers like Loren Eiseley offer a world view that is inclusive of the whole of creation, recognizes nature's value in and of itself, witnesses to human embeddedness in the history and processes of the natural world, and hints at something more than nature. From the perspective of Christian spirituality I contend that it is at this moment of self-transcendence when the encounter with nature merges with one's deep desire for union with God.

Love of Nature and Love of God

Athanasius' Life of Antony

Thus far this essay has focused on the human-nature relationship. Leopold's Land Ethic offers a world view that recognizes the web of relationships that link creature to creature as well as creature to inanimate creation. This intersecting complex of connections, according to Leopold, creates a community that he calls The Land. Leopold's Land Ethic clearly identifies *Homo sapiens* as a contributing member of this community. Building on Leopold's inclusive world view, Carolyn Merchant's partnership ethic introduces the need for the human community to be engaged in a process of attentive listening: listening to the needs of humans while also focused on an intense listening for and to the voices of the natural world. In order to actualize this particular type of listening, Merchant suggests that a more direct contact with the natural world is essential. Finally, "The Flow of the River," an essay by Loren Eiseley illustrates the transformative effects that can come from a direct experience of nature. Floating along the Platte River not only awakened Eiseley to the reality that humanity is embedded in nature, but, more importantly, an experience of this embedded-ness can open one to "seeing" beyond the limits of physical matter into the Mystery that lies beyond the material world. It is here that the human-nature relationship opens into and helps shape a God-human relationship. A correlation between Athanasius' *Life of Antony* and Eiseley's "The Flow of the River" offers an example of how the human-nature relationship and the God-human relationship can intersect and shape a stance towards life that supports an ecologically responsible life style whose single focus is union with God.

The *Life of Antony* is a hagiographical account of the spiritual journey of Antony, a fourth century monk living in the Egyptian desert. This story was written by Athanasius, bishop of Alexandria, shortly after Antony's death. In this hagiography[35] Athanasius recounts Antony's transformation from a young man of considerable wealth to a spiritual giant, living as a hermit deep in the Egyptian desert. It is Athanasius' understanding of spiritual transformation, with its focus on the contemplation of God, that sets up the parallels with Eiseley's own transformation.

In brief, Antony's spiritual transformation took place in three stages: call, withdrawal, and return. Antony's experience of 'call' came as he listened to the gospel passage in Matthew where the Lord says, "If you would be perfect, go, sell what you possess and give to the poor and you will have treasure in heaven" (Matt 19:20). This experience of invitation set Antony on a spiritual path in which he would gradually withdraw from society, practice the discipline (*askēsis*),[36] suffer unspeakable torments from the demons of temptation, and finally come to a profound encounter with the Lord. Through this 'school of purification' Antony came to the practice of contemplation. By remaining faithful to the practice of keeping his thoughts always on the Lord, Antony was able to hear the voice of Jesus, to know the nearness of the Lord.

> [T]he Lord did not forget the wrestling of Antony, but came to his aid. For when he looked up he saw the roof being opened, as it seemed, and a certain beam of light descending toward him. Suddenly the demons vanished from view, the pain of his body ceased instantly, and the building was once more intact. Aware of the assistance and both breathing more easily and relieved from the sufferings, Antony entreated the vision that appeared saying, "Where were you? Why didn't you appear in the beginning, so that you could stop my distresses?" And a voice came to him: "I was here, Antony, but I waited to watch your struggle. And now, since you persevered and were not defeated,

35. A hagiography is a biography of a holy person who is portrayed in larger than life proportions whose purpose is broader than simply recalling the life of the main character. Usually these stories are designed to teach specific aspects of Christian life and sanctity.

36. For Antony this was a life of fasting, constant prayer, reading of scriptures, keeping a close check on his thoughts, and celibacy.

> I will be your helper forever, and I will make you famous every-
> where." On hearing this, he stood up and prayed, and he was so
> strengthened that he felt that his body contained more might
> than before.[37]

Antony's time of withdrawal taught him the art of attentive listening. While it was Antony's choice to be faithful in wrestling with the
demons, it was God's faithful presence that provided the strength to stay
the course. God's invitation to come apart in order to come to know the
Lord was, for Antony, a source of profound inspiration and strength,
the fruits of which are most clearly seen in the third stage of his spiritual
transformation, the return.

To understand the full impact of Athanasius' description of the
third stage of the spiritual journey, it is important to know that twenty
years of Antony's period of withdrawal were spent sealed in a cave in
the desert. During this time, his friends would bring him bread and water, but, according to Athanasius, Antony never left the cave. One would
assume that twenty years spent in isolation and fasting would have left
Antony unrecognizable, emaciated, even near death. Athanasius' account was exactly the opposite.

> And when they beheld him they were amazed to see that his
> body had maintained its former condition, neither fat from
> lack of exercise, nor emaciated from fasting and combat with
> demons, but was just as they had known him prior to his with-
> drawal. The state of his soul was one of purity, for it was not con-
> stricted by grief, nor relaxed by pleasure, not affected by either
> laughter or dejection.[38]

Antony returned from this period of withdrawal a whole and healthy
person, recognizable to all who saw him. His mental and physical conditions reflect that the man who emerged from the cave was the same
as the one who entered the cave some twenty years earlier. Athanasius
goes on to explain that he was able to respond to the people in selfless
acts of service. His remarkable state of good health was less a reflection of his perseverance than his turning, full-faced, toward God in a
gesture of prayer and contemplative listening. Antony's well-being was
caused by years of facing toward God, listening for and responding to

---

37. Athanasius, *Life of Antony*, 10. Hereafter abbreviated *VA* (*Vita Antonii*).
Numerals indicate the paragraph being cited.

38. Athanasius, *VA*, 14.

the movements of God in the midst of his struggles. While Antony's struggles with the demons constituted a significant stage in his spiritual transformation, contemplative prayer is the focus of Athansius' understanding of the spiritual journey. This attitude of contemplative listening also offers a means for linking the *Life of Antony* with Loren Eiseley's "The Flow of the River."

Life of Antony and "The Flow of the River"

In the previous section I discussed Athanasius' understanding of the spiritual life as recorded in his *Life of Antony* as a process of call, withdrawal, and return. I also showed that this pattern offers the potential for change or self-transcendence, specifically a turning from one's personal struggles to an attentive listening stance towards God. In this final section I will draw a correlation[39] between the spiritual life described by Athanasius and Loren Eiseley's experience and reflections while floating on the Platte River. This correlation will highlight the fact that although these two experiences were quite different, there are enough points of intersection in the two works to support the idea that the discipline of contemplative listening can lead to a transformative moment.

Call

Both Antony and Eiscly experienced a call, an invitation to come apart into something that was not familiar. For Antony, the experience came through the hearing and reflecting on a specific passage in the gospels. His entire life began to change from its focus on the household to the practice of the discipline.[40] Athanasius' use of the expressions "immediately Antony went out"[41] and "he could not remain any longer"[42] suggests that there was a sense of urgency associated with the call. The call Antony received was clear, direct and so strong that he was compelled to respond.

---

39. I am basing this correlation on David Tracy's notion of mutual critical correlation. See Tracy, *Blessed Rage for Order.*

40. Athanasius, *VA*, 3.

41. Ibid., 2.

42. Ibid., 3.

The same type of urgency was also expressed by Eiseley. "The weaving net of water murmuring and little in the shallows on its way to the Gulf stirred me . . . with a new idea."[43] Here Eiseley indicates that it was something outside himself, the water, that was drawing him to engage in a behavior that was out of the ordinary for him. The urgency of the call was best illustrated when Eiseley states, "[A] great desire to stretch out and go with this gently insistent water began to pluck at me."[44] For Eiseley, too, the experience of call was clear, deep, and insistent, though not without risk.

Withdrawal

Responding to the Lord's call to leave everything and follow him, Antony engaged in a process of withdrawal that began on the outskirts of the city and ended deep in the Egyptian desert. This separation took Antony further from what was familiar and comfortable and deeper into the unknown. To stress the extraordinary nature of this response, Athanasius wrote, "[N]o monk knows at all the great desert."[45] While this statement makes the point that Antony initiated what would be called desert monasticism, it does not begin to express the extreme conditions of the desert itself. The desert is not safe. Belden Lane describes the desert as a place of lawlessness; a place that reduces a person to a "rawboned simplicity; a place where the structures that give shape and meaning to life do not exist."[46] While the desert provided Antony the solitude he sought, and clearly was the place where he transitioned from his former life into something quite different, he did place his physical and mental well being at risk. Yet, despite the desert's multiple uncertainties and dangers, Antony embraced the spiritual journey he was called to travel. Antony's fidelity to the spiritual process stripped him of every concern but for his simplest needs for survival, leaving him open and vulnerable to the movement of God. It was this combination of "rawboned simplicity" and Divine action that turned a potentially deadly encounter with the desert into a deep conversion, a radical turning towards God.

43. Eiseley, "Flow of the River," 18.
44. Ibid.
45. Athanasius, *VA*, 3.
46. Lane, *Solace of Fierce Landscapes*, 38.

Loren Eiseley's process of withdrawal also involved risk and the facing of deep fears. As he stood at the water's edge, feeling the urge to enter the water, he was compelled to deal with his own demons. Unlike Antony's temptations,[47] Eiseley had to face both his fear of drowning and the innate dangers of the Platte River itself.

> In addition to the fact that I was a nonswimmer, this "inch deep" river was treacherous with holes and quicksands. Death was not precisely infrequent along its wandering and illusory channels. Like all broad wastes of this kind, where neither water nor land quite prevails, its thickets were lonely and untraversed. A man in trouble would cry out in vain.[48]

Despite his fears and the huge risks, Eiseley simply entered the water. Encountering his fears created an openness to an adventure that left him vulnerable to an extraordinary and transformative event, a oneness with the water.

> I was streaming alive through the hot and working ferment of the sun, or oozing secretively through shady thickets. I *was* water and the unspeakable alchemies that gestate and take shape in water, the slimy jellies that under the enormous magnification of the sun writhe and whip upward as great barbeled fish mouths, or sink indistinctly back into the murk out of which they arose.[49]

Through this self-transcending moment Eiseley "saw" the essential link all of life has with water.

> Turtle and fish and the pinpoint chirpings of individual frogs are all watery projections, concentrations—as man himself is a concentration—of that indescribable and liquid brew which is compounded in varying proportions of salt and sun and time.[50]

Like Antony, Eiseley's withdrawal into the unknown, risky though it was, drew him into a transformative experience that enhanced and further solidified his conviction that all of created matter is linked together.

---

47. According to Athanasius, Antony's temptations dealt with memories of his past possessions, concern for his sister, bonds, of kinship, love of money and glory, pleasures of food and the love of a woman. *VA*, 5.

48. Eiseley, "Flow of the River," 18.

49. Ibid., 19–20.

50. Ibid., 20.

Return

Antony and Eiseley emerged from their respective periods of withdrawal with a new awareness. Antony came out of his cave with a greater sensitivity to the transformative power of Christ's love and the role *askēsis* played in the process of spiritual transformation.[51] For the remainder of his years Antony stayed in the desert, teaching the practice of the discipline to those who sought him out. Even though he preferred his solitude, the patience and understanding he showed those who came to him gave a continual witness to the love of Christ he encountered in the desert and continues to experience throughout the rest of this life.

Eiseley, tottering out of the River, emerged with a great sense of humankind's basic connection with the rest of creation.

> As for men, those myriad little detached ponds with their own swarming corpuscular life, what were they but a way that water has of going about beyond the reach of rivers. I, too, was a microcosm of pouring rivulets and floating driftwood gnawed by the mysterious animalcules of my own creation. I was three-fourths water, rising and subsiding according to the hollow knocking in my veins: a minute pulse like the eternal pulse that lifts Himalayas and which, in the following systole, will carry them away.[52]

Eiseley returned from a period of withdrawal having listened intently to the water and the land in a way that enabled him to experience his own connections to their ancient story. Like Antony's, his experience, though uniquely personal, was intended to be shared with others. For the remainder of his life, Eiseley continued to write essays that reflected his own experience of the web of life, of humanity's interconnections with the rest of creation.

In addition to a related call-withdrawal-return experience there is one more important similarity between Antony and Eiseley that needs to be highlighted here. Though clearly responding to a call from God, Antony's initial focus was on his struggles with the demons. Through his wrestling his focus was purified and rotated so that his gaze fell completely on the love of God. This change of attention from struggle to attentive listening to the Lord is the heart of Athanasius' story of Antony's

---

51. Athanasius, *VA*, 14.
52. Eiseley, "Flow of the River," 20.

life and spiritual journey. While Antony's response was religious in nature, Eiseley's decision to follow the insistent urgings to enter the water had more to do with a scientist's curiosity. In fact, it is doubtful that Eiseley himself would have attached any religious significance to this experience. However, Eiseley concluded his reflections in "The Flow of the River" with the suggestion that a stilled and attentive listening to nature's own self-revelation can open on to "an apparition from that mysterious shadow world beyond nature, that final world which contains—if anything contains—the explanation of men and catfish and green leaves."[53] In the end Eiseley's focus, too, had shifted; his gaze was being drawn through a contemplation of creation to a veiled glimpse of the Face that lies beyond the natural world.

Finally, in the Christian ecological spirituality suggested in this essay, the human person is engaged in a spiritual quest that involves an attitude of contemplative listening. Given that the primary focus of a Christian's spiritual quest is God, this spirituality recognizes that one's contemplative attitude is first and foremost towards God. Yet, given that humans are embedded in the natural world and responsible to the whole of creation, the human contemplation of God takes place within the context of a long, loving look towards creation as well. In this ecological spirituality, a person's response to God's call for a dynamic relationship is inclusive of the human person's response to the needs of the natural world. There is one stance, contemplative in character, in which the Christian encounters God and the natural world and is transformed by both. This transformation places the human person in a compassionate response towards nature while intensifying one's quest for God.

Bibliography:

Athanasius. *The Life of Antony and the Letter to Marcellinus.* Translated with an introduction by Robert C. Gregg and a preface by William A. Clebsch. Mahwah, NJ: Paulist, 1980.

Burton-Christie, Douglas. "A Feeling for the Natural World: Spirituality and Contemporary Nature Writing." *Continuum* 2 (1993) 154–90.

Eiseley, Loren. "The Flow of the River." In *The Immense Journey*, 15–27. New York: Vintage, 1957.

53. Ibid., 27.

————. "The Secret of Life." In *The Immense Journey*, 195–210. New York: Vintage, 1957.

Fern, Richard L. *Nature, God, and Humanity: Envisioning an Ethics of Nature.* Cambridge: Cambridge University Press, 2002.

Lane, Belden C. *The Solace of Fierce Landscapes: Exploring Desert and Mountain Spirituality.* New York: Oxford University Press, 1998.

Leopold, Aldo. *A Sand County Almanac: And Sketches Here and There.* New York: Ballantine, 1970.

————. *A Sand County Almanac: With Essays on Conservation from Round River.* New York: Ballantine, 1990.

Meine, Curt. "Building 'The Land Ethic.'" In *Companion to "A Sand County Almanac": Interpretative and Critical Essays,* edited by J. Baird Callicott, 172–85. Madison: University of Wisconsin Press, 1987.

Merchant, Carolyn. *Earthcare: Women and the Environment.* New York: Routledge, 1995.

————. "Partnership with Nature." The Second Annual Ian L. McHarg Lecture given at the Landscape Architecture and Regional Planning Graduate School of Fine Arts, University of Pennsylvania in Philadelphia, Pennsylvania, February 7, 2000.

————. *Reinventing Eden: The Fate of Nature in Western Culture.* New York: Routledge, 2003.

Oelschlaeger, Max. *The Idea of Wilderness: From Prehistory to the Age of Ecology.* New Haven, CT: Yale University Press, 1991.

Schneiders, Sandra. "The Study of Christian Spirituality: Contours and Dynamics of a Discipline." *Christian Spirituality Bulletin* 6 (1998) 1, 3–12.

Tracy, David. *Blessed Rage for Order: The New Pluralism in Theology.* New York: Seabury, 1975.

White, Lynn. "The Historical Roots of Our Ecologic Crisis." In *This Sacred Earth: Religion, Nature, Environment,* edited by Roger S. Gottlieb, 184–93. New York: Routledge, 1996.

Index